# Learn Raspberry Pi Programming with Python

**Wolfram Donat**

## Learn Raspberry Pi Programming with Python

ISBN-13 (pbk): 978-1-4302-6424-8

ISBN-13 (electronic): 978-1-4302-6425-5

President and Publisher: Paul Manning
Lead Editor: Michelle Lowman
Technical Reviewer: Chaim Krause
Development Editor: Anne Marie Walker
Editorial Board: Steve Anglin, Mark Beckner, Ewan Buckingham, Gary Cornell, Louise Corrigan, Jim DeWolf, Jonathan Gennick, Jonathan Hassell, Robert Hutchinson, Michelle Lowman, James Markham, Matthew Moodie, Jeff Olson, Jeffrey Pepper, Douglas Pundick, Ben Renow-Clarke, Dominic Shakeshaft, Gwenan Spearing, Matt Wade, Steve Weiss
Coordinating Editor: Kevin Shea
Copy Editor: Roger LeBlanc
Compositor: SPi Global
Indexer: SPi Global
Artist: SPi Global
Cover Designer: Anna Ishchenko

Distributed to the book trade worldwide by Springer Science+Business Media New York, 233 Spring Street, 6th Floor, New York, NY 10013. Phone 1-800-SPRINGER, fax (201) 348-4505, e-mail orders-ny@springer-sbm.com, or visit www.springeronline.com. Apress Media, LLC is a California LLC and the sole member (owner) is Springer Science + Business Media Finance Inc (SSBM Finance Inc). SSBM Finance Inc is a Delaware corporation.

For information on translations, please e-mail rights@apress.com, or visit www.apress.com.

Apress and friends of ED books may be purchased in bulk for academic, corporate, or promotional use. eBook versions and licenses are also available for most titles. For more information, reference our Special Bulk Sales–eBook Licensing web page at www.apress.com/bulk-sales.

Any source code or other supplementary material referenced by the author in this text is available to readers at www.apress.com/9781430265627. For detailed information about how to locate your book's source code, go to www.apress.com/source-code/.

*To Becky and Reed*

*Thank you for your patience and support when I disappear for hours, days, and weeks at a time, building all manner of off-the-wall things and then writing about them.*

# Contents at a Glance

# Contents

# About the Author

**Wolfram Donat** is tallish, with hair and four limbs attached in approximately the correct locations. He is a Computer Engineer, author and programmer, with interests in robotics, animatronics, automation and embedded systems. He wrote his first BASIC program on a Commodore VIC-20, more years ago than he cares to admit.

He currently lives in Anchorage, Alaska, with his wife, son, and menagerie of animals.

# About the Technical Reviewer

**Chaim Krause** presently lives in Leavenworth, Kansas, where the U.S. Army employs him as a Simulation Specialist. In his spare time, he likes to play PC games and occasionally develops his own. He has recently taken up the sport of golf to spend more time with his significant other, Ivana. Although he holds a BA in Political Science from the University of Chicago, Chaim is an autodidact when it comes to computers, programming, and electronics. He wrote his first computer game in BASIC on a Tandy Model I Level I and stored the program on a cassette tape. Amateur radio introduced him to electronics, while the Arduino and the Raspberry Pi provided a medium to combine computing, programming, and electronics into one hobby.

# Acknowledgments

Writing a book may be a solitary procedure, but it certainly can't be done without help. A lot of work by a lot of people went into this enterprise, and they all have my deepest appreciation. My thanks to Kevin for keeping things moving smoothly, to Anne Marie for figuring out what I was *trying* to say, and to Roger LeBlanc for making it look like I know what I'm doing. Thanks to Chaim, the tech reviewer, for making sure the stuff I wrote actually runs and does what it's supposed to. And thanks to Michelle, for taking notice of me in the first place.

Last but definitely not least, thanks to Becky and Reed. This one's for you.

# Introduction

In 2006, when Eben Upton and the other founders of the Raspberry Pi Foundation looked at the state of Computer Science (CS) programs in universities, they were dismayed. Computer science programs were being reduced to "CS 101: How To Operate Microsoft Word" and "CS 203: Optimize Your Facebook Page." Nobody, they realized, was learning how to *program* any more, least of all before they entered college. So they hatched a plan—create a small, cheap computer that kids could learn to program on, like the Amigas, Spectrums, and Commodore 64s of yesteryear. They put an ARM processor on a board, gave it (eventually) 512 MB of RAM and a VideoCore GPU, and allowed users to interface with it using a USB keyboard, mouse, and an HDMI output port. To make it easy to program, they designed it so that its main programming language would be Python—a powerful, easy-to-learn scripting language. And thus the Raspberry Pi was born.

I wrote my first program in BASIC on a Commodore VIC 20, lo these many years ago. At 5 KB of RAM, it had less computing power than many of today's microcontrollers, but I was still able to write a simple maze game on it, saving my progress as I went on a cassette-tape drive. In the years since, I've traversed my way through the different computing platforms, from Windows 3.1, to Macintosh OS 8, to a little bit of Linux. It had been a long time since I was truly excited by a computer; the Pi was a breath of fresh air in a somewhat stale computing environment. Not only was it small and cheap, but it was easy to get it to interact with the physical world—a real boon for anybody interested in designing physical systems. So when I heard about its release, I signed up like about a trillion other hobbyists/hackers/engineers and waited impatiently for mine to be delivered. Then I started building stuff with it and never looked back.

If you bought a Pi but aren't sure how to get started with it, this book is for you.

If you bought a Pi but aren't sure what to do with it, this book is for you.

If you're *considering* buying a Pi but haven't yet because you keep thinking, "Why should I? It's not like I can do anything cool with it, right?", then this book is *definitely* for you.

This book isn't meant to be a textbook on Python, nor is it an exhaustive exploration of the Raspberry Pi and everything it can do. But it is meant to be a fun, getting-started guide to this neat little computer. I hope that after you work your way through the book, you'll get a sense of all the things that are possible with the Pi when you combine it with a little ingenuity and creativity on your part.

If you want to work through the projects here in order, feel free. If you'd rather skip around, doing those that interest you, you're welcome to do that as well. Along the way, I hope you'll develop a familiarity with both Python and the Pi that will enable you to continue on, building projects as you go, and perhaps inspiring others along the way. Above all, I hope you enjoy the book and its projects. It was truly a blast to write.

Happy computing!

# CHAPTER 1

■ ■ ■

# Introducing the Raspberry Pi

So you've got yourself a Raspberry Pi mini computer. Now what? Perhaps you're familiar with the Pi and its architecture, but you're wondering what to do with it. Perhaps you have some experience with computers but aren't familiar with Linux or Raspbian, the Pi's default operating system. Perhaps you're already a Linux geek, but you don't know how to program in Python and thought it would be a good time to learn. Perhaps you have absolutely *no* experience with computers beyond clicking the Start button, checking your email, and surfing the web, but you heard about this "Raspberry Pie" thingamabob and decided to see what all the ruckus was about.

Whatever the case may be, welcome! You're about to join a club—not a particularly exclusive one, I'm afraid, since all it takes to join is about $35 US plus shipping—but a club nonetheless. As a member, you'll be able to discuss *package managers, ARM11 processors,* and *dot config files* intelligently with anyone who will listen. You'll know about drivers and APIs. You'll become familiar with servos, LEDs, and cameras-on-a-chip. And, perhaps most importantly, you'll be able to connect to your new mini computer, program it in one of many different programming languages (though this book deals exclusively with Python), build projects, and interface those projects with the Pi, enabling it to interact with the physical world and do some very cool things.

With this book, I hereby induct you into this club. Your experience doesn't matter because I'll take you step by step through the process of setting up your Pi so that you can work with it with a minimum of headaches. I'll try to give you a solid background in Linux so that you understand what's going on behind the scenes, and I'll devote a long chapter on introducing you to Python, the scripting language that all the fashionable geeks are scripting in. Google uses it, NASA uses it, and the Book of Faces uses it. Let's face it, Perl is *so* yesterday. I will also devote a chapter introducing you to the nuts and bolts of building electronics projects—something many technical and programming books either gloss over or neglect completely. There are safety factors to consider (I very nearly had a small explosion when I shorted out a battery pack, for instance) as well as just good building practice. For example, you'll learn how to make a good solder joint and how to avoid slicing your index finger off with an X-ACTO knife, as well as the difference between a 40Ω and a 40KΩ resistor.

Of course, if you're already familiar with all those things, feel free to skip ahead to the good stuff: the projects. All of them can be constructed in a weekend or so (or a month or two, depending on your motivation level and length of your honey-do list), and all are programmed in Python. I'll give you a shopping list of parts at the beginning of each project, with places to get the parts, and then we'll dive right in. They don't necessarily build on each other, nor are they in any particular order of complexity; if you want to build the Cat Entertainer and skip the Home Media Server, it's perfectly all right.

What kind of projects can you do with a Pi? You'd be surprised: the Pi's small size belies its impressive computing power. It has been used for everything from web servers to car computers (*carputers*) to cluster computing, when hooked up in large groups. I hope that after you finish this book you'll have not only some more ideas, but the skills necessary to put those ideas into practice.

Whatever your reason for picking up this book, your main objective should be to have fun and learn something! I'll do what I can to lead the way.

# The History of Raspberry Pi

It may seem to the casual observer that the Raspberry Pi is very new; many blog posts still treat it that way, and there's a surprisingly huge number of people who have no idea what it is. A good number of online articles still begin with something along the lines of, "The Raspberry Pi is a small, credit-card-sized computer that hobbyists have begun using for…". This is in stark contrast to, say, the Arduino; most people up on current events have at least *heard* of the Arduino, even if they have no idea what it is or what it's used for, because it has been around since 2005 and has gained a loyal—and vocal—following among hobbyists, geeks, and do-it-yourselfers worldwide.

---

## THE ARDUINO

For those who don't know, the Arduino is a microcontroller platform, mounted on a board that plugs easily into most computers. It allows the user to program the onboard Atmega chip to do various things using a C-like programming language, in programs called *sketches*. A typical Arduino sketch might look like this:

```
#include <Servo.h>
void setup()
{
    myservo.attach(9)
}
void loop()
{
    myservo.write(95);
    delay(100);
    myservo.write(150);
    delay(100);
}
```

This repeatedly moves a connected servomotor (a small motor that can be precisely controlled via software) back and forth, with one-second delays.

Although not as powerful as the Pi, the Arduino has done a lot to make electronics projects in general (and microcontrollers specifically) more accessible to the general public. I talk about how the Arduino and the Raspberry Pi complement each other well in Chapter 14.

---

The Raspberry Pi, while not brand new, *has* been around for a few years. Its creators—Eben Upton, Rob Mullins, Jack Lang, and Alan Mycroft—first floated the idea of a cheap PC in 2006. Based at the University of Cambridge in the United Kingdom, they were concerned that the demise of cheap personal computers like the Commodore 64, the Amiga, and the Spectrum were adversely affecting young people's ability to program. With desktop and laptop computers costing hundreds—if not thousands—of dollars, kids and teenagers were forbidden from practicing programming on the family's main machine.

At the same time, the creators realized that many university computer science curricula had been reduced to "Microsoft Word 101" and "How to create a web page." The four creators wanted to raise the programming knowledge bar of incoming students, and thus perhaps computer science and engineering courses would become a bit more robust.

Obviously, a cheaper computer was necessary. They played around with microcontrollers and various chips, breadboards, and PCBs, but it wasn't until 2008 that the idea became more feasible. Chips were becoming smaller, cheaper, and more powerful thanks to the explosion in mobile devices. These chips enabled them to plan a device that would be capable of supporting multimedia, not just command-line programming, which they felt was important. (See Figure 1-1.) Young people were more likely to be interested in a media-capable device, and thus more likely to try programming on one.

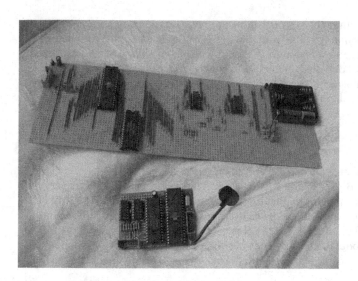

***Figure 1-1.*** *Eben Upton's 2006 Raspberry Pi prototype (image ©Raspberry Pi Foundation)*

In 2008, the original four creators, along with Pete Lomas and David Braben, formed the Raspberry Pi Foundation (the Foundation), and three years later the first mass-produced Pi rolled off the assembly line.

---

■ **Note**  The name *Raspberry Pi* is a nod to the number of microcomputers named after fruit in the early days, such as Apple and Tangerine, and the *Pi* comes from the Python scripting language.

---

Within a year, the Foundation had sold over one million units. The founding members have said many times that they were dumbfounded by the explosive interest in their device. Their original goal of putting a cheap, programmable device in the hands of educators and their students has come to fruition. However, it has become much more than that. Apparently, they were not the only ones who were missing the ability to program on a cheaper machine; hobbyists around the world flooded element14, Premier Farnell, and RS Electronics with orders—to the point that people who pre-ordered their Pi (such as yours truly) had to wait up to six months for supply to catch up with demand. Many customers may have been current or former programmers, eager to play with a new, small, powerful computer. (I first learned to program in BASIC on the Commodore VIC-20, with an impressive 20 KB of RAM in . . . well, a long time ago.)

But there were (and are) an infinite number of other uses for the Pi, as it says on the Raspberry Pi Foundation's About Us page:

> *We've had enormous interest, support and help from the educational community, and we've been delighted and a little humbled by the number of enquiries from agencies and people far away from our original targets for the device. Developing countries are interested in the Raspberry Pi as productivity devices in areas that simply can't afford the power and hardware needed to run a traditional desktop PC; hospitals and museums have contacted us to find out about using the Raspberry Pi to drive display devices. Parents of severely disabled kids have talked to us about monitoring and accessibility applications; and there seem to be a million and one people out there with hot soldering irons who want to make a robot.*

Luckily, supply has securely caught up with demand. There is no waiting period to buy a Pi anymore, and there is no longer a limit of one per customer. There is a "buy one give one" program in the works, in which the Raspberry Pi Foundation plans to donate a Pi to an educational organization for every Pi sold. The recent release of the Raspberry Pi camera board, a small camera-on-a-chip that plugs directly into the Pi and enables the user to take both still pictures and video, promises to open up even more possibilities for this little computer. And since the founders actively encourage other companies to copy their paradigm, it's anybody's guess what's coming next.

## Exploring the Pi Board

So what exactly is on the board? It's pretty darn small, so what can possibly fit on there?

There are two models of Pi: model A and model B. (See Figure 1-2 for a look at the model B.) The two are very similar, with model B having a few more features (and a slightly higher price) than model A. Model A has 256 MB of RAM; model B has 512 MB. Model A has one USB port, while model B has two. Finally, model A has no Ethernet port, while the B has one. You can still order one or the other; model A is $25 US as of this writing, while model B is $35 US. For the slight difference in price, I suggest getting model B. The difference between one and two USB ports can be huge, and the ability to plug into a hardwired Ethernet cable can make things such as updates and connecting to the board in a small, ad-hoc network much simpler.

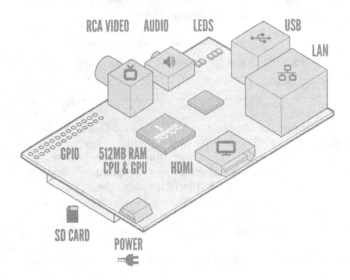

*Figure 1-2.* The Raspberry Pi Model B (image ©Raspberry Pi Foundation)

The Pi (from here on, we'll assume you have model B) measures 85.6 millimeters (mm) by 56 mm by 21 mm (yes, it's obviously not made in America), with some overlap for the ports and the SD card. Referring to Figure 1-2 and moving counterclockwise around the card, I'll explain the components in detail in the following sections.

## The SD Card

As you can see in Figure 1-2, a lot is packed into the card's small space. One of the Pi's greatest space-saving features is that there's no real hard drive like in your desktop or laptop; the SD card acts like a solid state drive (SSD). You can change the size of that drive merely by switching SD cards, within reason. You must use at least a 2-GB card, and at least 4 GB is recommended if you want to add any real software to your drive image. (You do.) Cards up to 32 GB have been tested and work, but they are not guaranteed, so be sure you back up your drive often if you decide to go with a bazillion-GB card.

## The Power Port

The power port is merely a 5V micro-USB input, similar to what you see with many cell phones or tablets. As a matter of fact, a cell-phone charger is one of the most common ways to power your Pi. (See Figure 1-3.)

**Figure 1-3.** *Common USB power adapter*

A word of warning, however: **The Raspberry Pi has no onboard power regulator!** If you're used to using the Arduino, you know that you can safely power it with up to 9V and go on your merry way. If you try that with the Pi, you'll have yourself a nice paperweight. Don't go above 5V— if you're not sure what your charger puts out, measure it with a multimeter. Better yet, all web sites that sell the Pi also sell a variety of chargers guaranteed to work with it. Me? I use the old charger that came with my Blackberry Torch. (Yes, I owned a Blackberry. Don't judge me.)

In case you were thinking of asking: Yes, you can power the Pi with batteries, though performance can get funky as they discharge and power levels drop below 5V. Probably the easiest way to do it is to use a 9V battery or a bank of 4 AA batteries and funnel it through a voltage regulator, or use a battery pack such as those found in Remote Control cars. I'll discuss that as well in chapters where the project involves a mobile Pi.

## The HDMI Port

The Pi is equipped with an HDMI (High Definition Multimedia Interface) output port, and many argue that this is truly where the Pi comes into its own, because it's able to output high-definition 1080p graphics, with 1 gigapixel/second processing power. The onboard GPU can do Blu-ray quality playback, using OpenGL and OpenVG libraries supplied on-chip.

## The Ethernet and USB Ports

The Ethernet and USB ports (on the model B board, anyway) are both supplied via the onboard LAN9512 chip. According to the 9512's datasheet, it's a high-speed USB 2.0 hub with a 10/100 Ethernet controller. This little chip is only 8 mm to a side, but it's capable of 480 Mbps USB 2.0 speeds and fully-integrated 10BASE-T and 100-BASETX Ethernet support. I know this description is a lot of technical gobbledygook, but what it means is that almost anything you can plug into your desktop machine can be plugged into your Pi, from your router to a webcam to a USB hub to an external hard drive (HDD.)

## The Audio and RCA Video Jacks

Audio and RCA video jacks are also on the board. The Pi does support sound over its HDMI output, but should you want to plug in headphones, it has a standard 3.5-mm audio jack. Should you want to use a microphone, most USB mics will work, assuming they're Linux-compatible. As for video: the Pi doesn't support VGA output, but the RCA jack sends video to any connected RCA video device—useful if you have a pair of self-contained video goggles like the MyVu device.

## The GPIO Pins

Perhaps the most overlooked part of the Pi are the GPIO (General Purpose Input Output) pins. These pins allow you to connect the Pi to any number of physical extensions, from LEDs and servomotors to motor controllers and extension boards like the large Gertboard, which will be introduced and discussed in Chapter 13. With a normal desktop or laptop computer, this would require some serious fiddling, either with USB drivers or accessing the (perhaps nonexistent) serial port and doing some serious low-level programming magic. But the Raspberry Pi comes with libraries pre-installed that allow you to access the pins using Python, C, or C++. Additional libraries also exist if you don't happen to like the official, preloaded versions. This means that you can connect up to eight servos to the Pi right out of the box—enough to control a quadruped robot, for example.

## The System on a Chip

The most important piece on the board is the chip in the middle, also referred to as an *SoC*, or *System on a Chip*. The Pi's chip is a Broadcom PCM2835 with an ARM11 processor running at 700 MHz and a Videocore4 GPU. The chip can be overclocked to at least 800 MHz without a problem; indeed, the latest generation of preloaded SD cards offer an overclocking option right from the `raspi-config` file. The fastest of the presets will take your processor up to 1 GHz, with an *on-demand* function available to prevent your chip from overheating. According to the Foundation, the result of all that overclocking equals 52-64 percent faster operations.

---

■ **Note** For more information on overclocking, see the article "Introducing turbo mode: up to 50 percent more performance for free" at `http://www.raspberrypi.org/archives/2008`.

---

What all this means is that the Pi's computing power makes it about equal to a 300-MHz Pentium 2, but with the graphics capabilities of a first-generation Xbox. Not bad for a system about the size of a credit card that costs less than $50 US. It also means that because the Pi is both small *and* powerful, it can go places and do things that previously only laptops dared to go and do.

## Comparing Raspberry Pi to Similar Devices

And what, you may ask, makes the Raspberry Pi better than other small microcomputers like the Arduino and the Beagleboard line of devices? The answer to that is that the Pi isn't necessarily better; each of these devices fills a particular niche, and it can be difficult to compare them. Arduinos are awesome for creating simple projects, and even controlling a very simple robot. In many cases, using a Pi to do what you could do with an Arduino would be overkill, pure and simple. As for the other computers like the Beagleboard, the main difference is price. A close relative to the Pi is the Beaglebone, but the Bone's manufacturer's suggested retail price (MSRP) is $89—more than twice the Pi's price. And purchasing the Raspberry Pi means you're supporting a charitable organization aiming to put cheap computers in the hands of schoolchildren worldwide, so there's that, too.

I think you would agree that now is as good a time as any to take the Pi out of its box, if you haven't already. Just read on before you start it up.

# Hardware Requirements of the Pi

Let's take a quick look at what the Pi's requirements are, and then we'll start it up.

## Connecting to Power

I already mentioned power; the Pi needs 5V—no more, no less. Again, because it bears repeating: **The Pi has no onboard voltage regulator!** You can't plug in a 9V battery or wall wart and expect it to work. Either use something like a cell-phone charger that puts out 5V (most of them do), or get a good power supply from an online electronics store or from the place where you bought the Pi. The power supply will also need to supply *at least* 500 milliamps (mA), and preferably more like 1 amp (A). If it sources only 500 mA, be prepared for some funky behavior, like the mouse and keyboard not working when the wireless adapter is plugged in. I recommend 1A.

## Adding a Monitor

The next peripheral you'll need, at least at first, is a monitor with either HDMI or DVI capabilities. If all you have is DVI input, that's all right, because HDMI-to-DVI converters are everywhere. After you've got it set up and all the necessary software is installed, you can run the Pi in a *headless* configuration. What that means is that you can log into it from another computer with either SSH (Secure Shell) or even a VNC (Virtual Network Computing) client. But at first, you'll need a monitor so that you can see what you're doing. Baby steps.

## Adding a USB Hub

You're probably going to want a USB hub at some point. Model B has two USB ports, which means you can plug in a keyboard and a mouse, and you'll be sitting pretty. However, if you want to go wireless (and at some point you will, trust me), you're going to need at least three USB ports, one of which is for your wireless USB dongle. That means you're going to need a hub.

Performance can get sticky when you add a hub, because some USB hubs have been shown to work *much* better than others when it comes to working together with the Pi. Perhaps the most important necessary feature is that the hub is externally powered; this will prevent your Pi from having to attempt to provide enough power to whatever power-sucking device you've decided to plug in that day. This is a problem that will come up with your wireless USB adapter. (See the section "Using a Wireless USB Dongle.") In any case, if you're unsure whether your hub is compatible and don't have a spare hub floating around the house to try, the best place to research the matter is often in the Raspberry Pi forums (http://www.raspberrypi.org/phpBB3). It's here that users like you have tried umpteen different brands and reported back about which ones work, which ones don't, and which ones require a little tweaking. Luckily, hubs are relatively inexpensive. If the one you try first doesn't seem to work, there's a good chance you'll find another use for it somewhere.

The one I use is a Belkin F5U407 4-port Ultra Mini Hub (shown in Figure 1-4).

*Figure 1-4.  The Belkin F5U407 USB hub*

However, here is where you should do as I say, not as I do, since it turns out that my particular hub is *not* externally powered. I purchased this one because it was small and fit in my robot parts box. If size is an issue for you, this particular hub might be a good fit for you. As it happens, I've had no problems running everything I need to with it, so feel free to copy my success with it.

## Using a Wireless USB Dongle

The last piece of hardware you're going to need is a wireless USB dongle. When you're first setting up the Pi, it's almost always a good idea to keep it hardwired to your Internet connection as long as possible. This is because a hard connection is *always* faster than a WiFi one, and you'll probably be downloading packages, updates, and libraries—all sorts of good stuff. In fact, if you plan to use the same Pi for several different projects (which is definitely an option, even though they're so cheap), you'll most likely plug it in again for each successive download you need. It'll save a lot of time.

But eventually you'll want or need to go wireless; after all, part of the Pi's allure is its compact size and portability, which is wasted if it's dragging an Ethernet cable behind it like a ball and chain. So you'll need a wireless adapter.

And this, my friends, is where configuring your Pi can get very sticky. WiFi support on ARM Linux can be "patchy," as the Foundation so eloquently puts it; without some sort of direction, you could spend months and hundreds of dollars trying out different dongles, all to no avail. Some adapters can make the Pi crash, others won't connect to a network. It may not source enough power through its onboard USB ports to power certain adapters, but it often has problems using a USB adapter that is connected via a hub. (For this reason if no other, it's *always* a good idea to plug the wireless adapter into one of the Pi's onboard ports and plug your hub into the other. Then your mouse and keyboard are connected via the hub, rather than the dongle.)

Fortunately, the Pi community has (collectively) spent those hundreds of dollars and months testing out all of those adapters, and it has published the results on the forums. It turns out that the Pi plays well with adapters using the Ralink RTL8188CUS chipset.

Unfortunately, you may have noticed that determining what chipset a certain adapter uses is no easy task, even if you're in the store, physically inspecting its packaging (spoken from experience). For whatever reason, wireless USB adapter chipsets are not commonly advertised. But again, the Pi community has experimented and determined that the following two adapters work very well with the Pi:

- Edimax EW-7811Un

- Ralink RT5370

Both are available on Amazon.com for very reasonable prices (less than $10 US).

As you can see in Figure 1-5, the Edimax adapter is small; it's so small, in fact, that it's actually quite easy to lose. (Not that *I* would lose track of a wireless adapter. But *you* might.)

**Figure 1-5.** *An Edimax adapter*

If you've purchased your adapter and have a working power supply, hub, monitor, mouse, and keyboard, you're ready to start setting up your Pi.

# The Pi Operating System

The Raspberry Pi's default operating system (OS)—the one it's designed to use—is Linux. If you're not familiar with the Linux operating system, don't worry—we'll peek under the hood in Chapter 2. For now, though, know that Linux comes in several flavors, or *distributions*: Ubuntu (one of the most popular), Debian, Mint, Red Hat, Fedora, and a few other, more obscure varieties. The Pi uses a version of Debian called, appropriately enough, *Raspbian*.

Because the Pi doesn't have a hard drive, you must download and copy a disk image to an SD card. That image is what the Pi will use to boot, and it will also act as memory/RAM. Almost any size will do, as long as it's at least 2 GB, and more than 4 GB is preferred if you plan on loading any appreciable amount of extra software onto the card. (You do.) As mentioned earlier, cards up to 32 GB have been tested; beyond that, your results may be kind of sketchy. It's recommended that you use a brand-name card, and it should be a *class 4*, which denotes the speed of the card.

## Formatting the Card

Your first task is to format the card so that your Pi can read it. Insert the SD card into your computer, and do the following:

- **For Windows users:** Download the formatting tool program from the SD Association at `https://www.sdcard.org/downloads/formatter_4/eula_windows/`. Install it, using all the default settings, and start it up. Set the "FORMAT SIZE ADJUSTMENT" option to "ON" in the tool's Options menu, make sure you have the right SD card selected, and click "Format."

- **For Mac users:** Download the Mac version of the formatting tool from `https://www.sdcard.org/downloads/formatter_4/eula_mac/`. Install the tool with all the default settings by double-clicking the downloaded `.pkg` file. Once it's installed, open it and select the "Overwrite Format" option. Make sure you have the right SD card selected, and click "Format."

## Using NOOBS

Now that the card is formatted correctly, you can put the operating system on it. Most users can use the Pi Foundation's NOOBS (New Out Of Box Software) from `http://www.raspberrypi.org/downloads`. The NOOBS system, upon first boot, will actually present you with a choice of operating systems to install, including two versions of XBMC (Xbox Media Center), Pidora, and Raspbian. For the purposes of this book and the subsequent chapters, we're going to install Raspbian.

Once you've downloaded NOOBS—and be aware that it's a hefty 1.1-GB download—unzip it using the extraction utility of your choice (Windows: right-click, "Extract all"; Mac: double-click). Then copy the extracted files onto your SD card.

That's it. Your Pi is now ready to boot.

# Connecting the Peripherals

Ready to connect all those wonderful components? Not so fast, Kemo Sabe. There's a preferred order to connecting the peripherals. It may seem weird, but it's *possible* (even if highly unlikely) that connecting power, the monitor, and the other parts in the wrong order could cause a voltage spike and fry your board. So get used to hooking things up in this order, and save yourself potential headaches down the line. The order is as follows:

1. Insert the SD card.

2. Connect the monitor.

3. Connect the USB peripherals (keyboard, mouse, and/or hub).

4. Connect the Ethernet cable.

5. Connect the power.

As a matter of fact, the most critical detail to remember here is to hook up the power last. You can probably fudge on the others, but power should always be last.

There's no on/off switch; as soon as you plug in the power, LEDs should start lighting up, and you should see a rainbow screen on your monitor.

# Configuring the Pi

When you start up the Pi for the first time with the NOOBS card, you'll see a selection box with six choices: Archlinux, OpenELEC, Pidora, RISC OS, RaspBMC, and Raspbian. Select Raspbian with your mouse, and click the "Install OS" button at the top left of the window. Click "yes" to confirm in the pop-up box that follows, and then wait while the image is written to your SD card. It might be worth watching because the progress window has a few tips you can read while you wait.

When it's done, click "OK" and the Pi will reboot to a black screen and crawling lines of text. When it's finished, you'll be greeted with the Software Configuration Tool (`raspi-config`). This gives you some additional options, such as expanding the file system (always a good idea), changing the user password, and even overclocking. Select whichever option you'd like to change with the arrow keys, and press Tab and then Enter to activate your choice. Definitely enable the camera because you'll be using it later. Overclocking is fine, but be aware that it *can* shorten your Pi's lifetime. The `raspi-config` menu allows you to overclock up to 1 GHz, but if you want to play it safe and stable, don't go any higher than 900 MHz.

Advanced options include setting a hostname and memory splitting. Play with these as you like, but definitely enable the SSH access because we'll be using this later as well. Remember, at this stage, you can't really damage anything. If you brick your card (make it unusable), simply use the SDCard tool to reformat it and copy NOOBS onto it again. Then you can start fresh. Later, you may want to be more careful, but I'll show you how to back up your card so that you don't lose any of your settings if you do something foolish.

When you're done playing with `raspi-config`, select "Finish" and press Enter.

Once Raspbian is installed, you'll probably want a normal desktop environment. No, you don't really *need* one, but I think we can all agree it's nice to see one, especially if you're new to Linux and the sight of a command-line interface gives you the willies. If you didn't choose to boot directly to Desktop in the `raspi-config` utility, type $ pi when prompted for your user name, and type

```
$ raspberry
```

for the password to log in to the Pi. After that, if you want to start a desktop environment, type

```
$ startx
```

at the prompt. You shall soon be greeted with a standard desktop, complete with a huge picture of a raspberry (as shown in Figure 1-6). The icons along the left side of the screen are programs, preloaded on the Pi, that are used most often. Their arrangement may vary from what you see in the image because distributions change and yours is most likely updated from the one I'm using as I write this. However, you'll probably have LXTterminal (for command-line interfacing), Midori (the Pi's native web browser), the Pi Store, IDLE (for Python work), Debian Reference, and maybe one or two others.

*Figure 1-6.* *The home (desktop) screen on the Raspberry Pi*

Your Pi is now up and running. Congratulations, and give yourself a pat on the back! Enjoy, but don't get too comfy. Your next task should be to make sure everything is up to date. Most Linux distributions release updates and upgrades regularly, and Raspbian is no different. There's a good chance there have been several important upgrades to the software and possibly even the kernel between the time when the Pi Foundation made the NOOBS image available for download and today.

To update the Pi, at the prompt type

```
$ sudo apt-get update
```

You'll see lines of text flow smoothly by as the Pi refreshes its software list. When it finishes, the "$" prompt will return. At this point, type

```
$ sudo apt-get upgrade
```

Lines of text should scroll by again. If new software is ready to be downloaded, the Pi will ask you if you want to download and install it. Press Enter (the default option). When it finishes and returns you to the $ prompt, everything should be at the latest version. Depending on what was updated, you may be prompted to restart. If so, reboot, restart the desktop by typing

```
$ startx
```

and you'll be back to the home screen.

## Shutting Down the Pi

Before we begin our Linux discussion, let's discuss shutdown. As a matter of fact, shutting down the Pi is unnecessary; it's such a low-power device that the designers just expect that you'll leave it running. You *can* shut it down, though, and in the interest of saving a little money and perhaps your Pi, I suggest you shut it down when you're done using it. Since there's no "Off" switch, the Pi is actually designed to be powered off simply by unplugging it, and nothing bad is supposed to happen (assuming you've saved your work, aren't in the middle of something, and so on). But just unplugging it makes many of us computer types cringe, so let me teach you the true, *proper* shutdown method. Open the terminal, and at the prompt, type

```
$ sudo shutdown -r now
```

This takes the processor through the proper shutdown sequence, killing running processes, stopping threads, and so on. When it's finished, it should take you back to the black, text-only startup page, if it doesn't actually power down the Pi. Once you're at that page, it's truly safe to unplug it.

## Summary

You've now been introduced to the Pi, installed its operating system, and updated it to within an inch of its life. You've also been introduced to the raspi-config tool, and you have even played a bit with the command-line interface (CLI). It's time to take a look at Linux.

# CHAPTER 2

■ ■ ■

# Linux by the Seat of Your Pants

Raspberry Pi uses Linux as its standard operating system, so that means if you don't know anything about this awesome OS, you're going to have to learn. Don't worry—I'll try to make this as painless as possible.

Whatever your preconceptions about Linux are, you can probably disregard them. Since its inception, Linux has always been regarded as the "geek's OS," associated with images of button-up-short-sleeve-shirt-clad pencil-necks hammering away on a keyboard while the screen fills with text and somewhere, deep in the basement, a row of tape-driven computer hard-drive cabinets spin to life. (See Figure 2-1.) In the background, a 20-sided die rolls across the table, and there is the soft muttering of an argument: "No, Han shot first!"

*Figure 2-1.* The Linux users' playground (©2006 Marcin Wichary)

However, fear not. While some of us still heartily embrace that culture and all that it stands for, that doesn't mean *you* have to. Linux has come a long way since it was first introduced, and it is now not only a real powerhouse of an operating system, but also extremely user friendly (at least, most of its distributions are). The most popular flavors of Linux are Ubuntu and Mint. Both are visually so similar to Windows and Mac that many people find switching to them fun and easy. Another popular version of Linux is Debian, which is the distribution that the Pi's operating system, Raspbian, is based on. When it first began, Debian was the only distribution of Linux that was truly "open"—allowing any developer and user to contribute. It still remains the largest distributor of Linux that is not a commercial entity.

Okay, enough horn-tooting. In order to really use the Pi, you'll need at least a basic understanding of Linux and how it works. So let's get started.

---

## THE LINUX STORY

Linux is an operating system loosely based on the Unix operating system. It has always been free and open-source, and it was first released in 1991 by its creator, Linus Torvalds. It is written in the C programming language and was originally designed to run on Intel's x86-based computers. In the intervening 20+ years, it has been ported to every imaginable device, from mainframes and supercomputers to tablets, televisions, and video game consoles. The Android operating system is built on the Linux *kernel*—the nugget of code on which an operating system is built.

Like most computer software, Linux was not born in a black hole. It owes its beginning to operating systems and kernels such as Unix, BSD, GNU, and MINIX. In fact, Torvalds has said on occasion that if the GNU kernel had been complete or if BSD had been available in the early 90s, he probably would not have written his own kernel. He began his work on the kernel with MINIX and eventually added many GNU software applications. He also switched his licensing to the GNU GPL, which states that code can be reused as long as it is released under a similar license.

In the following years, Linux spread, both in user acceptance and in devices. With all of the aforementioned devices running Linux, it is the most widely adopted operating system in the world.

---

# Getting Started with Linux on the Pi

To interact with your Pi, you're going to be doing a lot of work with the terminal—also called the *command-line interface*. With your Raspberry Pi desktop up and running, double-click the terminal icon to start it. Because you're already logged in, you won't be asked for a user name and password; rather, the prompt will show something like this:

```
pi@raspberrypi / $
```

This is the command-line interface (CLI). (See Figure 2-2.) It tells you that you are the user "pi," logged in to the machine "raspberrypi," in the home directory.

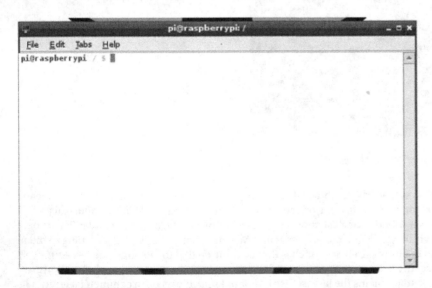

***Figure 2-2.*** *The Raspberry Pi terminal*

If you were in a different directory, the prompt would display that directory, such as

```
pi@raspberrypi:~/gpio $
```

## Linux Files and the File System

As an operating system, Linux is completely built around files and the file system. A file is any piece of information—be it text, image, video, or other—that is identified by a file name and a location. That location, also called a *directory path*, helps keep each file completely distinguishable from all others, because the location is technically part of the file name. For example,

```
/wdonat/Desktop/MyFiles/file.txt
```

is different from

```
/wdonat/Desktop/MyOtherFiles/file.txt.
```

File names are also case sensitive, which means that /file.txt is different from /FILE.txt, which is different from /File.txt. There are five categories of files that will become familiar to you:

- User data files: containing information you create, such as text files or images

- System data files containing information used by the system, such as logons, passwords, and so on

- Directory files, also called *folders*, which can contain files and other directories. Directories contained within directories are called *subdirectories*, and they can be nested almost as far down as you care to contemplate

- Special files representing hardware devices or some placeholder used by the OS

- Executable files, which are programs or shell scripts that contain instructions for the operating system

The entire file system in Linux is contained within one root folder, represented by a single /. Within that folder are subfolders, such as bin/, home/, proc/, var/, and dev/. Each has more subdirectories in it. In fact, if you could zoom out and look at the file system in a 3-dimensional sort of way, it would look similar to a giant, upside-down tree. The /home/ folder is your default home directory, and each user has one on a Linux (and Unix) system. Within that directory, you are free to create, execute, and delete files. If you need to manipulate, edit, or delete system files, you may need to either log in as the *root user* or execute the command sudo.

## Root User vs. sudo

In every Linux installation, there is a user, designated as the root, who is able to administer all files on the system, including system-level files. Most user accounts can't edit files in the /var/ directory, for example, but the root user can. Because of this power and the potential to misuse it (even accidentally), Linux users don't log in as root unless it's absolutely necessary; when they do, they log in, do what they need to, and log out again. There is a saying among Linux geeks: "Only noobs log in as root"; in other words, only neophytes log in and stay logged in as the root user.

There is a shortcut for logging in as a root user, however: sudo. sudo stands for **super user do**, and it simply tells the system to execute the command as if you were the root user. The system will ask for the root password and then execute the command. Again, the system does not double-check with you to see if you really want to do that, so when you're using sudo, be doubly careful you know the result of the command you just typed before you press Enter!

# Commands

To get around in the Linux CLI, you navigate through the file system using commands such as cd and ls. Commands to run programs are run from the terminal as well. Common commands you'll be using on a regular basis and should learn are included in Table 2-1.

***Table 2-1.*** *Common Linux Commands*

| Command | Meaning |
| --- | --- |
| ls | list files in current directory |
| cd | change directory |
| pwd | print working directory |
| rm *filename* | remove *filename* |
| mkdir *directoryname* | make directory with *directoryname* |
| rmdir *directoryname* | remove empty directory |
| cat *textfile* | display contents of *textfile* in the terminal |
| mv *oldfile newfile* | move (rename) *oldfile* to *newfile* |
| cp *oldfile newfile* | copy *oldfile* to *newfile* |
| man *command* | display manual of *command* |
| date | read system date/time |
| echo | echo what is typed back in the terminal |
| grep | search program that uses regular expressions |
| sudo | perform as root user |
| ./*program* | run *program* |
| exit | quit terminal session |

Most of the commands listed in Table 2-1 are self-explanatory, though some require explanation:

- man: Without a doubt, this is the most important command. If you are unsure of what a particular command does or what parameters/flags it uses, typing **man *command*** into your terminal brings up the Unix manual page with all of the information you'd ever want to know. When you bring up a page, it normally starts with the name of the command, followed by a synopsis of its various permutations, a detailed description of the command, all of its options and flags, and what those options and flags do. While you're in the manual view, just press Enter to scroll, and press *q* to return to the terminal.

- ls: This command lists the files in whatever directory you happen to be in; using flags like -l and -a includes information such as file permissions and modification dates. When you use the -l flag, the first part of every entry shows as something like this

```
drwxr-xr-x
```

- In this case, this means that the entry is a directory (d); the Owner can read, write, and execute files; Group members can read and execute files; and All Users can read and execute files. In most of our work with the Pi, you will be the owner of the files, so file permissions shouldn't affect you too much. There will be times, however, when you need to make a file executable; this is what the chmod command is for, but we'll get to that in another chapter—such as the chapter dealing with the home media server. ls has some other very useful flags as well. ls -F lists the current files in the directory, but with a "/" after all the contents that are themselves a directory. ls -a lists all the files, including the "hidden" files (those whose names begin with a period (.) or a double period (..), which normally doesn't show in a standard ls display).

- cd directory name: This command takes you to the directory you named, just as you would assume. A few special directory names include cd ~, which takes you to your home directory (the "~", or tilde, signifies your home directory), and cd ../, which takes you up one directory in the folder structure. In other words, if you're in the ~/Desktop/MyFiles/ directory, typing

  cd ../

  would place you in the ~/Desktop/ directory, typing

  cd ../../

  would place you in your home directory (~/), and typing

  cd ../MyOtherFiles/

  would take you out of the MyFiles directory on your desktop and put you in the MyOtherFiles directory on your desktop.

---

■ **Tip**  If you simply type cd and press Enter, you'll be taken back to your home directory, no matter where you are.

---

- pwd: This is a good command to know. When you're lost, pwd simply tells you what directory you're in, with the answer given as the path from the root directory. It is especially useful when you're four or five folders deep within a directory structure that may have repeated folder names, like

  /Users/wdonat/Desktop/MyApplication/bin/samples/Linux/bin/

  and the terminal prompt simply reads

  pi@raspberrypi /bin $

- rm: Using the command rm is like dragging a file into the trash, with one important difference: for all intents and purposes, you can't undo it, so be sure you really want to delete that file!

- mkdir **and** rmdir: The commands mkdir and rmdir create and delete directories. The caveat with rmdir is that the directory must be empty or the operating system will not allow you to remove it. You can, however, use the -p option with rmdir, which will remove a folder's (also empty) parent folders. For instance, typing

  rmdir -p /foo/bar/this_directory

will delete `this_directory/`, `bar/`, and `foo/`, in that order.

- `mv` **and** `cp`: The commands `mv` and `cp`, while fairly straightforward, can take some getting used to. `mv` doesn't *move* a file so much as it *renames* it while destroying the old file in the process: Typing

  ```
  mv myfile.txt myfile2.txt
  ```

  will rename `myfile.txt` to `myfile2.txt`.

In the `mv` command structure, you can specify directory levels, so in a sense you can `mv` a file from one folder to another. For instance, say you have a file named `myfile.txt` in the `MyFiles` folder on your desktop. You can move and rename it (from within the folder) by typing

```
mv myfile.txt ../MyOtherFiles/myfile2.txt
```

`myfile.txt` will be gone from your current directory, while a copy of it, named `myfile2.txt`, will appear in the `MyOtherFiles` folder on your desktop.

`cp` is similar to `mv`, but it copies rather than renames, so you don't lose the original file. Again, you can specify directory levels, so `cp` is handy for copying across folders. For example, typing

```
cp myfile.txt ../myfile.txt
```

places a copy of `myfile.txt` on your desktop (assuming you were still in the `Desktop/MyFiles/` directory.)

- `cat`: Using `cat` is a fast way to preview a file, like a text file, without actually opening it in a text editor. Typing `cat filename` will show you the contents of the file in your terminal, even if it's not a text file. (Try performing `cat` on an image file and you'll see a bunch of gibberish.) If you want to preview the file line by line rather than outputting the entire file at once into your terminal, use the `more` command. This will fill the screen with the first batch of text, and pressing the Enter key will advance through the file, one line at a time.

- `date`: Using `date` (without an argument) simply prints the system's date and time to the terminal. With an argument, it allows you to set that date and time.

- `echo`: This command merely echoes what you type back to you in the terminal. This is not a terribly useful command in the terminal, but when you write shell scripts (prescripted sets of commands that are run in the terminal), it is similar to a computer programming language's `print` statement.

- `grep`: Though `man` is probably the most important of these commands, `grep` is probably the most powerful. It is a search program that can search files and directories, using whatever input you give it in the form of regular expressions, and "pipe" that output to the screen or to another file. Its use of regular expressions is what makes it so powerful; if you're not familiar with them, a regular expression is a sequence of characters that form a search pattern, and often that sequence of characters seems like a foreign language. As a quick example,

  ```
  grep ^a.ple fruitlist.txt
  ```

  will search `fruitlist.txt` for all lines that begin with an "a," followed a single character, followed by "ple" and print those results to the screen. Using the "`|`" or *pipe*, allows you to send those results to different output, such as a text file. `grep`'s power and complexity is such that you could write chapters about it; for now, just be aware that it exists.

- ./filename: This command to run an executable file is pretty simple. Note that this works only on files that are executable, by your user name; it'll give you an error if the file doesn't have the correct permissions or simply isn't an executable file.

- exit: The final important command is simply exit—this stops whatever job is running in the terminal (also called a *shell*) and closes the terminal itself.

## Exercise: Navigating in the Linux File System

Let's practice moving around Linux's file system with the command line in the following introductory exercise. Start by opening a terminal prompt (command-line prompt) by double-clicking the LXTerminal icon on the Pi's desktop (which is shown in Figure 2-3).

LXTerminal

**Figure 2-3.**  *The LXTerminal icon on the desktop*

When it opens, make sure you're in the home directory by typing

cd ~

and then type

pwd

The terminal should print out

/home/pi

Now make a directory by typing

mkdir mydirectory

and then, without entering it, make a subdirectory within it by typing

mkdir mydirectory/mysubdirectory

If you now type **ls**, you should see mydirectory listed as an available directory. You can now type

cd mydirectory/mysubdirectory

and you'll be in your newly created subdirectory.

Let's test the echo function. In the terminal, type

```
echo "Hello, world!"
```

and the terminal should respond with

```
Hello, world!
```

True to its name, echo merely repeats the arguments you give it. However, you can "echo" something to other output formats as well; the default simply happens to be the screen. For instance, you can create a text file by using echo and the '>' operator. Type

```
echo "This is my first text file" > file.txt
```

If you then list the contents of your directory by typing ls, you'll see file.txt listed. Go ahead and create another text file called file2.txt by typing

```
echo "This is another file" > file2.txt
```

Now rename your first file to file1.txt by typing

```
mv file.txt file1.txt
```

If you now list the contents of the current directory, you'll see file1.txt and file2.txt.
Next, let's copy file1.txt to the directory one level up in the folder structure. Type

```
cp file1.txt ../file1.txt
```

Let's move file2.txt to our home directory, by typing

```
mv file2.txt ~/file2.txt
```

If you now list the contents of your home directory by typing

```
ls ../../
```

you'll see that file2.txt is there, while it has disappeared from your current directory. Congratulations! You've now successfully accomplished the most common file operations in the Linux command line, or shell!
Speaking of shells, Linux has several available in most distributions.

# Shells in Linux

Shells in Linux have names like the *Bourne shell*, the *C shell*, and the *Korn shell*. A shell is simply a text-based interface between the user and the operating system, allowing the user to execute commands directly to the file system. Each shell has its pros and cons, but it would be misleading to say that one is better than another. They are each simply different ways of doing the same thing. The *Bourne-again shell*, also referred to as *bash*, was written as a replacement for the Bourne shell and is the default on most Linux flavors, including the Pi's Raspbian. It can be identified with its login prompt, the "$." Bash has some keyboard shortcuts that can become very handy if you do a lot of editing and file manipulations in the terminal, as we will in our projects. (See Table 2-2.)

**Table 2-2.** *Bash Keyboard Shortcuts*

| Key or Key Combination | Function |
| --- | --- |
| Ctrl + A | Move cursor to beginning of line |
| Ctrl + C | Stop currently-executing process |
| Ctrl + D | Log out—equivalent to typing **exit** |
| Ctrl + E | Move cursor to end of line |
| Ctrl + H | Delete character in front of cursor |
| Ctrl + L | Clear terminal |
| Ctrl + R | Search command history |
| Ctrl + Z | Suspend a program |
| Arrow Left/Right | Move cursor left/right one character |
| Arrow Up/Down | Scrolls through previous commands |
| Shift + PageUp/PageDown | Move one page up or down in terminal output |
| Tab | Command or file name completion |
| Tab Tab | Shows all command or file name possibilities |

Again, most of the shortcuts are self-explanatory, but the last two bear some additional explanations:

- Tab: Pressing the Tab key when you're in the middle of typing a long file name will either complete the file name for you or offer you a list of choices. For example, if you are in the /Desktop/MyFiles/ directory and would like to quickly scan the myextralongfilename.txt file, simply type cat myextr and then press Tab. Bash will fill in the file name for you, assuming there are no other files with similar beginnings. If there are others that start with myextr, bash will make an error sound; in this case, press Tab again to see a list of choices.

- Tab Tab: This shortcut works with commands as well. In your terminal, type l and press the Tab key twice. Bash will respond with all available commands that start with "*l.*" (It can be a fairly long list.) You can repeat the process by adding one letter at a time and pressing Tab twice again—the shell will fill in all possible commands or files, giving you a preview of all possible outcomes.

# Package Managers

When you need to install a program from an online source in Windows, you normally download an .exe or .msi file, double-click it, and follow the instructions to install the program. Similarly, if you're using a Mac, you download a .dmg file and either copy the extracted file onto your hard drive or use the included installation package.

Linux, however, is a little different. Linux keeps track of its software using a package-management system, or *package manager*. The package manager is used to download, install, upgrade, configure, and remove programs for the operating system. Most package managers maintain an internal database of installed software as well as all dependencies and conflicts to prevent problems when installing software. Package managers vary by distribution. Debian (and the Pi) use *aptitude*, while Fedora uses the RPM package manager, and Puppy Linux uses PETget. If you have experience playing downloaded games, you may be familiar with Steam games; you may be surprised to learn that Steam's interface is a variant of a package manager. Most package managers have both command-line and graphics interfaces. Ubuntu, for instance, uses the Synaptic front end for its aptitude manager.

Like Ubuntu, the Raspberry Pi uses the aptitude package manager, and you'll probably do most of your work with it in the terminal. The common command to use to install a piece of software is

```
sudo apt-get install package name
```

which instructs the manager to do the following:

1. Determine which of its software sources, or *repositories*, has the requested file.

2. Contact that repository and determine what dependencies are necessary.

3. Download and install those dependencies.

4. Download and install the requested software.

If this seems easy, it should—it's supposed to be. You may run into problems when you request a piece of software not included in your installed repositories, but even this is normally an easy fix. If this should happen, just type

```
sudo add-apt repository repository name
```

into your terminal. When that's done, type

```
sudo apt-get update
```

to let your package manager know about the new repository, and then type

```
sudo apt-get install package name
```

again. Luckily, the default repositories included in Raspbian hold most of the software you'll ever need, so (for this book, anyway) you probably won't run into this problem.

## Text Editors

Unlike Windows and Mac—which have Notepad, Wordpad, and Textedit—Linux has several possibilities when it comes to text editors. There is a standard editor installed on most distributions, called gedit. Not only is it rather lightweight, it is also not included on the Pi. The Pi's built-in text editor, Leafpad, is decent. And you may also find yourself getting comfortable with nano—another text editor that is pre-installed on the Pi and has a very intuitive interface. But if you do any serious programming work on the Pi, you may eventually want to upgrade to one of Linux's two powerhouses: vi or emacs.

Both vi and emacs are not only powerful editors, they can be used as IDEs (Integrated Development Environments) as well, with keyword text coloring/syntax highlighting and word completion. Both are extensible and customizable; emacs, for instance, has over 2,000 built-in commands, while vi can be customized with its many ports and clones. In fact, one of vi's clones, Vim (Vi Improved), is included with almost every Linux distribution and is the one I'll discuss here because it is more of an IDE than its predecessor, vi. Emacs can be user-programmable with Lisp extensions, but there is a clone of vi for every sense of aesthetic you may have.

There is, however, a sort of war going on between emacs and Vim. Linux and Unix users strongly prefer one or the other, and they will get surprisingly animated when discussing/arguing the pros and cons of each. As a conscientious writer, I will introduce you to both programs here, but as a die-hard emacs user, I will do my best to sway your choice away from the swill that is Vim. As we discuss programs and scripts throughout the book, I won't mention how they're written, merely what the end result looks like. You may even decide you like the Pi's Leafpad, which is perfectly all right as well.

## Vim vs. emacs vs. nano

Vim is a modal editor. It has two modes: *insert* and *normal*. In insert mode, your keystrokes become part of the document. Normal mode is used to control the editing session. For example, if you type an "i" while in normal mode, it switches you to insert mode. If you then type an "**i**" again, an "*i*" will be placed at the cursor's position, exactly as you would expect a text editor to operate. By switching back and forth between these two modes, you create and edit your document.

Emacs, on the other hand, has a more intuitive interface. You can move throughout the document using the arrow keys, and when you press a key, you can expect it to appear wherever the cursor happens to be. Special commands, like copy/paste, save, and so forth are called by pressing the Control key, followed by a sequence of others, usually starting with the "x." So, for instance, if you wanted to save the current document, you would press Ctrl-x, then Ctrl-s, highlighted in the emacs menu as C-x C-s.

Nano, on the *other* other hand, is more intuitive than both of the others. You enter text as you would in any other editor, and the commands you use are always shown at the bottom of the screen.

If you would like to experiment with one or all three of them (always a good idea before you make up your mind one way or the other), make sure you have all of them installed. To do that, start by typing

```
sudo apt-get install emacs
```

and

```
sudo apt-get install vim
```

Vim should be preinstalled on the Pi, as is nano; emacs, however, is not. Be aware that it's a rather large download, so installing it and its dependencies may take a little while. Go have a cup of coffee or eat dinner, and when you come back it should be waiting for you.

## Using Vim

As I said, vim is a modal editor, meaning that you switch in and out of Insert and Normal modes. To start a test file, navigate to your desktop and type

```
vim testfile.txt
```

Rather than opening another window, vim opens in the terminal, which can get confusing if you're not used to it. You should be faced with a window not unlike the one in Figure 2-4.

**Figure 2-4.** *Blank vim file*

Vim opens in Normal mode, meaning that you cannot edit the file right away. To do so, you must enter Insert mode by typing "**i**." The word "INSERT" will appear at the bottom left—a handy way of reminding you whether you're in Insert or Normal mode. When you're done typing, press the Esc key to return to Normal mode. In Normal mode, you can move around the document with the arrow keys, just as you can in Insert mode, but you can't change or add anything until you type "**i**." To save a file, make sure you're in Normal mode by pressing the Esc key at least once. Then type "**:w**" (without the quotes) and press Enter. To save and exit at the same time, type "**:x**"(again, without quotes) and press Enter. Obviously, if you're in Insert mode when you type these characters, all you'll succeed in doing is adding **:w** or **:x** to your document.

Vim takes a lot of getting used to, and many people have trouble adjusting to the two different modes of operation. If you decide you like it, there are many tutorials online to teach you to use it to its full potential.

## Using Emacs

Emacs (to me, at least) is a bit more intuitive than Vim, particularly when you're first starting to use it. To start, open a terminal and navigate to where you want your test file, such as the desktop. Once there, type

```
emacs testfile.txt
```

Emacs will look for `testfile.txt`, open it if it exists, and create it and open it if it doesn't. You'll be faced with a blank pane, like the one you see in Figure 2-5.

**Figure 2-5.** *Emacs opening screen*

You can start typing immediately. Table 2-3 lists the most common commands in emacs.

**Table 2-3.** *Common Commands in emacs*

| Command | Keystroke(s) |
|---------|--------------|
| Open/New | Ctrl+x + Ctrl+f |
| Close | Ctrl+x + Ctrl+c |
| Save | Ctrl+x + Ctrl+s |
| Cut | Ctrl+w |
| Copy | Alt+w |
| Paste | Ctrl+y |
| Jump to beginning of line | Ctrl+a |
| Jump to end of line | Ctrl+e |
| Start/end select | Ctrl+space |

So, for instance, if you want to move a line of text, move your cursor to the beginning of the line. Press Ctrl and the space bar—the status text at the bottom left of the window will read "Mark activated." Then move your cursor to the end of the line with Ctrl and "**e**." The status text will disappear. Now cut the selected text by pressing Ctrl+w, move your cursor to where you want to paste it, and press Ctrl+y.

It does take some getting used to, so if you decide you like emacs, there are many tutorials online that can take you through the process of learning the keystrokes. Once you learn it, it can be very powerful, but always remember this: If you get confused, remember that most if not all of these commands are accessible from the menu.

## Using nano

As mentioned earlier, nano is probably the easiest of the three editors to use and get used to. To start a file in nano, simply type

```
nano testfile.txt
```

into your terminal, and you should be greeted by a screen like the one in Figure 2-6. As with the other two editors, if the specified file exists, nano will open it; if it doesn't exist, nano will create it for you.

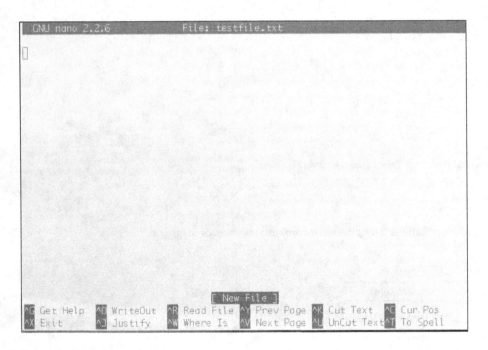

**Figure 2-6.** *nano opening screen*

As you can see in Figure 2-6, common commands are listed at the bottom, with the caret character (^) signifying the Ctrl key. To save a file, type Ctrl+X to exit. You'll be asked if you want to save the file, and under what name. In general, type "**Y**" and then Enter to save the file you've opened or created.

## Leafpad

The other editor I should describe is Leafpad—the full-featured (if lightweight), GUI-based text editor that comes preinstalled on the Pi. To open it, click the icon at the extreme lower left of the Pi's desktop, and then select "Accessories" and then "Leafpad." (See Figure 2-7.)

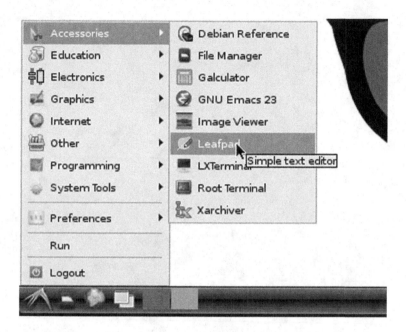

***Figure 2-7.*** *Opening Leafpad*

As you'll see, it looks like most editors you're used to, such as Textedit or Notepad. If you're comfortable using it, by all means, please do. I don't mention it much only because its one main drawback is that it is usable only if you're working on the Pi's graphic desktop. If you're remotely logged in to the Pi and are working solely through the command line, Leafpad is inaccessible.

# Summary

This concludes your introduction to Linux. While it in no way makes you an expert, it should give you a healthy appreciation for all that this powerful OS can do. You learned the basics of how to navigate through your file system using only the command line, and you were introduced to the shell. You've also been introduced to the choices of text editors you have available to you and have hopefully chosen one that you are comfortable with. Once you've muddled around with it on your Pi enough, you may find yourself installing Linux on one or more of your other machines. It's okay—I won't tell anybody.

In the next chapter, I'll do my best to give you a solid introduction to Python.

# CHAPTER 3

■ ■ ■

# Introducing Python

You may remember from the first chapter that the impetus behind the creation of the Raspberry Pi was to make programming more accessible for everyone, particularly kids. To that end, the creators wanted to release a relatively powerful computer that wouldn't cost a lot of money and one that anyone could simply connect to a keyboard, mouse, and monitor and start programming.

Another facet of that creation was to make programming easier, and for that reason Eben Upton and his companions decided to include Python as an integral part of the Pi's operating system. Python, they reasoned, was a powerful language, yet it was simple enough for someone without any programming experience to pick up quickly.

In this chapter, I'll give you a quick-and-dirty introduction to Python, walking you through the process of creating a few scripts, running them, and along the way learning some of the basics of this powerful language. I'll assume that you have at least a passing knowledge of what Python is and perhaps a slight bit of knowledge of programming, but no more than that, because—let's face it—that's why you bought this book.

## Scripting vs. a Programming Language

Python is a scripting language. Some may quibble over whether it's a *programming* language or a *scripting* language, but to keep the strict technocrats happy, we'll call it a scripting language.

A scripting language differs from a true programming language in a few ways. As you read the following comparisons, take note of the italics:

- Programming languages are compiled, unlike scripting languages. Common languages like C, C++, and Java must be compiled by a compiler. The compilation process results in a file of machine code, unreadable by humans, that the computer can read and follow. When you write a program in C and compile it, the resulting .o file is what is read by the computer. One of the side effects/results of this is that programming languages *may* produce faster programs—both because the compilation only happens once and because the compiler often optimizes the code during the compilation process, making it faster than it would be as originally written.

  Scripting languages, on the other hand, are read, interpreted, and acted upon each time you run them. They don't produce a compiled file, and the instructions are followed exactly as written. If you write sloppy code, you get sloppy results. For this reason, scripting languages *can* result in slower programs.

- Programming/compiled languages *most often* run directly on top of the hardware on which they are written. When you write and compile a program in C++, the resulting code is executed directly by the processor on your desktop machine.

  Scripting languages most often run "inside" another program—one that takes care of the compiling step just mentioned. PHP, a common scripting language, runs inside the PHP scripting engine. Bash scripts run inside the bash shell, which you were introduced to in the previous chapter.

- Programming languages *tend to be* more complex and difficult to learn.

  Scripting languages can be more readable, are less syntax-strict, and are less intimidating to nonprogrammers.

  For this reason alone, scripting languages are often taught in introductory programming courses in schools, and students are not introduced to stricter languages like C or Java until they have mastered the basics of programming.

However, the lines between the two have become so blurred in the past few years as to almost completely make the distinctions between the two disappear. To enumerate:

- While it is true that strict programming languages are compiled and scripting languages are not, advances in processor speeds and memory management in today's computers have almost made the speed advantages of compiled languages obsolete. A program written to perform a certain task in C and one written in Python may both do so with almost negligible differences in speed. Certain tasks may indeed be faster, but not all.

- Yes, scripting languages run inside another program. However, Java is considered a "true" programming language, because it must be compiled when run, but it runs inside the Java Virtual Machine on each device. This, in fact, is why Java is so portable: the code is transferable, as long as a version of the Virtual Machine is running on your specific device. C# is also a compiled language, but it runs inside another programming environment.

- Okay, I can't really argue with the fact that programming languages *tend to be* more complex and difficult to learn, and scripting languages *do* tend to be easier to read and learn, with fewer syntax rules and more English-like context. Take, for example, the following two ways to print "Hello, world!" to the screen.

In C++, you use this:

```
#include <iostream>
using namespace std;
int main() {
    cout << "Hello, world!" << endl;
    return 0;
}
```

In Python, you use this:

```
print "Hello, world!"
```

Of course, there are exceptions; I have seen Python scripts that were almost illegible. Likewise, there are some *very* readable C programs floating about. But in general, scripts can be easier for the novice programmer to learn, and they can be just as powerful.

Yes, you can program the Pi in C, C++, and even Java or (if you're particularly masochistic) in assembly language. But now that you know and have seen the difference between programming and scripting languages, wouldn't you much rather use Python?

Using Python to program the Pi means that many people who would never dream of programming a computer can pick up a Raspberry Pi and do something really cool with it, like build one of the projects presented in this book, without learning a difficult language. This is, after all, why the Pi exists: to make programming accessible to more students, and for that reason Python comes preinstalled on the Pi.

# The Python Philosophy

In the world of scripting languages, Python is a relative newcomer to the scene, though not as recent as many people believe. It was developed in the late 1980s, perhaps 15 years after the conception of Unix.

It was implemented in December 1989 by its principal author, Guido Van Rossum. He has remained active in Python's development and progress, and his contributions to the language have been rewarded by the Python community, which gifted him with the title Benevolent Dictator For Life (BDFL).

Python's philosophy has always been to make code readable and accessible. That philosophy has been summed up in Python's "PEP 20 (The Zen Of Python)" document, which reads as follows:

- Beautiful is better than ugly.

- Explicit is better than implicit.

- Simple is better than complex.

- Complex is better than complicated.

- Flat is better than nested.

- Sparse is better than dense.

- Readability counts.

- Special cases aren't special enough to break the rules.

- Although practicality beats purity.

- Errors should never pass silently.

- Unless explicitly silenced.

- In the face of ambiguity, refuse the temptation to guess.

- There should be one—and preferably only one—obvious way to do it.

- Although that way may not be obvious at first unless you're Dutch.

- Now is better than never.

- Although never is often better than *right* now.

- If the implementation is hard to explain, it's a bad idea.

- If the implementation is easy to explain, it may be a good idea.

- Namespaces are one honking great idea—let's do more of those!

In addition to these commandments, Python has a "batteries included" mindset, which means that whatever strange task you need to do in Python, chances are good that a module already exists to do just that, so you don't have to reinvent the wheel.

# Getting Started with Python

Let's get started. There are three ways to run Python on your Pi: using the built-in interpreter IDLE, in a terminal window, or as a script. We'll begin by using IDLE.

## Running Python Using IDLE

The IDLE interpreter is a sort of "sandbox" where you can work with Python interactively without having to write whole scripts to see what they do. The name IDLE stands for "Integrated DeveLopment Environment," but it also pays homage to Eric Idle, one of the founding members of the British comedy group Monty Python. (See the sidebar "Get Me a Shrubbery!")

Because it's the most user-friendly way of trying out code, let's use IDLE first. Double-click the icon on your desktop (shown in Figure 3-1), and you should be greeted by a window like Figure 3-2.

**Figure 3-1.** *The IDLE icon*

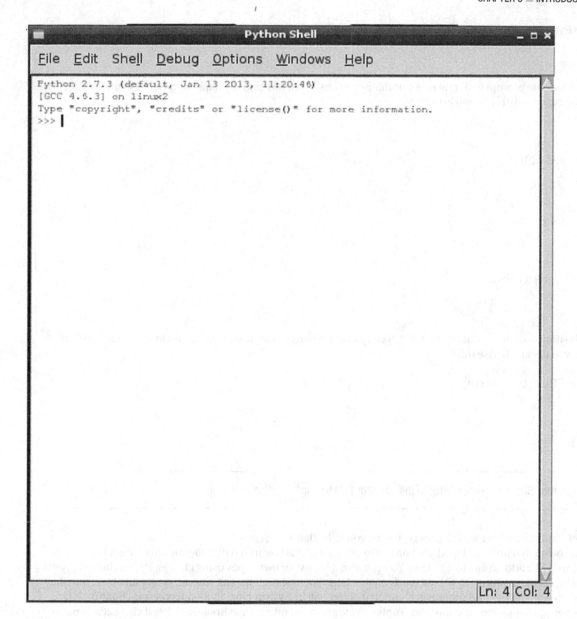

```
Python Shell                                              _ □ ✕

File   Edit   Shell   Debug   Options   Windows   Help

Python 2.7.3 (default, Jan 13 2013, 11:20:46)
[GCC 4.6.3] on linux2
Type "copyright", "credits" or "license()" for more information.
>>> |




















                                                              Ln: 4 Col: 4
```

***Figure 3-2.*** *The IDLE window*

To follow the great programming tradition, let's start with the first program a programmer ever writes in any language. At the prompt, type

```
>>> print "Hello, world!"
```

and press Enter. You should immediately be greeted with

```
Hello, world!
```

This is Python's print statement, whose default output is to the screen. Now type

```
>>> x=4
```

and press Enter. The prompt will return, but nothing happens. What has actually happened is that Python's interpreter has now associated x with 4. If you now type

```
>>> x
```

you'll be greeted with

4

Likewise, if you type

```
>>> print x
```

you'll again be greeted with

4

This illustrates another cool aspect of Python: *dynamic typing*. In languages like C, you must define a variable's type before you declare it, like this:

```
string x = "This is a string";
```

or

```
int x = 5;
```

---

■ **Note**    See the "Strings" section later in this chapter for more information on strings.

---

Python "knows" that x is an `int` (integer) when you tell it that x = 5.

Despite being dynamically typed, Python is *strongly typed*. This means it will throw an error rather than allow you to do things like add an `int` to a `string`. You can also define your own types using classes; Python fully supports object-oriented programming (OOP). I'll touch on that later, but in short it means you can create an object that may be a mix of integers, strings and other types, and that object will be its own type. Python has several built-in data types: Numbers, Strings, Lists, Dictionaries, Tuples, Files, and a few others (like Booleans). We'll visit each of these briefly later in the chapter.

Moving forward, let's try playing with some variables and operations inside of IDLE. Typing

```
>>> print x+5
```

will return 9; however, typing

```
>>> x + "dad"
```

results in an error. In this vein, however, typing

```
>>> "DAD" + "hello"
```

gives you

```
'DADhello'
```

because, to Python, adding strings is the same as concatenating them. If you'd like to make a list, enclose it in square brackets:

```
>>> y = ['rest', 1234, 'sleep']
```

Also, a dictionary—a type of file made up of associated keys and key values—is enclosed in curly braces:

```
>>> z = {'food' : 'spam' , 'taste' : 'yum'}
```

---

■ **Note**    Keys and key values are an integral part of Python dictionaries. They're just linked pairs of values. For example, in the z dictionary in the preceding code example, 'food' and 'spam' are a key and a key value, respectively. Likewise, 'taste' and 'yum' are a key and a key value. To use a dictionary, you input its key, and the associated key value is returned.

---

## GET ME A SHRUBBERY!

Python is *not* named after the snake; rather, its creator, van Rossum, named it after the BBC comedy troupe Monty Python, of whom he is a huge fan. As a result, Monty Python references abound in the language. The traditional "foo" and "bar" used to illustrate code in other programs become "spam" and "eggs" in Python examples. You'll see references to "Brian," "ni," and "shrubbery," all of which should make perfect sense to you if you are a fan of Monty Python. Even the interpreter, IDLE, is named after M.P. member Eric Idle. If you are not familiar with their work, I urge you to put down this book and go watch some of their sketches. I heartily recommend *The Dead Parrot Sketch* and *The Ministry of Silly Walks*. It's not necessary to be familiar with their work to learn the language, but it may help increase your enjoyment of it.

## Running Python Using the Terminal

Let's quickly visit another way of using Python, which is to use the terminal. Open the terminal on your Pi's desktop, and at the prompt type **Python**. You'll be greeted with the same introductory text as that which opens the IDLE window and the same interactive >>> prompt. At this point, you can issue the same commands as discussed in the preceding section "Running Python Using IDLE," and get the same results.

# Running Python Using Scripts

The problem with both IDLE and the terminal is that you can't write true "scripts." As soon as you close the window, any variables you've declared disappear, and there's no way to save your work. The last method of writing Python, in a text editor, addresses that problem. You can write a full-length program, save it with a .py extension, and then run it from a terminal.

Let's write a very short script using Leafpad, the Pi's native text editor. Open it from the Accessories menu (as shown in Figure 3-3).

***Figure 3-3.*** *Opening Leafpad*

In the resulting window, type the following:

```
x = 4
y = x +2
print y
```

Save it to your desktop as test.py. Now open a terminal and navigate to your desktop by typing

```
cd ~/Desktop
```

You can now run your script by typing

```
python test.py
```

You should be rewarded with the number 6. Congratulations! You've just written, saved, and run your first Python script!

When you write the scripts in this book, feel free to use any text editor you wish. If you're comfortable using Leafpad, by all means use it. I tend to use nano or emacs, the terminal-based editors, because I often log in to my Pi remotely, and Leafpad can't be run in a remote login session. For that reason, I'll tell you to edit a file like so:

```
sudo nano spam-and-eggs.py
```

but use whichever editor you wish.

Next, let's look at each data type briefly and see what you can do with each.

## Exploring Python's Data Types

As mentioned earlier, Python provides you with several built-in data types. In the following sections, you'll learn about Numbers, Strings, Lists, Dictionaries, Tuples, and Files.

## Numbers

Numbers seem self-explanatory, and indeed, if you have any programming experience you'll recognize Python's number types: integers, shorts, longs, floats, and others. Python has expression operators that allow you to perform calculations on those numbers; these include +, - , / and *, %; comparison operators such as >, >=, and !=, or, and and; and many others.

All of these operators are built in, but you can *import* others by using another of Python's great characteristics: importing *modules*. Modules are extra libraries you can import into your script that add to Python's native functionality. In this respect, Python is much like Java: if you want to do something, chances are *very* good that a library exists to make it easier. For example, if you want to parse text, such as web pages, you can check out the Beautiful Soup module. Need to log in to a remote computer (and you will, with some projects)? Import the telnetlib module and everything you need is available. And for numbers, the math module has all sorts of mathematical functions that add to Python's number functionality. You can try it for yourself: in an IDLE session, type

```
>>> abs(-16)
```

and you should get the result 16. That's because the absolute value function (I discuss the topic of functions in its own section later in this chapter) is already contained in Python's default libraries. However, typing

```
>>> ceil(16.7)
```

will return an error, because the ceiling function is *not* in those default libraries. It must be imported. Now type

```
>>> import math
>>> math.ceil(16.7)
```

and the terminal will return 17.0,—the *ceiling* of x, or the smallest integer greater than x. While you may not need to use the ceiling function, simply importing the math module gives you all kinds of extra functionality, such as logarithmic and trigonometric functions and angular conversions, all with just one line of code.

# Strings

In Python, a string is defined as an ordered collection of characters used to represent text-based information. Python doesn't have a char type like C and other languages; a single character is simply a one-character string. Strings can contain anything viewable as text: letters, numbers, punctuation, program names, and so on. This means, of course, that

```
>>> x = 4
```

and

```
>>> x = "4"
```

are *not* the same thing. You can add 3 to the first example of x, but if you tried it with the second example, Python would give an error—*that* x points to a string with a value of 4, not an integer, because the 4 is enclosed in quotes. Python does not distinguish between single and double quotes; you can enclose a string in either, and it will be recognized as a string. This has a nice side effect: you can enclose a quote character of the other type inside a string without having to escape with a backslash as you would have to in C. For example:

```
>>> "Brian's"
```

gives you

```
"Brian's"
```

without any escape characters needed.

There are some basic string operations you will probably use many times in your Python career, such as len (the length of a string), concatenation, iteration, indexing, and slicing (Python's equivalent of the substring operation). To illustrate, type the following bits of code into an IDLE session and see that the results match the output of what you see here:

```
>>> len('shrubbery')
9
```

'shrubbery' is 9 characters long.

```
>>> 'spam ' + 'and ' + 'eggs'
'spam and eggs'
```

'spam ', 'and ', and 'eggs' are concatenated

```
>>> title = "Meaning of Life"
>>> for c in title: print c,
...
M e a n i n g   o f   L i f e
```

For every character in 'title', print it.

```
>>> s = "spam"
>>>s[0], s[2]
('s', 'a')
```

The first ([0]) and third ([2]) characters of "spam" are 's' and 'a'.

```
>>> s[1:3]
'pa'
```

The second through the fourth characters are 'pa'. (When naming a range of characters in a string, the first parameter is inclusive, the second is not.)

You can also convert to and from string objects for those times when you have an integer that is currently typed as a string, like "4", and you need to square it. To do that, it's as simple as typing

```
>>> int("4") ** 2
16
```

You can convert to and from ASCII code, format with escape characters like %d and %s, convert from uppercase to lowercase, and a whole host of other operations, just with Python's built-in string library.

## Lists

Lists, along with dictionaries, are arguably the most powerful of Python's built-in data types. They are actually collections of other data types and incredibly flexible. They can be changed in place, grow and shrink on demand, and contain and be contained in other kinds of objects.

If you have experience with other programming languages, you might recognize Python lists as equivalent to arrays of pointers in, say, C. As a matter of fact, lists are actually arrays in C inside the Python interpreter. As such, they can be collections of any other type of object, since their contained pointer objects can be pointing to literally any other data type, including other lists. They are also indexable—as fast as indexing a C array. They can grow and shrink in-place like C++ and C#'s lists; they can be sliced, diced, concatenated—pretty much anything you do with strings, you can do with lists.

To create a list, you declare it with square brackets ( [ ] ) like so:

```
>>> l = [1, 2, 3, 4, 5]
```

or

```
>>> shrubbery = ["spam", 1, 2, 3, "56"]
```

after which you can play all sorts of games with them, like concatenating and so on:

```
>>> l + shrubbery
[1, 2, 3, 4, 5, 'spam', 1, 2, 3, '56']

>>> len (shrubbery)
5

>>> for x in l: print x,
...
1 2 3 4 5

>>> shrubbery[3]
3
```

(You may notice here that lists, like arrays, are indexed starting from 0.) By using index and slice operations, you can change lists in place as a combination delete and insert:

```
>>> cast = ["John", "Eric", "Terry", "Graham", "Michael"]
>>> cast [0:2] = ["Cleese", "Idle", "Gilliam"]
>>> cast
['Cleese', 'Idle', 'Gilliam', 'Graham', 'Michael']
```

Lists also allow you to use function calls that are associated with and specific to them, like append, sort, reverse, and pop. For an updated list (no pun intended!) of list's functions, type

```
>>> help(list)
```

for an up-to-date breakdown of everything available.

---

■ **Note**  Python's help function is extremely useful. If you don't know how to do something or what's available, typing **help(<confusing object>)** at the prompt can aid you immensely. (See the sidebar "Python Help.")

---

## PYTHON HELP

If you ever get stuck in Python, its online documentation is a very useful resource. Point your browser to http://docs.python.org/2/library/stdtypes.html, and you can read about all of the standard data types available to you and how to use them. Likewise, http://docs.python.org/2/library/functions.html will show you all of the functions that are always available to you to use. Its built-in help function is also very thorough. To try it, in an IDLE session, type

```
import string
```

and then

```
help (string)
```

You'll be rewarded with everything you ever wanted to know about strings.

# Dictionaries

Like lists, Python dictionaries are extremely flexible collections of objects. Dictionaries differ in that, unlike lists, they are unordered; you can access items of a list by their index, but items in a dictionary are accessed by *key*. In other words, dictionaries contain key-value pairs; requesting the key will return the value associated with that key. For example, in the following dictionary, the value 'spam' can be accessed by its key, 'food':

```
>>> dict = {'food' : 'spam', 'drink' : 'beer'}
>>> dict['food']
'spam'
```

Like lists, dictionaries can be nested:

```
>>> dict2 = {'food' : {'ham' : 1, 'eggs' : 2}}
```

The means the key 'food' has an associated key value of {'ham':1, 'eggs':2}, which is itself a dictionary. Dictionaries have certain method calls specific to them:

```
>>> dict.keys()
['food', 'drink']
```

This lists all of the keys in dict.

```
>>> dict.has_key('food')
True
```

This returns 'True' if dict contains the key 'food', and returns 'False' otherwise. Dictionaries can be changed in place

```
>>> dict['food'] = ['eggs']
>>> dict
{'food' : ['eggs'], 'drink' : 'beer'}
```

This changes the key value of 'food' from 'spam' to 'eggs'. (Here, you'll notice that 'eggs', aside from being a normal item, is also a one-item list.)

---

■ **Note**    Keys do not always need to be strings, as you've seen here. You can use any immutable objects as keys; if you happen to use integers, the dictionary behaves more like a list—that is, is indexable (by integer key.)

---

## Tuples and Files

The last major data types I'll mention here are tuples and files. Tuples are collections of other objects that cannot be changed, and files refer to the interface to file objects on your computer.

Tuples are ordered collections of objects. They are very much like lists, but unlike lists, they can't be changed in place and are written with parentheses, not square brackets, like this:

```
>>> t = (0, 'words', 23, [1, 2, 3])
```

Here, t contains two integers, a string and a list. You can nest tuples, index them, slice them, and do pretty much everything else you can do with a list.

So why are there tuples if they're almost exactly like lists? The most commonly accepted answer to that is because they're immutable—they can't be changed. By declaring a collection of objects as a tuple rather than a list, you ensure that that collection won't be changed somewhere else in your program. It's sort of like declaring something as a const in C—if you try to change it later, the compiler will give you an error.

Recall that I talked about files in Chapter 2, so the notion should be familiar to you. Python has a built-in function, open, that creates a file object that links to a file sitting in your computer's memory. File objects are a bit different than the other types, as they are really nothing more than a collection of functions that can be called on those external files. Those functions include read, write, open, close, and various parsing functions for text files. To illustrate, the following lines open a file test.txt (or create it if it doesn't exist already) for writing, writes a line of text to it (complete with a newline escape character), and then closes the file:

```
>>> myfile = open ('test.txt', 'w')
>>> myfile.write ('hello there, text file!\n')
>>> myfile.close()
```

All this happens within whatever directory you happen to be in when you execute the lines.

Note, however, that as written, if test.txt already exists, its contents will be overwritten by the myfile.write() call. If you want to *append* to the file rather than overwrite it, use an 'a' flag when you open it rather than a 'w'.

Once you have a file open, you can read from and write to it, bearing in mind that you can only read string objects from file objects. This simply means that you must convert all objects in the file to their "real" data types before you perform any operations on them; if myfile.readline() returns '456', you must convert that 456 to an integer with int() if you want to perform calculations on it.

File operations are very useful, because they allow you to create and write to text files, but they're a bit beyond the scope of this introductory chapter. We'll revisit them later as we use them in projects.

As you can see, Python's built-in data types can do anything a true "programming language" can do—sometimes more easily and more economically. By combining the types, you can do some truly powerful processes with Python, as you'll see next.

# Programming with Python

Now that you've seen the data types, let's investigate how to use them in actual programs. To create a Python program, you must exit the interpreter and open a text editor, such as emacs or the Pi's Leafpad. After you create the program, save it with a ".py" extension. You'll then be able to run it by typing

```
$ python myprogram.py
```

Python is unique among programming languages in its syntax in that it blocks out code using whitespace or indentation blocks. Languages like C enclose a block of code such as an if statement within curly braces; Python uses a colon and indentation to delineate the block.

Code in C looks like this:

```
if (x == 4)
{
    printf ("x is equal to four\n");
    printf ("Nothing more to do here.");
}
printf ("The if statement is now over.");
```

The same code in Python looks like this:

```
if x == 4 :
    print "x is equal to four"
    print "Nothing more to do here."
print "The if statement is now over."
```

You may notice two additional details about the Python program. First, the parentheses in the if statement are not necessary. In Python, parentheses are optional, but in most cases it's considered good programming practice to use them, as it enhances your code readability. You'll also notice that most other languages end their lines of code with a semicolon; Python does not. This may take some getting used to, but it is a nice change to not have a program fail to compile because you've got a misplaced or missing semicolon somewhere in it. In Python, the end of the line is the end of the statement—that simple.

You've seen statements already, such as

```
x = 4
y = "This is a string."
```

As mentioned earlier, Python doesn't require declarations telling it that x is an integer and y is a string—it just *knows*. These statements are known as *assignments*, where the value on the right is assigned to the variable on the left. There are various variable naming conventions in different languages, but the best advice I can give you is to just pick a convention and stick with it. If you prefer Pascal case (ThisIsAVariable), use it; if you prefer camelback (thisIsAVariable), use that one. Just be consistent—you'll thank yourself later. In any case, an assignment does just that: assigns a value to a variable, whether that variable is a number, string, list, or something else. It's the simplest of the programming functions.

# IF tests

The next programming functionality we'll look at is the if statement and its derivatives—elif and else. Just as you'd expect, if performs a test and then selects from alternatives based on those test results. The most basic if statement looks like this:

```
>>> if 1:
...     print 'true'
...
True
```

'1' is the same as the Boolean "true," so the preceding statement will always print "true."

---

■ **Note**  When you type the if statement at the Python prompt in your terminal (or IDLE) and end it with a colon, the next prompt will always be the ellipsis (. . .), meaning Python is expecting an indented block. If you're done with the indented block, just press Enter again to end it. If you're writing a program in a text editor, make sure you indent the blocks you need to indent.

---

From here on, I'll format the code as if it were in a text editor and print the output as if you had run the script. A more complicated test uses elif and else, such as the following:

```
x = 'spam'
if x == 'eggs':
    print "eggs are better when they're green!"
elif x == 'ham':
    print 'this little piggy stayed home!'
else:
    print "Spam is a wonderful thing!"
```

Obviously, this code outputs "Spam is a wonderful thing!" When the program is executed, the computer checks the first if. If that statement is determined to be true, it executes the indented block directly after it. If that statement is false, it skips the indented block and looks for an elif, which it then evaluates. Again, if it's determined to be true, or if there is no elif, the computer executes the following block; if not, it skips that block and looks for another elif or an else.

Three points here are important enough to mention: First, remember that if an if statement is determined to be false, *nothing* in the following indented block is executed—the computer jumps straight to the next unindented line.

Second, Python, like other languages, uses the double equal signs to indicate a test for equality. A single equal sign is used for assignments; a double is a test. I mention this because every programmer—and I do mean *every* programmer—has, at some point, used a single equals sign in an if statement, and their program has done all sorts of funky, unexpected things as a result. You'll do it too, but I hope to save you at least a little exasperation ahead of time.

Third, Python ignores blank lines and spaces (except at the interactive prompt and indented blocks, of course) and comments. This is important because it frees you to make sure your code is readable to other programmers, even if that other programmer is you at a later date.

---

■ **Note** Comments in Python are preceded with a "#"; the program ignores anything on that line after it.

---

Readability in your code is a big deal; expect me to drum that into your head regularly. Would you rather attempt to debug the preceding program or something like this:

```
x='this is a test'
if x=='this is not a test':
    print"This is not "+x+" nor is it a test"
    print 89*2/34+5
else:
    print x+" and I'm glad "+x+str(345*43/2)
print"there are very few spaces in this program"
```

While you can certainly read the second one, it's no fun, and after hundreds of lines of code with no spaces, blank lines or comments, your eyes will thank you—trust me. Look at the difference just in the second-to-last line if you use spaces:

```
print x + " and I'm glad " + x + str(345 * 43 / 2)
```

You're allowed to use white spaces; use them liberally.

The last part of the if statement I want to mention is the Boolean operators. In a truth test, X and Y is true if both X and Y are true. X or Y is true if either X or Y is true, and not X is true if X is false. Python uses the words, rather than C or C++'s &&, ||, or ! operators. Learn these operators; they'll come in very handy.

# Loops

Normally, a program is executed from top to bottom, one line at a time. However, certain statements can cause the program execution to jump all over the place; these *control-flow statements* include if/thens and loops.

The simplest loop is probably a block of code, executed a fixed number of times, such as

```
for x in range (0, 10):
    print "hello"
```

This simply prints

```
hello
hello
hello
hello
hello
hello
hello
hello
hello
hello
```

You can also use for loops to iterate through a string, or even a list:

```
for x in "Camelot":
    print "Ni!"
```

```
Ni!
Ni!
Ni!
Ni!
Ni!
Ni!
Ni!
```

or, to iterate through and print the characters themselves:

```
for x in "Camelot":
    print x
```

```
C
a
m
e
l
o
t
```

Although the for loop's syntax is a bit different than that of C or Java, once you get used to it, using the syntax becomes second nature.

The other loop statement is the while statement. This statement evaluates a condition and continues to execute the indented block as long as that statement is true:

```
x = 0
while (x < 10):
    print x
    x = x + 1
```

```
0
1
2
```

```
3
4
5
6
7
8
9
```

Unlike what you may have expected, this code never prints "10," because x is incremented after it's printed. On the tenth iteration, the interpreter prints "9" and then increments x to 10. At this point, the while condition is no longer true, so the code inside the block is never executed.

While statements are useful if you're waiting for a particular event to happen, like a keypress or a user pressing "Q" to exit. An example of this follows:

```
while True:
    var = raw_input ("Enter something, or 'q' to quit: ")
    print var
    if var == 'q':
        break
```

Two details to note about this script: first, in Python 2.x, the command raw_input is used to get input from a user. In Python 3.x, that command has changed to simply input. Second, remember the break command. This command literally breaks you out of the loop you happen to be in. So in this case, the while portion of the loop makes it go forever, but if the check var == 'q' returns true, the script breaks out of the loop and ends the program.

## Functions

Functions allow you, the programmer, to reuse code. They allow you to be more efficient. In general, if you find you need to perform a specific task in your code more than twice, that task is a likely candidate for a function.

Suppose you write a simple program that computes the area and perimeter of a rectangle. It asks the user to input the rectangle's height and width, and then performs the necessary calculations. One the simplest ways to do this is to create a function that takes as input parameters the rectangle's height and width. It then prints the rectangle's area and perimeter and returns to the program. To do this, we use a compound statement block, beginning with the def assignment. The def assignment is how we define a function, with the syntax def functionname (firstparameter, secondparameter):

```
def AreaPerimeter (height, width):
    height = int(height)
    width = int(width)
    area = height * width
    perimeter = (2 * height) + (2 * width)
    print "The area is: " + area
    print "The perimeter is: " + perimeter
    return

while True:
    h = raw_input ("Enter height: ")
    w = raw_input ("Enter width: ")
    AreaPerimeter (h, w)
```

This little program simply takes the numbers you feed it and returns the calculations. While this may not be the *best* example (you could just calculate on the fly with less code), it illustrates the idea of code reuse. With this function, no matter where in the program you need to calculate area or perimeter, all you need to do is call `AreaPerimeter` with the two parameters of `"height"` and `"width"` and it's done for you.

One point to note here: `raw_input` always returns a string, even if you enter numbers. That's why the `height` and `width` variables in `AreaPerimeter` must be converted to `int`s before any calculations can be performed.

Python's functions are slightly different in a few ways from methods, functions, and procedures in other languages, if you're familiar with other languages. For one thing, in Python all functions are *call-by-reference*. Without getting too deep into programming-speak, this means that when you pass a parameter to a function, you really only pass a pointer to a variable, not the variable itself. This has the effect of tending to make Python more memory friendly—you're not copying entire lists willy-nilly and passing them back and forth to functions, for example. Instead, if a function takes a list as a parameter, you pass it the memory location of the first item of the list, and it does what it needs to based on that location and item.

Another interesting aspect of functions is that they are executable statements. This means that a function definition can actually be declared and called within an `if` statement, for example. While not normal, it's legal (and sometimes useful) to be able to do this. `def`s can be nested inside loops, other `def`s, and even lists and dictionaries.

We'll visit functions again as we go through the projects; for now, be aware that they exist, and they are extremely useful parts of any program you write.

## Objects and Object-Oriented Programming

Another important item I want to address in this Python introduction is its native ability to run object-oriented code. While object-oriented programming (OOP) can be an advanced topic, and is probably beyond the scope of this book, it's an important enough topic to brush over lightly, methinks.

OOP is a paradigm in which program data is split up into a mix of *objects* and functions or methods. An object is a data type—normally a collection of data types like integers, strings, and so forth. Objects are normally part of *classes*, which have associated methods that act on members of that class.

Perhaps the easiest way to illustrate this is with an example using shapes. In this example, a *shape* is a class of objects. That class has associated values, such as `name` and `numberOfSides`. That class also has associated methods, like `findArea` or `findPerimeter`.

The `shape` class has subclasses, which are more specific. A `square` is a shape object, with the value `shapeType` equal to `square`, and `numberOfSides` equal to 4. Its `findArea` method takes the `numberOfSides` value and squares it. Meanwhile, a `triangle` object has different values for `name`, `shapeType`, and `numberOfSides`, and its `findArea` method is different.

This example, while a quick introduction to objects, also illustrates the concept of inheritance—an integral part of OOP. The `triangle` object *inherits* its name, `numberOfSides`, and `findArea` parts from its *parent* class, `shape` (though those parts have different values and implementations). If an object inherits from the `shape` class, it will also inherit those parts. It may not necessarily *use* those parts, but it has them. It may have additional parts (the `circle` object may have a `radius` value, for instance), but it will always have those parts.

If you start to use classes in your programming, Python is simpler to understand than its counterparts like C++ or Java. You can pretty much name any object or method with the following syntax: `object.attribute`, whether that attribute is an object or a method. If you have a `circle` object named `holyGrail`, its radius is `holyGrail.radius`. A square named `unexplodedScotsman` has an area defined by `unexplodedScotsman.findArea`.

Like I said, OOP is beyond the scope of this book. Like functions, however, it can be extremely useful, especially in longer, more intricate programs. Feel free to investigate further as you progress in your Python studies. You'll find that Python is a very versatile language as well, even allowing you to perform functional and other advanced programming tasks.

# Summary

In this chapter, I gave you a brief but practical introduction to Python, starting with a little of its history and then continuing with how to interact with the Python prompt, helping you learn some of its data types, and then showing you a little bit of script writing using an editor. Don't worry if you can't take all this information in at once; there's a lot to learn here, and I'll explain what I'm doing as we progress through the projects in the book.

In the next chapter, we'll take a look at Electronics 101. You're going to be building projects, after all, and before you do, you should have a basic grasp of the concepts of electricity, power, and various electronic parts and gizmos.

# CHAPTER 4

■ ■ ■

# Electronics at 100 MPH

You bought this book to learn to program using Python and to learn about the Raspberry Pi. You also want to build some cool projects, learn how the Pi runs Linux, and learn how you can use Python to interface with the Pi and various add-ons.

Well, we're going to get to that, but before we do I need to explain some other essential prerequisites—namely, the rules of electronics and electricity, tools, safety, and some how-tos. They may not be the most sexy topics, but any book that deals with building electronics projects should have at least one chapter that deals with concepts like *Ohm's Law* and *How To Solder*, and the fact that, yes, it's entirely possible to *electrocute yourself with a 9V battery*. *(See sidebar.)* Not to mention that I wouldn't want my readers to suffer any bodily injury because I didn't do enough safety instruction. So, please, at least skim this chapter, and take some notes if this information is completely new to you. If you finish the chapter and feel the need to protect yourself by dressing in a manner similar to Figure 4-1, that is perfectly all right.

***Figure 4-1.*** *Possible lab safety outfit*

---

**THE DARWIN AWARDS**

If you're not aware of them already, the Darwin Awards are humorous awards bestowed yearly upon those members of the human race who have managed to remove themselves from the gene pool, either through death or sterilization, due to their own stupidity. Past winners have included thieves electrocuting themselves while stealing copper wire from electrical substations, drivers who have switched places with their passengers while driving at highway speeds, and drug users injecting poppy seeds into their veins.

The 9V battery electrocution incident took place when a Navy sailor, in an attempt to measure his body's electrical resistance, stuck the pointed probes of his 9V multimeter into his thumbs, making his blood a perfect conductor. The current traveled across his heart, disrupting his heartbeat and killing him.

You can read more of the Darwin Awards at their website: www.darwinawards.com.

---

# Basic Electricity Concepts

> *. . . and he spake, and spake thusly: "There shall be one law, and that law is of Ohm, and it is that V is equal to I times R."*

OK, I know this quote is somewhat cheesy; however, Ohm's Law is indeed the first thing any electrical engineering student learns, and it affects everything you do in electronics. It means that the total voltage (V; measured in volts) at any point in a circuit is equal to the product of the current (I; measured in amps) times the resistance (R; measured in ohms). The *I* stands for *Inductance*, which is why it's an I, not a C. So if you have a 200-ohm resistor that has 0.045 amps moving through it, the voltage across that resistor is equal to 9V. Like any good algebraic equation, it's interchangeable:

$$V = I \times R \quad I = V \div R \quad R = V \div I$$

The other important variable in a circuit is power, signified by *P* and measured in watts. Power is equal to voltage times current, voltage squared divided by resistance, or current squared times resistance. If this is confusing, use the diagram in Figure 4-2 to better envision the relationships.

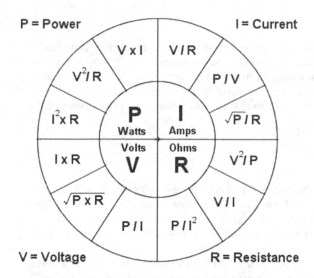

P = Power    I = Current

V = Voltage    R = Resistance

**Figure 4-2.** *Common electrical equations*

As an example, a common way of illustrating the different electrical concepts is with water and different sized pipes. In a "water circuit," the water power is provided by a pump. In an electrical circuit, the power is provided by a *battery*. In a water circuit, the pump takes water at low pressure, increases the pressure, and sends the water on its way around the circuit. In an electrical circuit, the battery takes "low pressure" *voltage*, increases its volts, and sends it on its way around the circuit. In both cases, the *current* means the flow—of either electrons or water—around the circuit. The *resistance* of the circuit is analogous to how large the water pipe is. If the pipe is large, it offers less resistance to the water flowing through it. In a circuit, if the wire has less resistance it allows the electrons to flow freely. This, in turn, affects the *power*.

Power increases with resistance and current. Think of power as the "speed" of the electricity; if you have a certain amount of water flowing from the end of a hose and you hold your finger over the end, increasing the resistance, the speed of the water increases. Increasing the resistance of the circuit increases the power. There are byproducts to this, of course. Partially blocking the end of a hose increases the friction at the mouth of the hose, and thus the heat. Likewise, increasing the resistance of a circuit often means increased heat. Heat is bad for circuits, especially fragile items like integrated circuits (ICs), so many electronic components that produce heat (because of internal resistance, among other reasons) often have a heat sink built in to dissipate the heat they create.

At its most fundamental, electricity is nothing more than electrons moving back and forth, along a wire or some other path. That path is always the *path of least resistance*. Given the choice of two ways to travel, electrons will always take the easiest path, whether it's through a wire, a screwdriver, or a human torso. Your goal, when working with these electrons, is to ensure that the easiest path does not involve your body. You won't always be successful; I've been shocked more times than I can count. *(In fact, in addition to the multiple electric shocks I've experienced with batteries and power supplies, I've actually been struck by lightning three times.)* A conscientious experimenter should try to reduce these incidents, if for no other reason than they can *hurt*! Rubber gloves can help (though wearing them all the time is a bit impractical), as can rubber boots or rubber-soled shoes. The reason rubber boots are a good idea, in addition to them being extremely fashionable, is that electrons always want to connect to ground. That "ground" may be a power ground, like the terminal of a battery; a chassis ground, like an engine block in a car; or the actual *ground*, called an *earth ground*.

With the electricity basics under your belt, let's talk about the tools you'll need to build your projects.

# Required Tools for Robotics

All engineers need good tools, and as a budding hobbyist/experimenter/engineer, you're no exception. That dented, banged-up screwdriver sitting in your kitchen's junk drawer may be fine for prying staples out of the wall, but if you try to use it for any delicate work on your projects, you're just asking for trouble. Likewise, a pair of wire cutters with huge gaps in the teeth won't do you any good when you're trying to reach inside a tiny opening and clip the red wire before the timer reaches zero. In order to build cool things, you need good tools. The following sections describe the necessary tools you should have.

## Screwdrivers

You need a good set of small, jeweler's screwdrivers. Spend the extra $10 and get a good quality set that will last you a long time, preferably one made out of hardened steel. The set should have at *least* three regular and three Phillips screwdrivers, with the regular sizes ranging from 3/64 of an inch to 1/8 of an inch, and the Phillips sizes including both #0 and #1. A good screwdriver is worth its weight in gold because it's less likely to strip the screw or develop a damaged tip that fails to grip the screw at all.

In addition, make sure you have on hand a regular, standard-sized screwdriver and a Phillips #2, because you're apt to be assembling/disassembling ordinary-sized items as well as miniature ones. I suggest you get a ratcheting screwdriver with a set of different bits, and you'll be prepared for most if not all of your projects.

## Pliers and Wire Strippers

Again, spend the money on good pliers and wire strippers, because you get what you pay for. You will definitely need a good pair of needle-nosed pliers (shown in Figure 4-3) that can be used as tweezers or to bend parts to fit.

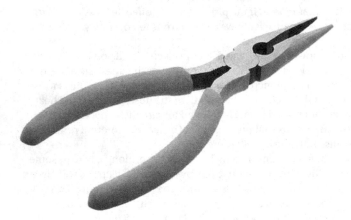

***Figure 4-3.*** *Needle-nosed pliers*

You can probably get away without a regular pair of pliers, though I wouldn't recommend it. Take good care of your pliers, and they'll take good care of you. It's difficult to bend wire or cut contacts with a pair of pliers that have gaps in them or don't close correctly.

You'll also need some wire strippers. Yes, you can use the cutters attached to your pliers to carefully score wire insulation and strip it, but when you have to do that repeatedly every time you need a wire end, it gets tedious *really* fast. Get some wire strippers, and save yourself the headache. Either the kind shown in Figure 4-4 or the kind shown in Figure 4-5 will work— just be sure you know how to use them.

*Figure 4-4.* Wire strippers, version 1

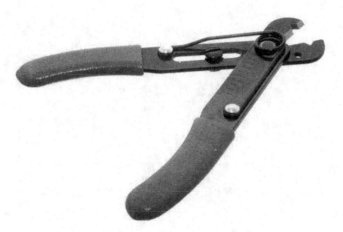

*Figure 4-5.* Wire strippers, version 2

I actually use both, because although I appreciate being able to choose my wire size in the pair shown in Figure 4-4, I often come across odd-sized wire that doesn't fit in any of that model's pre-sized holes. That's where the strippers shown in Figure 4-5 come into play.

## Wire Cutters

You'll need two types of cutters: regular cutters (Figure 4-6) and fine cutters (Figure 4-7).

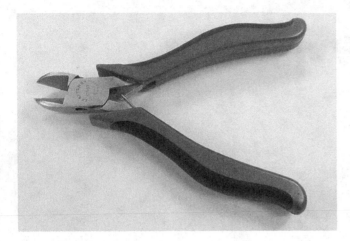

**Figure 4-6.** *Wire cutters*

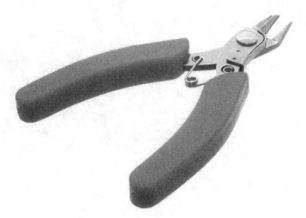

**Figure 4-7.** *Fine wire cutters*

The regular-sized cutters are great for everyday work, but the smaller cutters are invaluable when you have to snip tiny broken solder joints or the frayed ends of #24 gauge wire.

## Files

You won't need anything fancy when it comes to files—just a set of small files with varying *cuts*, or roughness. The finer cuts can be used for roughening a joint before soldering it or removing a bit of solder from a wire end before inserting it into a breadboard, while the rougher cuts can be used to reshape metal and plastic enclosures, increase hole sizes, and various other tasks.

## Magnifying Light

You'll be working with lots of very small objects, from resistors to wires to servo connections, and your eyes will get tired quickly. A good adjustable desk lamp with a magnifier built in is an incredibly valuable investment. The one I use is designed for use by jewelers and beaders, and the difference it makes when I'm trying to work with miniature pieces cannot be overstated. (See Figure 4-8.)

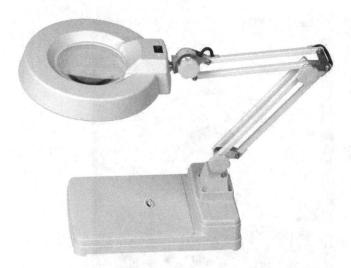

***Figure 4-8.*** *Magnifying light*

## Hot Glue Gun

At some point, you'll need to stick things to other things—like one servo to another, or a printed circuit board (PCB) to a robot's platform body—and it may not be feasible to use screws or bolts. One of the best ways to do this is with a hot glue gun. Ignore the stigma of scrapbooking and paper plate/macaroni designs, and get a good glue gun. Hot glue works surprisingly well in all sorts of applications—wood to plastic, plastic to plastic, wood to metal, and so on.

## Assorted Glues

Speaking of glue, you'll probably want to pick up an assortment of other, non-hot-glue-gun glues. Superglue is a must-have (get a brand-name version, though, not a store brand), as is modeling cement. I also have a stockpile of 5-minute epoxy and rubber cement and recently discovered Gorilla Glue to be one of the most awesome glues yet. You may also find a use for those cold-welding sticks—the ones where you mix two putty-like substances together to form a "clay" that hardens to a steel-like consistency.

Add "tape" to this list as well; get some regular transparent tape, some double-sided tape, masking tape, electrical tape, and—of course—duct tape.

## Multimeter

A multimeter measures different aspects of an electrical circuit—voltage across certain points, current, and resistance. (See Figure 4-9.) Whether you get an analog or a digital version is up to you, but be prepared to spend a little money, because a good multimeter is an incredibly valuable tool. It can be used to trace electrical shorts, ensure that you're using the correct voltage, and figure out how much resistance exists between two points in a circuit.

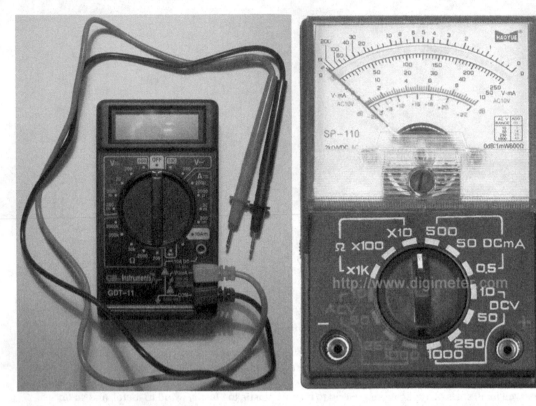

**Figure 4-9.** *Analog and digital multimeters (©www.digimeter.com)*

When choosing your multimeter, make sure it can measure both AC and DC voltage levels, because it's likely you'll be using both at some point. It should be able to measure resistance and continuity as well as current. The most important characteristic to look for, however, is ease of use. If you don't know how to use the multimeter, you won't use it, and you'd be wasting an important tool. So get one you like, that makes sense to you, and then spend some time with the manual learning how to use it.

# Power Supplies

When it comes to powering your experiments and projects, there are a few different routes you can take. Obviously, you'll often be using batteries or battery packs, and I'll talk about those for each specific project. However, when it comes to powering a prototype or just determining if a particular configuration works, you can't go wrong with a wall wart—the AC-to-DC converters that come with almost all electronic devices these days.

You can get an adjustable wall wart at an electronics store, which I recommend, but you can also haunt your local thrift store. Somewhere, buried in the back by the electronics, you may find a bin full of abandoned power supplies, for around a dollar apiece. You can either cut off the connector so you can plug it directly into your breadboard or get an adapter like the one in Figure 4-10.

*Figure 4-10.* *Power plug adapter*

I tend to pick up power supplies whenever I see them, or keep them when I throw a device away at home, so I have a pretty good assortment. Try to find at least a 9V and a 12V, with different current ratings, because these are common voltage sources. If your device runs well with your 12V source, for example, that means it'll probably run well in your car.

## Breadboard

A breadboard is another must-have when you're putting electronics together to see if everything works as it should. You can go full-out, with a deluxe model with power connections and meters and all sorts of bells and whistles (as shown in Figure 4-11).

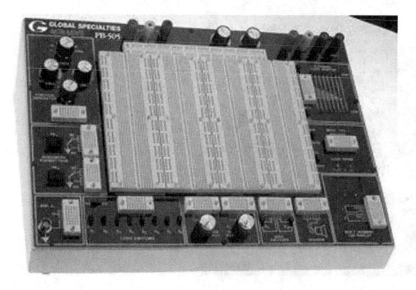

*Figure 4-11.* *Prototyping breadboard setup*

Or you can go with a more old-school version, like the one shown in Figure 4-12.

**Figure 4-12.** *Analog breadboard*

Either way, just be sure you can plug devices like resistors and ICs into it, and that you can connect those devices using jumper wires. And as your skills increase and your interests diversify, be prepared for your breadboard to someday look like the image in Figure 4-13.

**Figure 4-13.** *Breadboarding gone horribly wrong*

Yes, you'll be debugging that conglomeration of wires, and no, I can't help you. But I feel for you—I truly do.

## Power Strip

You'll need a power strip, but it doesn't have to be anything elaborate. It's just a good idea to have all of your electronics—desk lamp, soldering iron, Pi, and so on—plugged into one source so that you have a failsafe way to abort if you need to. One flip of a switch, and *everything* goes off. Get one with a surge protector built in if you can.

## Soldering Iron

Another critical tool on your list should be a soldering iron, and this is the one item you shouldn't skimp on when it comes to cost. The $9.99 iron you can get at your local department store might be all right for tinkering with some circuits around the house, but when you're a serious builder/hobbyist, you need a good quality, adjustable soldering iron. I have a Weller WES51 (shown in Figure 4-14).

***Figure 4-14.*** *Soldering station*

It's easily the best $100 I ever spent in my electronics career. Get one with a stand, adjustable heat, and tips you can swap. Trust me: your projects will thank you when you can use the correct temperature to make the solder melt without melting your circuit, or when you can use even heat to remove a bad solder joint.

While you're shopping for the iron, get a few soldering accessories as well. A solder-sucker (a hand-held vacuum pump that removes melted solder from joints) is a must-have, as is a helping-hands tool. (See Figure 4-15.)

***Figure 4-15.*** *Helping-hands tool*

A helping-hands tool comes in very handy when you need two hands to hold a connection and another two hands to solder that connection and you've burned your wife's fingers *one too many times* and your kid's nowhere to be found. You can even make your own out of stiff baling wire, alligator clips, and a wooden stand.

# General Safety Rules

Here is when I get to act like your mother and ask if you're being safe. After all, although we're building relatively innocuous projects in this book, you're still dealing with some components that can seriously hurt you. The tip of your soldering iron, for instance, averages around 450°F. Hot glue, even the low-temp variety, melts at about 250°F. Sure, programming is a fairly harmless activity, but you'll also be cutting, drilling, sanding, and doing any number of other tasks that have the capability to badly injure you. So, please—take this safety talk seriously.

## Working with Heat

Keep in mind at all times that you are surrounded by tools and components that can get *very* hot, and it would behoove you to remember which objects those are and treat them accordingly. As mentioned earlier, your soldering iron gets to around 450°F. But also the solder you're using melts at around 350°F, which means that the part you just soldered is *hot*! Give it a few seconds to cool before you touch it and see if your joint is solid. Wait until your hot glue cools to at least a gel-like state before you touch it. Speaking from personal experience: the worst thing about hot glue is that you can't just shake it off when you get it stuck to your finger. Instead, it stays right there on your finger and *sizzles*.

## Working With Sharp Objects

This should go without saying, but it's necessary to follow good safety practices when it comes to your cutting tools as well. That means

- Cut away from your body.

- Keep your tools sharp.

Cutting toward yourself, even lightly or for a very small cut, is simply asking for trouble. One slip with an X-ACTO knife and you could be committing *hara-kiri*, or at the very least heading to the emergency room for stitches. Believe me, stitches are no fun, particularly when the doctor injects an anesthetic into the cut. And if you lose a finger completely, robotics experimenting will immediately become at least 10 percent more difficult, because you will have only nine fingers to work with rather than 10—an immediate 10 percent cut.

Keep your blades sharp, because as any chef knows, a dull knife is a dangerous knife. If your utility knife blade is getting dull, switch it out for a new one. Same thing goes for your X-ACTO knife blade. A dull blade is much more likely to slip and cut you, while a sharp knife will simply cut deeper into whatever it is you're hacking away at.

## Wear Safety Glasses

Get a pair of safety glasses or goggles. This is not negotiable—if you don't have a pair, get one before you do any experimenting. Your sight is too important to lose it to a flying speck of metal from your wire snips or a spark from your grinding wheel. If you have a pair that is uncomfortable, get another pair—you're more likely to wear them if they're a comfortable fit. I prefer the safety glasses, but many people prefer the goggles that hold fast to your head with an elastic band, since they won't fall off. Whichever you prefer, take care of them to avoid scratches and breakage, and *wear them when you're working*.

## Fire Extinguishers at the Ready

Let me tell you a little story. When I was building my first little mobile robot with the Pi, I was using a Lithium Polymer (LiPo) battery for the first time. It was a small 11.1V, 1300mAh battery. I was connecting it to my servo motors, and I managed to short the negative and positive terminals together with an alligator clip.

Immediately after the loud *pop!* and the spark, the pack began to heat up incredibly fast, and the packaging started to swell. Thinking as fast as I could, I managed to disconnect the alligator clips, dropped the pack onto the middle of the floor and threw a glass of water onto the battery. I narrowly managed to escape an explosion, and I found out later that those LiPo batteries pack quite a punch.

The moral of this story is that although I used a glass of water, I had a fire extinguisher nearby that I was ready to use if I had needed to, and so should you. They're not expensive, and they're well worth the cost when it comes to possibly saving your house or workshop from a fire. Get an extinguisher, and be sure to keep it charged.

Also, be sure to learn how to use your fire extinguisher *before* you need it. Think of it as being like bear spray as you're hiking in the wilds of Alaska and need to fend off a bear. You would definitely practice using it before you go hiking, since it can be extremely difficult to read directions while running from an angry grizzly. Your fire extinguisher is similar—it can be very difficult to read and follow the instructions while your workshop is turning into a remake of *The Towering Inferno*. Become familiar with it, and hopefully you will never have to use it.

## Keep a First-Aid Kit Handy

Although this should go without saying, always have a first-aid kit nearby. You don't need a full Level 1 Emergency Kit that you could take on an Antarctic expedition, but a small, well-stocked kit should be somewhere in close proximity. The kit should contain some Band-Aids, alcohol, cotton swabs, and maybe a few other odds and ends. It's difficult to solder a joint when you're bleeding all over it.

## Work in a Ventilated Area

One important detail to remember when you're working is to keep your workshop well-ventilated, because you'll most likely be sanding, painting, sawing, and doing various other activities that can fill the air (and your lungs) with dangerous substances. You may not be painting enough to be too worried about paint fumes, but you'll definitely be around solder fumes, for instance. Solder contains lead—not much, but some—and lead is poisonous. If you come into contact with too much of it too often, it can lead to lead poisoning. Symptoms include abdominal pain, confusion, headache, and irritability. In severe cases, it can lead to seizures and even death, neither of which facilitate further robotics experimentation.

Even though you're unlikely to come into contact with enough lead to poison yourself while soldering, be aware that it *is* toxic. Don't breathe the fumes, and wash your hands thoroughly and often after touching soldered parts. You should work in a well-ventilated area, with windows open, or at least a fan going. Some experimenters hook up an old computer fan to a dryer-vent hose for a customized smoke-away solution.

# Organizing Your Workplace

As you progress in your experimenting endeavors by buying additional tools, parts, chips, boards, and so forth, you're going to need a way to organize it all. Keeping your work area organized could just as easily fall under safety, since having everything stored neatly in its place can eliminate workplace hazards as well.

At the very least, buy several sizes of sandwich baggies so that you can keep different parts separated, but when you pass the point of no return, look into storage solutions. I have had good luck in the beading section of my local craft store, since many resistors and LEDs are about the size of beads. My main storage looks like the image in Figure 4-16.

**Figure 4-16.** *Organized parts storage*

And I have various other plastic boxes and drawers for wheels, motors, batteries, ICs, and whatever else I need to store. Keeping in that vein, you may notice the labels in the picture. Buy a label maker! Easily another of my best purchases—you can label drawers, power supplies, cords, the children . . . the possibilities and uses are endless.

Keep your area clean. Not only is it much more efficient to find things when they're where they're supposed to be, but tripping over a power supply cord when holding an X-ACTO knife can be a dangerous incident. Get your tool or part from its place, use it, and then put it back. (This is another area where you may have to do as I say, not as I do. You'll be seeing pics of my workspace throughout the book, and I can't guarantee it'll always be the neatest space. I tend to spread out when I work. But you get the idea.)

# Bonus: Soldering Techniques

In this last section of this introductory electronics chapter, I'll give you a few tips on how to solder. Soldering is an art as much as a skill, and it *does* take practice. If you've never soldered before, your first joints are bound to be lumpy, ugly clumps, but improvement can be swift if you stick with it. No more than a few hours spent soldering components together for practice can make a huge difference when you do it for a real project.

Soldering basically breaks down to four steps: prepare your surfaces, tin if necessary, connect the parts, and heat them.

1. **Prepare your surfaces.** If you're connecting wires—to other wires or to another surface—strip the insulation off of the last half-inch or so and twirl the strands together to make a compact bunch. Other metal parts may need to be cleaned, and if it's a particularly smooth surface, roughing it with sandpaper may help the solder stick better to it.

2. **Tin if necessary.** Tinning a surface is simply melting a little solder onto it before you stick it to another surface. It's a good practice to get into when attaching wire to an IC leg, for instance. To tin a wire, heat it from the bottom with the soldering iron, and hold the solder to the top. When the wire gets hot enough, the solder will melt right into it.

3. **Connect the parts.** If you can, connect the parts mechanically—twist wires together, wrap wires around an IC leg, and so forth. If that's not possible, that's where your helping-hands tool comes into play—use it to hold the parts together.

4. **Heat the parts.** With a *clean* soldering iron tip, heat the joint while holding the solder to it. When the connection heats up enough, the solder will melt and flow onto the joint.

The last step is probably the most important. The tip of your iron should be clean; get in the habit of wiping it on a damp sponge whenever you finish a joint, and before you start another one. A clean tip will transfer heat better. You should also heat *the joint*, not the solder. *Don't* melt the solder onto the tip of the iron and then smear it onto the connection—you'll run the chance of making a cold solder joint (shown in Figure 4-17), which is bound to fail eventually. Remember: heat the parts, not the solder. If you have trouble getting the joint hot enough for the solder to melt onto it, you can melt a tiny bit of solder onto the tip of your iron before touching a joint, since the solder will transfer the heat more effectively. You should end up with a joint that looks like the one in Figure 4-18.

*Figure 4-17.* *A cold solder joint. Note the poor connection*

*Figure 4-18.* *A good solder joint*

Again, don't stress too much about your soldering skills or lack thereof. A little practice and you'll be soldering circuits like an expert.

Aside from just doing it, perhaps the best way to learn to solder well is to watch it, and the magic of YouTube now makes that possible. A quick search of "how to solder" brings up over 300,000 results. I can't pick any two or three that stand out, but if you watch a few you should get the idea. Makezine, an incredibly informative online blog, has a good page with resources on learning how to solder. It's located at http://makezine.com/2006/04/10/how-to-solder-resources/.

# Summary

After being introduced to some basic electricity principles, you learned your way around some of the common electronics tools in the lab, and learned the basics of how to use them safely. I also introduced you to soldering and pointed you in the direction of some resources to learn to do it better.

Let's gather our tools and head into the projects, starting with a simple one that doesn't require any tools—the WebBot.

# CHAPTER 5

■■■

# The Web Bot

As anyone who has spent any time at all online can tell you, there is a *lot* of information available on the Internet. According to Google's indexes, as of 2013 there are 4.04 billion web pages in existence. (See Figure 5-1.) Sure, a lot of those pages are probably cat pictures and pornography, but there are also hundreds of millions of pages with information on them. *Useful* information. It has been said that every piece of information that has been digitized exists somewhere on the Internet. It just has to be found—not an easy task when the Internet looks something like Figure 5-1.

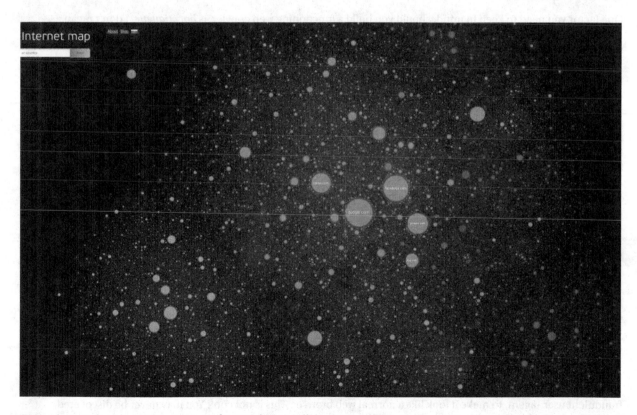

***Figure 5-1.***  *Visual map of the Internet (© 2013 http://internet-map.net, Ruslan Enikeev)*

Unfortunately, there's no way any one person could download and read all of the information he or she found interesting. Human beings just aren't that fast, and we have to eat and sleep and perform all sorts of inefficient, sometimes unpleasant, tasks like showering and working for a living.

Luckily, we can program computers to do some of the boring, repetitive tasks that we don't need to perform ourselves. This is one of the functions of a web bot: we can program the bot to crawl web pages, following links and downloading files as it goes. It's commonly just called a "bot," and knowing how to program and use one can be an incredibly useful skill. Need the stock reports when you wake up in the morning? Have your bot crawl the international indexes and have a spreadsheet waiting for you. Need to research all of the passenger manifests for the White Star Line that have been posted online, looking for your ancestor? Have your bot start with "White Star" in Google, and traverse all of the links from there. Or perhaps you want to locate all of Edgar Allan Poe's manuscripts that are currently available in the public domain; a bot can help with that as well, while you sleep.

Python is well-suited to doing the job of a web bot, also called—in this context—a *spider*. There are a few modules that need to be downloaded, and then you can program a fully functional bot to do your bidding, starting from whatever page you give it. Because traversing web pages and downloading information is not a terribly processor-intensive task, it is also a task well-suited to the Raspberry Pi. While your normal desktop machine handles more difficult computing tasks, the Pi can handle the light lifting required to download web pages, parse their text, and follow links to download files.

# Bot Etiquette

One factor you need to keep in mind, should you build a functioning web crawler, is *bot etiquette*. I don't mean etiquette in the sense of making sure that the bot's pinky is extended when drinking high tea. Rather, there are certain niceties you should observe when you program your bot to crawl sites.

One is to respect the robots.txt file. Most sites have this file in the root directory of the site. It's a simple text file that contains instructions for visiting bots and spiders. If the owner of the site does not want certain pages crawled and indexed, he can list those pages and directories in the text file, and courteous bots will accede to his requests. The file format is simple. It looks like this:

```
User-agent: *
Disallow: /examples/
Disallow: /private.html
```

This robots.txt file specifies that no bots (User-agent: *) may visit (crawl) any pages in the /examples/ folder, nor may they visit the page private.html. The robots.txt file is a standard mechanism by which web sites can restrict visits to certain pages. If you want your bot to be welcome at all sites, it's a good idea to follow those rules. I'll explain how to do that. If you choose to ignore those rules, you can often expect your bot (and all visits from your IP address) to be banned from the site in question.

Another piece of etiquette is controlling the speed of your bot's information requests. Because bots are computers, they can visit and download pages and files hundreds and thousands of times faster than humans can. For this reason, it is entirely possible for a bot to make so many requests to a site in such a short time that it can incapacitate a poorly configured web server. Therefore, it is polite to keep your bot's page requests to a manageable level; most site owners are fine with around 10 page requests per second—far more than can be done by hand, but not enough to bring down a server. Again, in Python, this can be done with a simple sleep() function.

Finally, it can often be problematic to fake your *user-agent identity*. A user-agent identity identifies visitors to a site. Firefox browsers have a certain user-agent, Internet Explorer has another, and bots have yet another. Because there are many sites that do not want bots to visit or crawl their pages at all, some bot-writers give their bots a fraudulent user -agent, to make it look like a normal web browser. This is not cool. You may never be discovered, but it's a matter of common decency—if you had pages you wanted kept private, you'd want others to respect those wishes as well. Do the same for other site owners. It's just part of being a good bot-writer and netizen. You may simulate a browser's user-agent if you are emulating a browser for other purposes, such as site testing or to find and download files (PDFs, mp3s, and so on) but not to crawl those sites.

# The Connections of the Web

Before we get to the business of programming our spider, you need to understand a bit about how the Internet operates. Yes, it's basically a giant computer network, but that network follows certain rules and uses certain protocols, and we need to utilize those protocols in order to do *anything* on the web, including using a spider.

## Web Communication Protocols

HyperText Transfer Protocol (HTTP) is the format in which most common web traffic is encapsulated. A protocol is simply an agreement between two communicating parties (in this case, computers) as to how that communication is to proceed. It includes information such as how data is addressed, how to determine whether errors have occurred during transmission (and how to handle those errors), how the information is to travel between the source and destination, and how that information is formatted. The "http" in front of most URLs (Uniform Resource Locators) defines the protocol used to request the page. Other common protocols used are TCP/IP (Transmission Control Protocol/Internet Protocol), UDP (User Datagram Protocol), SMTP (Simple Mail Transfer Protocol), and FTP (File Transfer Protocol). Which protocol is used depends on factors such as the traffic type, the speed of the requests, whether the data streams need to be served in order, and how forgiving of errors those streams can be.

When you request a web page with your browser, there's a good bit happening behind the scenes. Let's say you type `http://www.irrelevantcheetah.com` into your location bar. Your computer, knowing that it's using the HTTP protocol, first sends `www.irrelevantcheetah.com` to its local DNS (Domain Name System) server to determine to what Internet address it belongs. The DNS server responds with an IP address—let's say, 192.185.21.158. That is the address of the server that holds the web pages for that domain. The Domain Name System maps IP addresses to names, because it's much easier for you and me to remember "`www.irrelevantcheetah.com`" than it is to remember "192.185.21.158."

Now that your computer knows the IP address of the server, it initiates a TCP connection with that server, using a three-way "handshake." The server responds, and your computer asks for the page "index.html." The server responds and then closes the TCP connection.

Your browser then reads the coding on the page and displays it. If there are other parts of the page it needs, such as PHP code or images, it then requests those parts or images from the server and displays them as well.

## Web Page Formats

Most web pages are formatted in HTML—HyperText Markup Language. It's a form of XML (eXtensible Markup Language) that is pretty easy to read and parse, and it can be understood by most computers. Browsers are programmed to interpret the language of the pages and display those pages in a certain way. For instance, the tag pair `<html>` and `</html>` indicate that the page is in HTML. `<i>` and `</i>` indicate that the enclosed text is *italic*, while `<a>` and `</a>` indicate a *hyperlink*, which is normally displayed as blue and underlined. JavaScript is surrounded by `<script type="text/javascript"></script>` tags, and various other more involved tags surround various languages and scripts.

All of these tags and formats make browsing and reading raw web pages easy for humans. However, they have the effect of also making it easy for computers to parse those pages. After all, if your browser couldn't decode the pages, the Internet wouldn't exist in its current form. But you don't need a browser to request and read web pages—only to display them once you've got them. You can write a script to request web pages, read them, and do pre-scripted tasks with the pages' information—all without the interference of a human. Thus, you can automate the long, boring process of searching for particular links, pages and formatted documents and pass it to your Pi. Therein lies the web bot.

## A Request Example

For simplicity's sake, let's begin by saying we have requested the page `http://www.carbon111.com/links.html`. The page's text is pretty simple—it's a static page, after all, with no fancy web forms or dynamic content, and it looks pretty much like this:

```
<HTML>
<HEAD>
<TITLE>Links.html</TITLE>
</HEAD>
<BODY BACKGROUND="mainback.jpg" BGCOLOR="#000000"
 TEXT="#E2DBF5" LINK="#EE6000" VLINK="#BD7603" ALINK="#FFFAF0">
<br>
<H1 ALIGN="CENTER">My Favorite Sites and Resources</H1>
<br>
<H2>Comix, Art Gallerys and Points of Interest:</H2>
<DL>
<DT><A HREF="http://www.alessonislearned.com/index.html" TARGET="blank">
A Lesson Is Learned...</A>
<DD>Simply amazing! Great ideas, great execution. I love the depth of humanity
these two dig into. Not for the faint-of-heart ;)
   .
   .
   .
```

and so on, until the final closing `</HTML>` tag.

If a spider were receiving this page over a TCP connection, it would first learn that the page is formatted in HTML. It would then learn the page title, and it could start looking for a) content it has been tasked to find (such as `.mp3` or `.pdf` files) and b) links to other pages, which will be contained within `<A></A>` tags. A spider can also be programmed to follow links to a certain "depth"; in other words, you can specify whether or not the bot should follow links from linked pages or whether it should stop following links after the second layer. This is an important question, because it is possible that if you program too many layers, your spider could end up trawling (and downloading) the entire Internet—a critical problem if your bandwidth and storage are limited!

# Our Web Bot Concept

The concept behind our web bot is as follows: we'll start with a certain page, based on user input. Then we'll determine what files we are looking for—for example, are we looking for `.pdf` files of works in the public domain or freely available `.mp3`s by our favorite bands? That choice will be programmed into our bot as well.

The bot will then start at the beginning page and parse all of the text on the page. It will look for text contained within `<a href></a>` tags (hyperlinks.) If that hyperlink ends in a ".pdf" or ".mp3" or another chosen file type, we'll make a call to *wget* (a command-line downloading tool) to download the file to our local directory. If we can't find any links to our chosen file type, we'll start following the links that we *do* find, repeating the process for each of those links, as recursively as we determine beforehand. When we've gone as far as we want to, we should have a directory full of files, to be perused at our leisure. *That* is what a web bot is for—letting the computer do the busy work, while you sip a margarita and wait to enjoy the fruits of its labor.

# Parsing Web Pages

Parsing refers to the process a computer goes through when it "reads" a web page. At its most basic, a web page is nothing more than a data stream, consisting of bits and bytes (a byte is eight bits) that, when decoded, form numbers, letters, and symbols. A good parsing program not only can re-form that data stream into the correct symbols, it can read the re-formed stream and "understand" what it reads. A web bot needs to be able to parse the pages it loads, because those pages may/should contain links to the information it's programmed to retrieve. Python has several different text parser modules available, and I encourage you to experiment, but the one I have found the most useful is Beautiful Soup.

---

■ **Note**    Beautiful Soup is named after the Mock Turtle's song by Lewis Carroll (1855):

Beautiful soup, so rich and green

Waiting in a hot tureen!

Who for such dainties would not stoop?

Soup of the evening, beautiful soup!

Soup of the evening, beautiful soup!

---

Beautiful Soup (the Python library) has gone through several versions; as of this writing, it is on version 4, which works in both Python 2.x and 3.x.

Beautiful Soup's syntax is pretty basic. Once you've installed it by typing

```
sudo apt-get install python-bs4
```

you can start using it in your scripts. Open a Python prompt by typing **python** and try typing the following:

```
import BeautifulSoup
```

If you get an error message that says, "No module named BeautifulSoup," you're probably using the beta version of Beautiful Soup 4 (BS4)—the default version as of this writing. In that case, type

```
from bs4 import BeautifulSoup
```

Then continue to type:

```
import re
doc = ['<html><head><title>Page title</title></head>',
       '<body><p id="firstpara" align="center">This is paragraph <b>one</b>.',
       '<p id="secondpara" align="blah">This is paragraph <b>two</b>.',
       '</html>']
soup = BeautifulSoup(''.join(doc)) #that's two apostrophes, one after another, not a double quote
```

This loads the file named doc with what a web-page stream would look like—a long single stream of characters. Then soup loads the lines into a file that can be parsed by the library. If you were to type print soup at this point, it would look the same as the results of typing print doc. However, if you type

```
print soup.prettify()
```

you'll be rewarded with the page, redone in a more readable fashion. This is just an example of what Beautiful Soup can do; I'll go over it more when we get to programming the bot.

As an aside: the re module you import in the preceding example is used to evaluate regular expressions in text. Regular expressions, if you're not familiar with them, are an extremely versatile way to search through text and pick out strings and sequences of characters in ways that may not be immediately obvious to a human reader. A regular expression term can look like complete gibberish; a good example of a regular expression is the sequence (?<=-)\w+, which searches for a sequence of characters in a string that follows a hyphen. To try it out, open a Python prompt by typing **python** and then type

```
import re
m = re.search('(?<=-)\w+', 'free-bird')
m.group(0)
```

and you'll be rewarded with "bird."

While regular expressions are very helpful in terms of finding sequences of characters in text and strings, they're also not very intuitive and are far beyond the scope of this book. We won't be spending much time on them here. It's enough that you know they exist, and you can spend some time learning about them if they interest you.

# Coding with Python Modules

When it comes to using different Python modules when coding your web spider, you have quite a few options. Many open-source spiders already exist, and you could borrow from those, but it's a good learning experience to code the spider from the ground up.

Our spider will need to do several things in order to do what we need it to. It will need to initiate TCP connections and request pages, parse the received pages, download important files that it finds, and follow links that it comes across. Luckily, most of these are pretty simple tasks, so programming our spider should be relatively straightforward.

## Using the Mechanize Module

Probably the most-used module when it comes to automated web browsing, *mechanize* is both incredibly simple and incredibly complex. It is simple to use and can be set up with a few paltry lines of code, yet it is also packed with features that many users don't fully utilize. It's a great tool for automating tasks such as web-site testing: if you need to log into a site 50 times with 50 different username/password combinations, and then fill out an address form afterward, mechanize is your tool of choice. Another nice thing about it is that it does much of the work, such as initiating TCP connections and negotiating with the web server, behind the scenes so that you can concentrate on the downloading part.

To use mechanize in your script, you must first download and install it. If you've been following along, you still have a Python prompt open, but you'll need a regular command-line interface for this download and installation process. Here you have two options: you can exit from the Python entry mode, or you can open another terminal session. If you prefer to have only one terminal session open, exit from the Python prompt in your current window by typing Ctrl+d, which will return you to the normal terminal prompt. On the other hand, if you choose to open another terminal session, you can leave the Python session running, and everything you've typed so far will still be in memory.

Whichever option you decide, from a command-line prompt, enter

```
wget http://pypi.python.org/packages/source/m/mechanize/mechanize-0.2.5.tar.gz
```

when that's finished downloading, untar the file with

```
tar -xzvf mechanize-0.2.5.tar.gz
```

and navigate into the resulting folder by typing cd. Then run

```
sudo python setup.py install
```

Follow any onscreen instructions, and mechanize will be installed and ready to use.

## Parsing with Beautiful Soup

I mentioned parsing earlier; Beautiful Soup is still the best way to go. If you haven't done so already, enter

```
sudo apt-get install python-bs4
```

into a terminal and let the package manager do its work. It's ready to use immediately afterward. As I stated before, once you download the page, Beautiful Soup is responsible for finding links and passing them to the function we'll use for downloading, as well as setting aside those links that will be followed later.

As a result of this, however, it turns out that the job of finding links and determining what to download becomes mainly a problem with strings. In other words, links (and the text contained within them) are nothing but strings, and in our quest to unravel those links and follow them or download them, we'll be doing a lot of work with strings—work ranging from lstrip (removing the leftmost character) to append to split and various other methods from the string library. Perhaps the most interesting part of a web bot, after all, isn't the files it downloads; rather, it's the manipulations you have to do to get there.

## Downloading with the urllib Library

The last part of the puzzle here is the urllib library—specifically, its URLopener.retrieve() function. This function is used to download files, smoothly and without fuss. We'll pass it the name of our file and let it do its work.

To use urllib, you must first import it. Switch to the terminal with your Python prompt, if it's still open, or start another session by typing **python**. Then type

```
import urllib
```

to make it available for use.

The urllib library uses the following syntax:

```
image = urllib.URLopener()
image.retrieve ("http://www.website.com/imageFile.jpg", "imageFile.jpg")
```

where the first parameter sent to the URLopener.retrieve() function is the URL of the file, and the second parameter is the local file name that the file will be saved as. The second, file-name parameter obeys Linux file and directory conventions; if you give it the parameter "../../imageFile.jpg", imageFile.jpg will be saved two folders up in the directory tree. Likewise, passing it the parameter "pics/imageFile.jpg" will save it in the pics folder inside of the current directory (from which the script is running). However, the folder must already exist; retrieve() will not create the directory.

# Deciding What to Download

This can get kind of sticky because there *is* so much out there. Unfortunately (or fortunately, depending on your point of view), a good deal of it is copyrighted, so even if you find it for free, it's really not cool to just download it. Whatever you're looking for is out there.

That, however, is the topic for an entirely different book. For the time being, let's assume you're going to be looking for freely-available information, such as all works by Mark Twain that are in the public domain. That means you're probably going to be looking for .pdf, .txt, and possibly even .doc or .docx files. You might even want to widen your search parameters to include .mobi (Kindle) and .epub files, as well as .chm. These are all legitimate file formats that may contain the text of books you're looking for.

## Choosing a Starting Point

The next thing you're going to need is a starting point. You may be inclined to just say "Google!," but with tens of millions of search results from a simple search for "Mark Twain," you would probably be better off staying a bit more focused. Do a little groundwork *beforehand*, and save yourself (and your bot) hours of work later. If you can find an online archive of Twain's works, for example, that would be an excellent starting point. If you're looking for free music downloads, you may want to get a list together of blogs that feature new music files from up-and-coming bands, because many new artists give songs away to download free on those blogs in order to promote themselves and their music. Likewise, technical documents dealing with IEEE network specifications can probably be found on a technical site, or even a government one, with much more success than a wide Google search.

## Storing Your Files

You may also need a place to store your files, depending on the size of your Pi's SD card. That card acts as both RAM and a place for file storage, so if you're using a 32-GB card, you'll have lots of room for .pdf files. However, a 4-GB card may fill up rather quickly if you're downloading free documentary movie files. So you'll need an external USB hard drive—either a full-blown hard drive or a smaller flash drive.

Again, this is where some experimentation may come in handy, because some external drives won't work well with the Raspberry Pi. Because they're not particularly expensive these days, I would buy one or two medium-sized ones and give them a try. I'm currently using an 8-GB flash drive by DANE-ELEC (shown in Figure 5-2) without any problems.

**Figure 5-2.** *Common flash drive to store files*

(A note on accessing your jump drive via the command line: a connected drive such as a flash drive is accessible in the /media directory; that is,

```
cd /media
```

will get you to the directory where you should see your drive listed. You can then navigate into it and access its contents. You'll want to set up your Python script to save files to that directory—/media/PENDRIVE, for example, or /media/EnglebertHumperdinckLoveSongs. Probably the easiest way to do it is to save your webbot.py script in a directory on your external drive, and then run it from there.)

# Writing the Python Bot

Let's start writing some Python. The following code imports the necessary modules and uses Python's version of *input* (raw_input) to get a starting point (to which I've prepended the "http://" found in every web address). It then initiates a "browser" (with air quotes) with mechanize.Browser(). This code, in its final completed form, is listed at the end of this chapter. It's also available for download as webbot.py from the apress.com web site.

To start the process of writing your bot, use your text editor (either Leafpad or nano) and begin a new file, called webbot.py. Enter the following:

```
from bs4 import BeautifulSoup
import mechanize
import time
import urllib
import string

start = "http://" + raw_input ("Where would you like to start searching?\n")
br = mechanize.Browser()
r = br.open(start)
html = r.read()
```

Later we may need to fake a user-agent, depending on the sites we visit, but this code will work for now.

## Reading a String and Extracting All the Links

Once you've got a browser object, which is called br in the preceding code, you can do all sorts of tasks with it. We opened the start page requested from the user with br.open() and read it into one long string, html. Now we can use Beautiful Soup to read that string and extract all of the links from it by adding the following lines:

```
soup = BeautifulSoup(html)
for link in soup.find_all('a'):
    print (link.get('href'))
```

Now you can run the script to try it out. Save it and close it. Open a terminal session, and navigate to the same directory in which you created webbot.py. Then type

```
python webbot.py
```

to start the program, and type **example.com** when it asks where to start. It should return the following and then quit:

```
http://www.iana.org/domains/example
```

You've successfully read the contents of http://example.com, extracted the links (there's only one), and printed that link to the screen. This is an awesome start.

The next logical step is to instantiate a list of links, and add to that list whenever Beautiful Soup finds another link. You can then iterate over the list, opening each link with another browser object and repeating the process.

## Looking For and Downloading Files

Before we instantiate that list of links, however, there's one more function we need to create—the one that actually looks for and downloads files! So let's search the code on the page for a file type. We should probably go back and ask what sort of file we're looking for by adding the following code line at the beginning of the script, after the start line:

```
filetype = raw_input("What file type are you looking for?\n")
```

---

■ **Note** In case you're wondering, the \n at the end of the raw_input string in both of these cases is a carriage return. It doesn't get printed when the line is displayed. Rather, it sends the cursor to the beginning of the next line to wait for your input. It's not necessary—it just makes the output look a little prettier.

---

Now that we know what we're looking for, as we add each link to the list we can check to see if it's a link to a file that we want. If we're looking for .pdf files, for example, we can parse the link to see if it ends in pdf. If it does, we'll call URLopener.retrieve() and download the file. So open your copy of webbot.py again and replace the for block of code with the following:

```
for link in soup.find_all('a'):
    linkText = str(link)
    if filetype in linkText:
        #download file code here
```

You'll notice two elements in this little snippet of code. First, the str(link) bit has been added. Beautiful Soup finds each link in the page for us, but it returns it as a link object, which is sort of meaningless to non-Soup code. We need to convert it to a string in order to work with it and do all of our crafty manipulations. That's what calling the str() method does. In fact, Beautiful Soup provides a method to do this for us, but learning to parse a string with the str() function is important to learn here. As a matter of fact, that's why we used the line import string at the beginning of our code—so we can interact with string objects.

Second, once the link is a string, you can see how we can use Python's in call. Similar to C#'s String.contains() method, Python's in call simply searches the string to see if it contains the requested substring. So in our case, if we're looking for .pdf files, we can search the link text for that substring, "pdf". If it has it, it's a link we're interested in.

## Testing the Bot

To make testing our bot easier, I set up a page at http://www.irrelevantcheetah.com/browserimages.html to use for testing. It contains images, files, links, and various other HTML goodies. Using this page, we can start with something simple, like images. So let's modify our webbot.py code and make it look like this:

```
import mechanize
import time
from bs4 import BeautifulSoup
import string
import urllib
start = "http://www.irrelevantcheetah.com/browserimages.html"
filetype = raw_input ("What file type are you looking for?\n")
br = mechanize.Browser()
r = br.open(start)
html = r.read()
soup = BeautifulSoup(html)

for link in soup.find_all('a'):
    linkText = str(link)
    fileName = str(link.get('href'))
    if filetype in fileName:
        image = urllib.URLopener()
        linkGet = "http://www.irrelevantcheetah.com" + fileName
        filesave = string.lstrip(fileName, '/')
        image.retrieve (linkGet, filesave)
```

This last section of code starting with the for loop requires some explanation, methinks. The for loop iterates through all of the links that Beautiful Soup found for us. Then linkText converts those links to strings so that we can manipulate them. We then convert the *body* of the link (the actual file or page to which the link points) to a string as well, and check to see if it contains the file type we're looking for. If it does, we append it to the site's base URL, giving us linkGet.

The last two lines have to happen because of the retrieve() function. As you recall, that function takes two parameters: the URL of the file we're downloading, and the local name we'd like to save that file to. filesave takes the fileName we found earlier and removes the leading "/" from the name so that we can save it. If we didn't do this, the fileName we would try to save under would be—for example—/images/flower1.jpg. If we tried to save an image with that name, Linux would attempt to save flower.jpg to the /images folder, and then give us an error because the /images folder doesn't exist. By stripping the leading "/", the fileName becomes images/flower1.jpg, and as long as there's an images folder in our current directory (remember what I said about creating the directory first), the file will save without incident. Finally, the last line of code does the actual downloading, with the two parameters I already mentioned: linkGet and filesave.

If you create an images directory in your current directory and then run this script, answering "jpg" to the file type question, the images directory should fill up with 12 different images of flowers. Simple, eh? If, instead, you create a files directory and answer "pdf," you'll get 12 different (boring) PDFs in your files folder.

## Creating Directories and Instantiating a List

Now there are two more features we need to add to finish this bot. First, we aren't always going to know what directories we need to create ahead of time, so we need to find a way to parse the folder name from the link text and create the directory on the fly. Second, we need to create a list of links that link to other pages so that we can then visit those pages and repeat the download process. If we do this several times, we've got ourselves a real web bot, following links and downloading the files we want.

Let's do the second task first—instantiating the list of links we mentioned at the end of the section dealing with reading strings and extracting links. We can create a list at the beginning of the script, after the import statements, and add to it as we go. To create a list we simply use

```
linkList = []
```

To add to it, we add an elif block to our script:

```
if filetype in fileName:
    image = urllib.URLopener()
    linkGet = "http://www.irrelevantcheetah.com" + fileName
    filesave = string.lstrip(fileName, '/')
    image.retrieve (linkGet, filesave)

elif "htm" in fileName: #covers both ".htm" and ".html" files
    linkList.append(link)
```

That's it! If the fileName contains the type of link we're looking for, it gets retrieved. If it doesn't, but there's an "htm" in it, it gets appended to linkList—a list that we can then iterate through, one by one, opening each page and repeating the download process.

The fact that we're going to be repeating the download process many times should make you think of one element of coding: a *function*—also called a *method*. Remember, a function is used in code if there's a process you're going to be repeating over and over again. It makes for cleaner, simpler code, and it's also easier to write. Programmers, you'll find, are very efficient people. If we can code it once and reuse it, that's ever so much better than typing it over and over and over again. It's also a massive time-saver.

So let's start our downloading function by adding the following lines to our webbot.py script, after the linkList = [] line we added just a bit ago:

```
def downloadFiles (html, base, filetype, filelist):
    soup = BeautifulSoup (html)
    for link in soup.find_all('a'):
        linkText = str (link.get('href'))
        if filetype in linkText:
            image = urllib.URLopener()
            linkGet = base + linkText
            filesave = string.lstrip (linkText, "/")
            image.retrieve (linkGet, filesave)
        elif "htm" in linkText: #covers both "html" and "htm"
            linkList.append (link)
```

Now that we have our downloadFiles function, all we have left to do is parse our linkText to get the name of the directory we'll need to create.

Again, it's simple string manipulation, along with using the os module. The os module allows us to manipulate directories and files, regardless of what operating system we're running. First, we can add

```
import os
```

to our script, and then we can create a directory (if needed) by adding

```
os.makedirs().
```

You may remember that in order to simplify file saving, we need to have a local directory on our machine that matches the web directory in which our target files are stored. In order to see if we need a local directory, we need to first determine that directory name. In most (if not all) cases, that directory will be the first part of our linkText; for example, the directory name in /images/picture1.html is images. So the first step is to iterate through the linkText again, looking for slashes the same way we did to get the base of our web-site name, like this:

```
slashList = [i for i, ind in enumerate(linkText) if ind == '/']
directoryName = linkText[(slashList[0] + 1) : slashList[1]]
```

The preceding code creates a list of indices at which slashes are found in the linkText string. Then directoryName slices linkText to just the part between the first two slashes. (/images/picture1.html gets cut to images from our earlier example.)

The first line of that snippet bears some explanation because it's an important line of code. linkText is a string, and as such is *enumerable*; that is, the characters within it can be iterated over, one by one. slashList is a list of the positions (indices) in linkText where a slash is located. After the first line populates slashList, directoryName simply grabs the text contained between the first and second slashes.

The next two lines simply check to see if a directory exists that matches directoryName; if it doesn't, we create it.

```
if not os.path.exists(directoryName):
    os.makedirs(directoryName)
```

This completes our downloadProcess function, and with it our simple web bot. Give it a try by pointing it at http://www.irrelevantcheetah.com/browserimages.html and asking for either "jpg," "pdf," or "txt" file types, and watch it create folders and download files—all without your help.

Now that you get the idea, you can go crazy with it! Create directories, surf three (and more) levels deep, and see what your bot downloads for you while you're not looking! Half the fun is sometimes seeing what gets downloaded when you least expect it!

# The Final Code

Here you can see the final, lengthy code you've been typing in, bit by bit, if you've been following along as we progressed through the chapter. Again, if you don't want to type it all, it's available on Apress.com as webbot.py. However, I highly recommend you type it in, because learning code can be much more effective if you type it rather than simply copying and pasting it.

```python
import mechanize
import time
from bs4 import BeautifulSoup
import re
import urllib
import string
import os

def downloadProcess (html, base, filetype, linkList):
    "This does the actual file downloading."
    soup = BeautifulSoup(html)
    for link in soup.find_all('a'):
        linkText = str(link.get('href'))

        if filetype in linkText:
            slashList = [i for i, ind in enumerate(linkText) if ind == '/']
            directoryName = linkText[(slashList[0]+1):slashList[1]]
            if not os.path.exists(directoryName):
                os.makedirs(directoryName)

            image = urllib.URLopener()
            linkGet = base + linkText
            filesave = string.lstrip(linkText, "/")
            image.retrieve (linkGet, filesave)
        elif "htm" in linkText: #covers both "html" and "htm"
            linkList.append(link)

start = "http://" + raw_input ("Where would you like to start searching?\n")
filetype = raw_input ("What file type are you looking for?\n")

numSlash = start.count('/') #number of slashes in start-need to remove everything after third slash
slashList = [i for i, ind in enumerate(start) if ind == '/'] #list of indices of slashes

if (len(slashList) >= 3): #if there are 3 or more slashes, cut after 3
    third = slashList[2]
    base = start[:third] #base is everything up to third slash
else:
    base = start

br = mechanize.Browser()
r = br.open(start)
html = r.read()
linkList = [] #empty list of links
```

```
print "Parsing " + start
downloadProcess(html, base, filetype, linkList)

for leftover in linkList:
    time.sleep(0.1) #wait 0.1 seconds to avoid overloading server
    linkText = str(leftover.get('href'))
    print "Parsing " + base + linkText
    br = mechanize.Browser()
    r = br.open(base + linkText)
    html = r.read()
    linkList = []
    downloadProcess(html, base, filetype, linkList)
```

## Summary

In this chapter, you got a nice introduction to Python by writing a web bot, or spider, that can traverse the Internet for you and download files you find interesting, perhaps even while you sleep. You used a function or two, constructed and added to a list object, and even did some simple string manipulation.

In the next chapter, we'll transition away from the digital world and interact with a very physical phenomenon—the weather.

# CHAPTER 6

■ ■ ■

# The Weather Station

Since time immemorial, Man has been fascinated by the weather, asking questions such as: "Will it rain for our crops? Will it snow, so we can go skiing? Will a tornado carry our house to a fictitious country populated by supernatural women and flight-capable primates? We get some kind of weather every day: What's it going to be today?"

Forecasting the weather has not always been a scientific pursuit. People would pray to the rain gods for rain and to the sun gods for sunshine. If prayer didn't work, they would often visit a prophet or a seer, who professed the ability to look into the future and predict the path of a coming low-pressure system (though not in those particular words, of course).

Gradually, the science behind the weather was discovered, and we no longer had to rely on a magical rock for a forecast. (See Figure 6-1.) People attended school to become meteorologists and learn about weather fronts, storm surges, and other weather-related science information.

***Figure 6-1.*** *The weather stone (Image ©2010 Tom Knapp)*

Through all of these advances, a weather station was needed—a small, localized way of keeping up on current conditions. Even small weather stations normally give wind speed and direction, temperature, humidity, and relative barometric pressure. Each of these readings, when viewed in combination over the course of a day or two, can help you predict the weather for the immediate future.

Of course, the Raspberry Pi is perfect for creating this weather-station application. A lot of computational power is *not* required, but the ability to easily interact with a small network of sensors is. Some are connected to the Pi via I2C (Inter-Integrated Circuit), some are connected via pulse width modulation (PWM), and some are simply connected to the GPIO pins. By simply polling each sensor one by one in a round-robin style, we can gain an accurate picture of what the weather is doing at any given moment.

Let's start by gathering the parts required to build our weather station.

# A Shopping List of Parts

The weather station does not take a lot of parts, but fair warning: some of them are a bit more costly than you'd think, considering their size:

- Raspberry Pi and power adapter
- Digital compass/magnetometer (*https://www.sparkfun.com/products/10530*)
- Optical shaft encoder (*http://www.vexrobotics.com/276-2156.html*)
- Barometric pressure sensor (*https://www.adafruit.com/products/1603*)
- Digital thermometer (*https://www.adafruit.com/products/1638*)
- Small breadboard (*https://www.sparkfun.com/products/9567*)
- Square shaft from hardware store
- Pinwheel or similar fan-like device
- Lazy Susan bearing
- Thin wooden plate
- PVC pipe with cap, about 12 inches long, 1-2 inches in diameter
- Miscellaneous jumper wires, glue, screws

# Using the I2C Protocol

This project takes advantage of the I2C protocol for communicating with humidity and pressure sensors that you'll add to the Pi. While it's a relatively simple protocol, it can get a little confusing, so it's best to review it quickly before we start the building the station.

I2C enables a large number of devices to communicate on one circuit using only three wires: a data line, a clock line, and a ground wire. Each device is called a *node*, and there is usually one master node and many slaves. Each slave node has a 7-bit address, such as 0x77 or 0x43. When the master node needs to communicate with a particular slave, it begins by transmitting a "start" bit, followed by the slave's address, on the data line. That slave responds with an acknowledgment, while all other slaves ignore the rest of the message and go back to waiting for the next address pulse to be transmitted. The master and slave then communicate with each other, often switching between transmitting and receiving modes until all information has been transmitted.

I2C has been referred to as "the serial protocol on steroids," and it is most often used in applications where speed does not matter and the cost of parts needs to remain low. The Raspberry Pi has two pins, #3 and #5, that are preconfigured to be the I2C protocol's SDA (data) and SCL (clock) lines, respectively, so it can easily communicate with I2C devices. Two of the devices we'll be using (the barometer/altimeter and the magnetometer) are I2C devices, so we'll need to configure the Pi to make the I2C protocol work. Start by editing the /etc/modules file by typing

```
sudo nano /etc/modules
```

and add the lines

```
i2c-bcm2708
i2c-dev
```

to the end of the file, saving it when you're done. Then reboot your Pi with sudo shutdown -r now.

The Pi also has an I2C utility that makes it possible to see the devices that are currently connected. To install it, type

```
sudo apt-get install python-smbus
sudo apt-get install i2c-tools
```

You may also need to edit your blacklist file, if you have one. The blacklist.conf file is used by the Pi's kernel to prevent it from loading unnecessary modules, and it may exist only in earlier versions of the Raspbian OS. Later versions don't have any modules blocked. See if /etc/modprobe.d/raspi-blacklist.conf exists; if it does, comment out the following two lines:

```
#blacklist spi-bcm2708
#blacklist i2c-bcm2708
```

They are there to prevent the kernel from loading the I2C modules, and we need to load those modules, so we comment them out.

Now you can run the I2C utility tool called *i2cdetect* to make sure everything is working and see what devices are connected. Type the following line:

```
sudo i2cdetect -y 1
```

which should display the screen shown in Figure 6-2.

```
pi@raspberrypi ~/Documents/weather $ sudo i2cdetect -y 1
     0  1  2  3  4  5  6  7  8  9  a  b  c  d  e  f
00:          -- -- -- -- -- -- -- -- -- -- -- --
10: -- -- -- -- -- -- -- -- -- -- -- -- -- -- -- --
20: -- -- -- -- -- -- -- -- -- -- -- -- -- -- -- --
30: -- -- -- -- -- -- -- -- -- -- -- -- -- -- -- --
40: -- -- -- -- -- -- -- -- -- -- -- -- -- -- -- --
50: -- -- -- -- -- -- -- -- -- -- -- -- -- -- -- --
60: -- -- -- -- -- -- -- -- -- -- -- -- -- -- -- --
70: -- -- -- -- -- -- -- --
pi@raspberrypi ~/Documents/weather $ ▌
```

*Figure 6-2.* *The i2cdetect tool*

In this case, no devices are present, which makes sense, because we haven't plugged in any yet. But you now have the necessary tools installed and running correctly.

---

■ **Note**  If, by chance, you *do* have devices plugged in but nothing is showing, try typing `sudo i2cdetect -y 0` instead. The 1 or 0 flag depends on the Pi revision you happen to have. If you have the Pi revision 2, you'll use the 1 flag; otherwise, the 0 flag should work.

---

# Using an Anemometer

An important part of any weather station is the anemometer—the device that measures wind speed—because wind speed is an important factor in any weather forecasting. If it's a cold day (below 32°F or 0°C, for instance), the wind speed plays an important factor in how cold it *feels* (the wind chill). According to the National Weather Service's wind chill chart, a 15 MPH wind at 15° F makes it feel like 0° F, and a 20 MPH wind at 0° F makes it feel like 24 degrees below zero. Wind speed is important in this case in determining whether your extremities are going to freeze first or fall off first (both equally unappealing, if you ask me).

On the other hand, if it's not particularly cold out, the wind speed plays a part in how fast the next weather phenomenon is coming at you. At 2 MPH, that sunny day is going to take another few days to reach you; at 50 MPH, you have only minutes before the cyclone destroys your house.

An anemometer can be a fairly complicated device, with bearings and shafts and switches and so forth; ours, on the other hand, is relatively simple.

## Building the Anemometer

We'll be using a rotary shaft encoder, a rotating shaft, and some fins to measure the speed of the wind.

The rotary shaft encoder we're using from Vex robotics consists of a plastic disk with slits spaced evenly around its circumference. When power is applied, a small light shines through the slits in the disc and onto a photosensitive receptor on the other side. By counting the number of times the light is blocked by the disk (or, alternatively, the number of times the light shines through a slit) in a given span of time, it is possible to determine how fast the disc is spinning. It is also possible to determine how many times the disc has rotated, and this is, in fact, how rotary encoders are often used; if a rotary encoder is hooked to a robot's axle, it's a very good way of measuring how far the wheels connected to that axle have travelled, for instance. If the disc has 90 slits (as ours does), we know that one full rotation of the axle (one full wheel rotation) is 90 flashes of light onto the encoder's photo receptor. Thus, we can tell the robot, "Go forward 30 slits," and the wheel will advance exactly one-third of its circumference forward. If we know the circumference of the disc/wheel is 3 feet, we know the robot has just advanced 1 foot.

This may seem like a lot of unnecessary math, but it's important for you to understand how the encoder operates. Once we attach the fins to the rotating shaft, we *could* (theoretically) figure out wind speed based on the circumference of the fins and the speed of the shaft. However, my experience is that it's actually much easier to just experiment with known wind speeds and incorporate those speeds into our program, so that's what we'll do. To do that, you'll need a partner—somebody who can drive you around at predetermined, *sane* speeds while you take wind speed measurements. That means speeds of around 5-20 MPH, *not* 80.

To create your anemometer, peruse your local hardware store until you find a small, 1/8-inch square shaft that will fit in the square hole in the rotary encoder. (See Figure 6-3.)

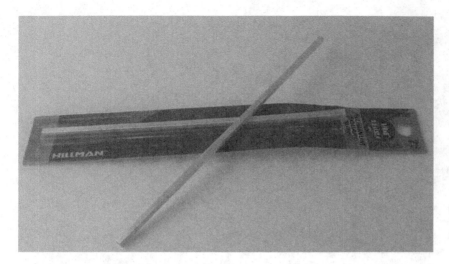

***Figure 6-3.*** *Square shaft*

---

■ **Note** As of this writing, a 1/8-inch shaft fits perfectly in the rotary encoder's hole.

---

Next, you'll need a pinwheel or something similar. I used the windmill portion of a science kit that you can buy at your local craft store (*http://amzn.to/1koelSW*, for instance). As you can see, the shaft fits perfectly in the windmill's hole, and the directional fin attaches easily to the back of the encoder. (See Figure 6-4.)

***Figure 6-4.*** *Encoder with wind vanes attached*

The entire mechanism needs to rotate; that is, it needs to be connected to a device that can spin on an axis, like a weather vane, so we can determine the wind's direction. This is where the Lazy Susan bearing set comes into play. First, cut two slots in the end of the PVC pipe into which your encoder will fit snugly (as shown in Figure 6-5).

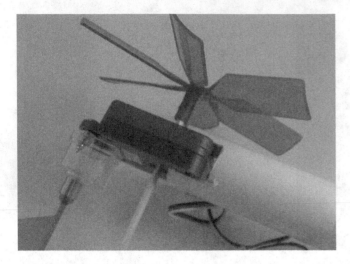

*Figure 6-5.* *Encoder in slot in PVC pipe*

Put the PVC cap on the other end of the pipe. Attach a light piece of wood to one side of the Lazy Susan bearing, and then, as near to the middle of the rotation axis as you can, attach the PVC pipe and cap with a screw from underneath. Figure 6-6 shows one way to determine the center of the axis of rotation.

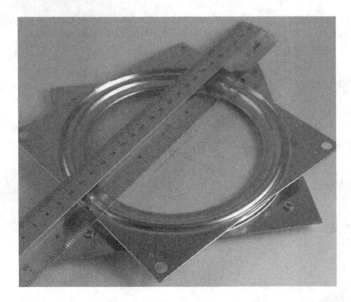

*Figure 6-6.* *Determining the platform center*

When you're done, you should have an assembly like the one shown in Figure 6-7.

***Figure 6-7.*** *Anemometer assembly*

## Connecting the Anemometer to the Pi

Now we need to hook up the anemometer to the Pi and measure rotation speeds. Connect the red wire of the encoder to the Pi's power pin (#2), the black wire to GND (#6), and the white wire to a GPIO pin of your choice. Let's use pin #8 for illustrative purposes.

As mentioned earlier, this encoder works by sending a HIGH signal every time a slit in the disc passes a certain point. We know that there are 90 slits in the disc, so every 90 HIGH signals one rotation of the shaft. So all we need to do is keep track of the HIGHs and how long it takes to get 90 of them, and we'll have rotation speed over time. If we track the time in seconds (as we will when using the time library), we'll have revolutions per second. So the code to read our encoder should be something like this:

```
import time
import RPi.GPIO as GPIO
GPIO.setmode(GPIO.BOARD)
GPIO.setup(8, GPIO.IN, pull_up_down=GPIO.PUD_DOWN)

prev_input = 0
total = 0
current = time.time()
```

```
while True:
    input = GPIO.input(8)
    if ((not prev_input) and input):
        print ("turning")
        total = total + 1
    prev_input = input
    if total == 90:
        print (1/(time.time() - current)), "revolutions per sec"
        total = 0
        current = time.time()
```

Everything interesting here happens in the while loop. Since we've begun by setting the prev_input to 0, a 1 (HIGH) as an input means that the disc is turning. In that case, we increment total, set prev_input to input, and continue the loop after checking to see if we've reached 90 HIGHs yet. If we have, that means we've gone exactly one revolution, so we can calculate and print revolutions per second (RPS) and reset total and current. To test this encoder code, connect the wires to your Pi, run the script, and manually spin the encoder wheel. You should see 90 iterations of the word "turning" and then a line with RPS displayed.

## Correlating Revolutions per Second with Wind Speed

If the encoder is working as it should, the only step left is to correlate revolutions per second with wind speed, and the easiest way to do that is with a friend and a car. With your anemometer held out the window and your Pi connected to your laptop via an ad-hoc network (see the sidebar), have your friend drive for a few minutes at 5 MPH while you run the encoder script; repeat the process at 10, 15, and 20 MPH until you have enough data to correlate wind speed with RPS.

When I drove around with my anemometer hanging out the window, I got the RPS readings shown in Table 6-1.

*Table 6-1.* *MPH correlated to RPS reading using an anemometer*

| MPH | RPS |
| --- | --- |
| 5 | 5.8 |
| 10 | 9.23 |
| 15 | 10.8 |
| 20 | 11.7 |

The correlation of MPH to RPS is obviously a logarithmic relationship, which means we can use a little algebra (eek!) to calculate wind speed based on revolutions per second.

If you plot these values on a graph, you get Figure 6-8.

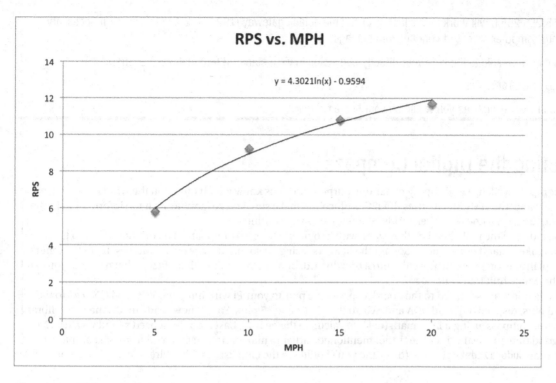

**Figure 6-8.** *RPS vs. MPH*

As you can see from the equation, the relationship between revolutions per second and wind speed is a logarithmic, not a linear, one. So we'll have to use the inverse logarithmic function, or $e^x$, to solve for wind speed in terms of revolutions per second. I don't want to bore you with the math, so just take my word for it that

$$\text{wind speed} = e^{((y+0.95)/4.3)}$$

We'll be able to substitute that calculation into our final program, as you'll soon see.

## HOOKING YOUR PI TO YOUR LAPTOP VIA AN AD-HOC NETWORK

If you're like me, most of the work I do with my Pi is headless—I SSH (Secure Shell) into it or run a VNC (Virtual Network Computing) server if I need to see the desktop, but I ordinarily don't have a monitor, mouse, or keyboard connected to it. This works well if you're connected to your home network, for instance, but what if there's no network around? Luckily, setting up a wired ad-hoc network between your Pi and a laptop is pretty simple. An ad-hoc is simply a network connection between the Pi and another computer, such as your laptop, with no router or hub in between.

The easiest way to set this up is to take note of your Pi's static IP address and adjust your laptop's Ethernet port to communicate with that address. Let's say your Pi has the address 192.168.2.42. Use a short Ethernet cable to connect your Pi directly to your laptop's Ethernet port. Now go into your laptop's network settings. Chances are your computer is set up to receive an address automatically from the router via DHCP (Dynamic Host Control Protocol). Change that method to Manual, and give your computer's network port an address that coincides with the Pi's subnet. In our example, a good address would be 192.168.2.10. If there are spots for it, fill in the subnet mask (255.255.255.0 will work in this instance) and the default gateway (192.168.2.1 in this case). If necessary, reboot your computer or restart your network manager.

You should now be able to log in to your directly-connected Pi via a standard terminal connection:

```
ssh -l pi 192.168.2.42
```

and you can work exactly as you would on your home network.

# Connecting the Digital Compass

The digital compass we'll use in this project has one purpose: to let us know which direction the wind is blowing. The one we're using, the HMC5883L, uses the I2C protocol, so make sure you're familiar with the information in the section "Using the I2C Protocol" earlier in this chapter before you continue.

Start by soldering the male headers that came with it to the HMC breakout board. The orientation is up to you; if you plan to make it standalone, you may want the headers facing up so that they're easy to access. If, on the other hand, you're planning on plugging the chip into a breadboard, by all means solder them facing down so that you can easily plug the whole unit into your board.

Once the headers are soldered to the board, connect the pins to your Pi with jumpers. VCC and GND go to the Pi's #2 and #6 pins, respectively, and SDA and SCL to the Pi's #3 and #5 pins. You're now ready to use the smbus library to read from the compass, using a little math (eek!) to calculate the bearing based on the sensed x- and y-values. Now would be a good time to use the i2cdetect tool mentioned earlier to make sure you can read from the compass. Run the tool by typing sudo i2cdetect -y 0 (or 1) and you should see the chip listed with address 0x1e. (See Figure 6-9.)

```
pi@raspberrypi ~/Documents/weather $ sudo i2cdetect -y 0
     0  1  2  3  4  5  6  7  8  9  a  b  c  d  e  f
00:          -- -- -- -- -- -- -- -- -- -- -- --
10: -- -- -- -- -- -- -- -- -- -- -- -- -- -- 1e --
20: -- -- -- -- -- -- -- -- -- -- -- -- -- -- -- --
30: -- -- -- -- -- -- -- -- -- -- -- -- -- -- -- --
40: -- -- -- -- -- -- -- -- -- -- -- -- -- -- -- --
50: -- -- -- -- -- -- -- -- -- -- -- -- -- -- -- --
60: 60 -- -- -- -- -- -- -- -- -- -- -- -- -- -- --
70: -- -- -- -- -- -- -- --
pi@raspberrypi ~/Documents/weather $ ▮
```

*Figure 6-9.* *Viewing the compass' I2C address*

If it doesn't appear, double-check your connections. (The other address you see listed in Figure 6-9, 0x60, is another I2C device I had plugged into my Pi.) When it shows up, start a new Python script to read from the device. We'll use the smbus library's I2C tools to read from and write to the sensor. First, start a directory on your Pi to keep all of your weather-station code together by typing

```
cd ~
mkdir weather
cd weather
```

Now that you've created a weather directory in your home folder and have navigated inside it, type the following code into your new Python script:

```
import smbus
import math

bus = smbus.SMBus(0)
address = 0x1e

def read_byte(adr):
    return bus.read_byte_data(address, adr)
def read_word(adr):
    high = bus. read_byte_data(address, adr)
    low = bus.read_byte_data(address, adr+1)
    val = (high << 8) + low
    return val

def read_word_2c(adr):
    val = read_word(adr)
    if (val >= 0x8000):
        return -((65535 - val) + 1)
    else:
        return val

def write_byte(adr, value):
    bus.write_byte_data(address, adr, value)

write_byte (0, 0b01110000)
write_byte (1, 0b00100000)
write_byte (2, 0b00000000)

scale = 0.92
x_offset = -39
y_offset = -100

x_out = (read_word_2c(3) - x_offset) * scale
y_out = (read_word_2c(7) - y_offset) * scale

bearing = math.atan2(y_out, x_out)
if bearing < 0:
    bearing += 2 * math.pi
print "Bearing: ", math.degrees(bearing)
```

After importing the correct libraries, this script sets up functions to read from and write to the sensor's address using the smbus library. The functions read_byte(), read_word(), read_word_2c(), and write_byte() are all used to read and write values (either single bytes or 8-bit values) to the sensor's I2C address. The three write_byte() lines write the values 112, 32, and 0 to the sensor to configure it for reading. These values are normally listed in the data sheet that comes with an I2C sensor.

■ **Note**   You may have also noticed that very often when you purchase a breakout board from either Adafruit or Sparkfun, those companies have example code available for that sensor. Check the "Documentation" link on each site whenever you purchase a part from them. As any programmer will tell you: if the work has been done already, there is no ·need to reinvent the wheel. Nor is there shame in using pre-existing code if it solves your problem for you.

The script then reads the current values of the x- and y-axis readings of the compass and calculates the sensor's bearing with the math library's `atan2()` (inverse tangent) function, first converting it to degrees with the library's `degrees()` function. The `x_offset` and `y_offset` values, however, are subject to change, depending on your current geographic location, and the best way to determine those values is to simply run the script.

Run the script, preferably with a working compass nearby, and compare the readings you get to the compass readings. (The side of the board with the soldered headers is the direction in which the board is "pointed.") You may have to tweak the offsets bit by bit to the get the bearing to register correctly. Once it's configured, you have a way to measure the wind's direction; we'll mount the compass to the anemometer's rotating shaft so that we can read the direction when we assemble the final weather station.

# Connecting the Temperature/Humidity Sensor

The temperature and humidity sensor we're using, the Sensirion SHT15, is one of the pricier parts in this build. However, it's also very easy to work with, because there's no I2C protocol involved. You'll first need to solder the included headers to it. Like the compass, the orientation of the headers is up to you. I tend to solder headers on with the board facing up, so I can see what each pin is as I plug the jumper wires into it. Of course, if I'm going to plug the unit into a breadboard, it means that I can't read the pins, but that's the tradeoff.

Once you've soldered the headers, complete the following steps:

1. Connect the VCC pin to the Pi's 5V pin (#2).

2. Connect the GND pin to the Pi's pin #6.

3. Connect the CLK pin to pin #7.

4. Connect the DATA pin to pin #11.

■ **Note**   With the pins labelled DATA and CLK, it'd be an understandable mistake to think this board runs on the I2C protocol, but it doesn't. The pins are just labelled that way.

In order to work with this sensor, you'll have to install the `rpiSht1x` python library by Luca Nobili. Inside your weather directory (or wherever you're working on your weather station code), download the `rpiSht1x` library by typing

```
wget http://bit.ly/1i4z4Lh --no-check-certificate
```

■ **Note**   You'll need to use the "`--no-check-certificate`" flag because I've shortened the link by using the link-shortening service `bitly.com` to make it easier for you to type. Ordinarily, when you download a file using wget, it just saves to your current directory, but renaming the link using `bitly.com` can lead to strange behavior when downloading. This flag corrects that problem.

When it's done downloading (which shouldn't take long, considering it's only an 8-KB download), you'll need to rename it so that you can expand it. Rename the downloaded file by typing

```
mv 1i4z4Lh rpiSht1x-1.2.tar.gz
```

and then expand the result by typing

```
tar -xvzf rpiSht1x-1.2.tar.gz
```

Then cd into the resulting directory (cd rpiSht1x-1.2) and run

```
sudo python setup.py install
```

You now have the library available to you, so let's try it out. With your SHT15 still connected as defined earlier, type the following code:

```
from sht1x.Sht1x import Sht1x as SHT1x
dataPin = 11
clkPin = 7
sht1x = SHT1x(dataPin, clkPin, SHT1x.GPIO_BOARD)

temperature = sht1x.read_temperature_C()
humidity = sht1x.read_humidity()
dewPoint = sht1x.calculate_dew_point(temperature, humidity)

temperature = temperature * 9 / 5 + 32    #use this if you'd like your temp in degrees F
print ("Temperature: {} Humidity: {} Dew Point: {}".format(temperature, humidity, dewPoint))
```

Save this code as sht.py and run it with sudo python sht.py. The script uses the functions defined in the Adafruit script—read_temperature_C(), read_humidity(), and calculate_dew_point()—to get the current values from the sensor, which we've connected to pins 7 and 11. Then it performs a quick conversion for those of us not using the metric system and displays the results.

You should get a line with your current conditions:

```
Temperature: 72.824 Humidity: 24.282517922 Dew Point: 1.22106391724
```

As you can see, it's a pretty self-explanatory library. Many of these libraries started their lives as written for the Arduino to communicate with them, and thankfully they've since been ported to run on the Pi. (See the side note regarding using existing code from earlier.)

# Connecting the Barometer

Perhaps one of the most interesting parts of the weather station is the BMP180 barometer chip, if only because changing air pressure is one of the best indicators as to what the weather is going to do next. In general, falling air pressure indicates a storm on the way and rising air pressure indicates good weather ahead. That is an oversimplification, of course, but that seems to be the case.

The BMP180 chip runs on the I2C protocol, so you'll have to wire it up to your Pi's SDA and SCL pins (pins #3 and #5) like you did with the compass. After soldering your headers to the board, connect VCC and GND to pins #1 and #6, and then SDA and SCL to pins #3 and #5, respectively.

**■ Note**  You're connecting the chip's power to the Pi's 3.3V, *not* the 5V. You want the chip to run on 3.3V logic so that it doesn't have a chance to damage the Pi's delicate 3.3V inputs.

To make sure everything is connected correctly, run sudo i2cdetect -y 0 and make sure the device shows up. It should show up as address 0x77, like in Figure 6-10.

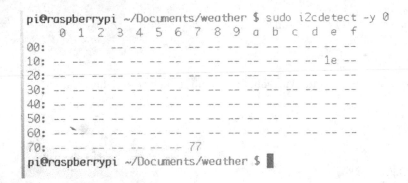

**Figure 6-10.**  *i2cdetect showing the 0x77 and 0x1e addresses in use*

**■ Note**  The 0x1e device in the screenshot in Figure 6-10 is the connected compass we're using.

Again, this device needs some external libraries to work. In this case, we'll be using Adafruit's excellent BMP085 libraries.

**■ Note**  The BMP180 chip's original version was the BMP085. Although it has since been replaced, the schematic and pinout of the chips is the same, so all libraries written for the BMP085 also work for the BMP180.

To grab the necessary library, in your terminal type

```
wget http://bit.ly/NJZOTr --no-check-certificate
```

As we did before, we'll need to rename the downloaded file so that we can use it. In this case, the file we downloaded is named NJZOTr. Rename it by typing

```
mv NJZOTr Adafruit_BMP085.py
```

There's nothing to install here, so we can jump right into using the library to communicate with the chip. In a new Python script in the same directory, enter the following:

```
from Adafruit_BMP085 import BMP085

bmp = BMP085(0x77)      #you may recognize the I2C address here!

temp = bmp.readTemperature()
temp = temp*9/5 + 32      #if you're not in one of the 99% of countries using Celsius
pressure = bmp.readPressure()
altitude = bmp.readAltitude()

print "Temperature:      %.2f F" % temp
print "Pressure:         %.2f hPa" %(pressure / 100.0)
print "Altitude:         %.2f" %altitude
```

As the script for the temperature sensor did, this little bit of code uses the prewritten library and its functions to read the necessary values from the barometer chip. When you run it, you should get something like Figure 6-11.

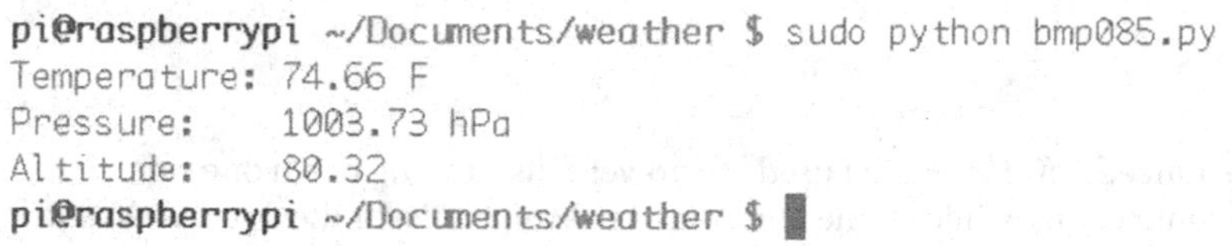

```
pi@raspberrypi ~/Documents/weather $ sudo python bmp085.py
Temperature: 74.66 F
Pressure:    1003.73 hPa
Altitude:    80.32
pi@raspberrypi ~/Documents/weather $
```

***Figure 6-11.*** *Output of BMP180 pressure sensor*

You can now read from all of your sensors, so it's time to put everything together!

# Connecting the Bits

An important part of building this weather station is putting everything (or at least the compass) on a rotating platform so that you can determine the wind's direction. As you can see in Figure 6-12, I put all of my chips on a single breadboard and connected it to the Pi so that it was easier for me to mount everything (Pi and breadboard) on a rotating platform. With a decent-sized platform on your Lazy Suzan bearing, this shouldn't be a problem.

*Figure 6-12.* *Breadboarded chips*

Looking at Figure 6-12, you may have noticed how I wired it: I used the power rails running down one side of the board for the positive (+) and negative (–) connections, while on the other side I used the rails for the data (SDA) and clock (SCL) lines for the I2C connections. It's the easiest way I've found to attach several different I2C devices to the Pi, since they share the clock and data lines.

With the anemometer mounted to your weather station base, you can now attach the Pi and the breadboarded compass, temperature sensor, and barometer chips. Because of the short leads from the rotary encoder, you may need to mount an additional breadboard to your anemometer mast, as you can see in the figure. Your finished assembly may look something like Figure 6-13. Power your Pi, and you're ready to receive weather updates.

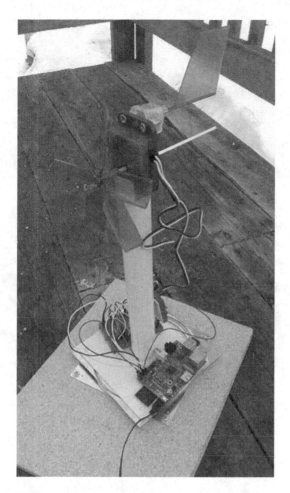

**Figure 6-13.** *Completed weather station*

We'll write the code so that the Pi queries each sensor every 30 seconds and displays the results to the screen. See the final code.

# The Final Code

The final code is available as weather.py from Apress.com.

```
import os
import time
from sht1x.Sht1x import Sht1x as SHT1x
import Rpi.GPIO as GPIO
from Adafruit_BMP085 import BMP085
import smbus
import math
```

```python
GPIO.setmode(GPIO.BOARD)
GPIO.setup(8, GPIO.IN, pull_up_down=GPIO.PUD_DOWN)

bus = smbus.SMBus(0)
address = 0x1e

def read_byte(adr):
    return bus.read_byte_data(address,adr)

def read_word(adr):
    high = bus.read_byte_data(address, adr)
    low = bus.read_byte_data(address, adr)
    val = (high << 8) + low
    return val

def read_word_2c(adr):
    val = read_word(adr)
    if (val >= 0x8000):
        return -((65535 - val) + 1)
    else:
        return val

def write_byte(adr, value):
    bus.write_byte_data(address, adr, value)

def checkTemp():
    dataPin = 11
    clkPin = 7
    sht1x = SHT1x(dataPin, clkPin, SHT1x.GPIO_BOARD)
    temp = sht1x.read_temperature_C()
    temp = temp*9/5 + 32        #if you want degrees F
    return temp

def checkHumidity():
    dataPin = 11
    clkPin = 7
    sht1x = SHT1x(dataPin, clkPin, SHT1x.GPIO_BOARD)
    humidity = sht1x.read_humidity()
    return humidity

def checkBarometer():
    bmp = BMP085(0x77)
    pressure = bmp.readPressure()
    pressure = pressure/100.0
    return pressure

def checkWindSpeed()
    prev_input = 0
    total = 0
    totalSpeed = 0
    current = time.time()
```

```
    for i in range(0, 900):
        input = GPIO.input(8)
        if ((not prev_input) and input):
            total = total + 1
        prev_input = input
        if total == 90:
            rps = (1/ (time.time()-current))
            speed = math.exp((rps + 0.95)/4.3)
            totalSpeed = totalSpeed + speed
            total = 0
            current = time.time()
    speed = totalSpeed / 10    #average speed out of ten turns
    return speed

def checkWindDirection()
    write_byte(0, 0b01110000)
    write_byte(0, 0b00100000)
    write_byte(0, 0b00000000)
    scale = 0.92
    x_offset = 106        #use the offsets you computed
    yoffset = -175        #use the offsets you computed
    x_out = (read_word_2c(3) - x_offset) * scale
    y_out = (read_word_2c(7) - y_offset) * scale
    direction = math.atan2(y_out, x_out)
    if (direction < 0):
        direction += 2 * math.pi
        direction = math.degrees(direction)
    return direction

#main program loop
while True:
    temp = checkTemp()
    humidity = checkHumidity()
    pressure = checkBarometer()
    speed = checkWindSpeed()
    direction = checkWindDirection()

    os.system("clear")
    print "Current Conditions"
    print "----------------------------------------"
    print "Temperature:         ", str(temp)
    print "Humidity:         ", str(humidity)
    print "Pressure:         ", str(pressure)
    print "Wind Speed:         ", str(speed)
    print "Wind Direction:  ", str(direction)

    time.sleep(30)
```

## Summary

In this chapter, you built a weather station from scratch and installed the necessary sensors to keep tabs on the weather goings-on, including barometric pressure, temperature, humidity, wind speed, and even wind direction. You've learned more about the I2C interface and should now have a good grasp of how to use Python functions to repeat tasks at a given interval. You've also done more fabrication here than any other project so far; now you can take a break because the next project, the media server, requires no construction whatsoever!

■ ■ ■

# CHAPTER 7

# The Media Server

The concept behind a media server is its ability to store all of your media files—music and movies—in one central location, and then stream them from that location to whatever device in your house you choose. These days, almost every media device (and some non-media devices) can hook up to a network—if not the Internet, then at least your home network. This means that all of these machines, except for perhaps the refrigerator, can become *clients*, streaming media files from a central *server*. This is standard networking language; the computer that stores files—whether they be media files, spreadsheets, or web pages—is called a *server*, and computers that request those files are called *clients*.

As it happens, the Pi is perfect to act as a server. That's because there's very little computing power necessary (an Arduino can actually be a media server, and it's about 100 times less powerful than the Pi), and storage space is not a problem, because you can stream media files from any connected storage device, such as an external hard drive. The Pi can stream files to any compatible device. "But it's a Linux box!" I hear some of you screaming from the back row. "I need to stream to my Windows laptop!" Not a problem—the software we'll use to act as the server allows Linux servers and Windows clients to play nicely together.

Regarding your media files, I'm going to assume you are an upstanding, law-abiding citizen who has paid for all of your movies and music and have amassed quite a collection the correct, *legal* way. Right? Right. Let's begin with the parts you'll need.

## A Shopping List of Parts

This project requires almost no parts. All you'll need is your Pi and an external USB hard drive large enough to store all of your files. The Pi should recognize most modern external drives, but I recommend that if you purchase a drive for this purpose, you plug it into the Pi and make sure everything works before you start transferring gigabytes of files to it to be streamed.

## Using an NTFS Drive

The USB hard drive you use needs to be formatted as an NTFS (New Technology File System) drive. NTFS is a Windows format that often requires some special handling in order to be compatible with Linux. FAT32 was the format most often used prior to NTFS, and Linux and Unix had no problems reading from it or writing to it, but FAT32 cannot handle file sizes over 4 GB—a limit easily exceeded by one high-definition movie file. Thus, we've moved to the NTFS format, which can handle file sizes up to 16 TB without breaking a sweat. FAT32 also had issues with total drive sizes; depending on the size of file clusters, it could only format a drive up to around 127 GB. NTFS formats, on the other hand, have a *theoretical* upper size limit of 256 TB with a 64-KB cluster—obviously much larger and more applicable to today's larger file and drive sizes.

File sizes are a common source of confusion with many users setting up a file/media server for the first time. Table 7-1 will help you make some sense of them.

**Table 7-1.** *Common file sizes*

| Type of file | File Type | Average Size |
|---|---|---|
| Song | mp3 | 5 MB |
| Music video | mp4, avi, mpg | 150 MB |
| Standard def movie | mp4, avi, mpg | 750 MB |
| High def movie (~1080p) | mp4, avi, mkv, mpg | > 1.5 GB |

Keep those sizes in mind as you look at your current music and video collection and shop around for a drive on which to store them. Also remember: 1024 KB equals 1 MB, 1024 MB equals 1 GB, 1024 GB equals 1 TB. (Yes, you can round to 1000 in most cases; it's a binary thing—$2^{10} = 1024$.) Luckily, storage prices are dropping steadily, and you can most likely pick up a 2-TB drive for under $150 US.

Because most drives purchased are preformatted with the NTFS format, let's make sure your Pi can read and write to it, by installing a program called NTFS-3g. Open a terminal, and install it by typing

```
sudo apt-get install ntfs-3g
```

NTFS-3g is an open source, read-write NTFS driver program for Linux, Android, Mac OSX, and various other systems. It comes preinstalled on most Linux systems, but not the Pi (as of this writing), which is why you'll need to add it.

Once NTFS-3g is installed, plug your drive into your Pi. You'll probably be greeted with a popup window asking what to do; just select "Open in File Manager" and continue. Once you know you can read it (by viewing its files), make sure you can write to it by opening a terminal and creating a directory (which is only for testing), like this:

```
cd ../../
cd media
ls
cd "My Book" (or whatever your drive is named—use ls to find the name)
mkdir test
```

If the test folder appears, you can move on. If not, make sure you installed NTFS-3g, and reboot the Pi if necessary.

You may have noticed the fact that "My Book" is in quotes in the preceding command. That's because while file names *can* contain spaces, you need to account for the spaces when you're using the command line. If you need to change directories (cd) to a folder called My Book, just typing the following line will give you a file not found error, because the OS looks for a folder named My and then stops looking:

```
cd My Book
```

The way to account for spaces in file names is to either use quotation marks around the name or escape the space with a backslash, like so:

```
cd My\ Book
```

We need to create a Media folder in the /media directory of the Pi, where we'll be storing all of our music and movie files. We can create subdirectories in there later, but for now we just want to make sure that every time we boot up our Pi, the external drive will get mounted to the same folder. This is because all of our other devices (clients) will be looking for that folder when we set them up, and we don't want to have to reconfigure them to ask for a different folder every time we boot our Pi. To create that folder, do it as a root user:

```
sudo mkdir /media/Media
```

To set the Media folder as a *mount point*, we need to edit a file called `fstab` and insert our drive's information. First, we need our drive's information. In your terminal, enter the following command:

```
sudo blkid
```

This will list all of the drives, both virtual and physical, currently connected to your Pi. The results of my `blkid`, for example, look like the screen shown in Figure 7-1.

```
pi@raspberrypi /media/My Book $ sudo blkid
/dev/mmcblk0p1: LABEL="RECOVERY" UUID="707B-AD5D" TYPE="vfat"
/dev/mmcblk0p5: SEC_TYPE="msdos" LABEL="boot" UUID="676B-0317" TYPE="vfat"
/dev/mmcblk0p6: UUID="0eb36e9e-40f5-47f4-a751-4e197c0dd7c8" TYPE="ext4"
/dev/sda1: LABEL="My Book" UUID="39D8-62EF" TYPE="vfat"
pi@raspberrypi /media/My Book $ 
```

***Figure 7-1.*** `blkid` *results*

As you can see, the disk mounted as /dev/sda1; "My Book," is the one we're interested in, and what we need is that disk's UUID (Universally Unique Identifier).

Now we need to open the `fstab` file by typing

```
sudo nano /etc/fstab
```

There will probably be a few lines already in the file. They follow this format:

```
Device name | Mount point | File system | Options | Dump options | File system check options
```

We need to add our external drive and mount point to the file, with the correct file system and options. So, as an example, for a fictitious NTFS-formatted drive, I would add the following (each separated by one tab):

```
UUID=39E4-56YT    /media/Media    ntfs-3g    auto,user,rw,exec    0    0
```

The first entry is your drive's UUID, the second is the folder we created earlier (which will become the mount point), the third is the volume type, and the last three are the necessary permissions and default options.

Once you've added to and saved your `fstab` file, mount all of the drives in it by typing

```
sudo mount -a
```

(which should force mount all drives listed in `fstab` if they're not mounted already), and you should hear your external drive spin up. Then see if it mounted correctly to the correct folder by typing the following, which lists all currently mounted drives:

```
df -h
```

If everything shows up correctly, you can move to the next step in the process, installing Samba.

# Installing Samba

As Samba's web site explains, "Samba runs on Unix platforms, but speaks to Windows clients like a native. It allows a Unix system to move into a Windows 'Network Neighborhood' without causing a stir. Windows users can happily access file and print services without knowing or caring that those services are being offered by a Unix host." The name *Samba* comes from the SMB (Server Message Block) protocol, which is a part of the CIFS (Common Internet File System) put out by Microsoft in its attempt to get along with other operating systems without causing an outright mutiny.

This program, then, is what we need to install on the Pi so that your collection of Windows boxes can receive media files as well as your collection of Macs and Linux boxes. It is preinstalled on many Linux distributions; the Pi, however, is not one of them. Installing it is as simple as typing

```
sudo apt-get install samba
```

---

## SAMBA AS A LIAISON

Once upon a time, computers all played nicely together. Networking was uncomplicated, and computers communicated easily over phone lines, with low baud rates and small messages. If you needed to talk to another computer, chances are it was over a BBS (Bulletin Board System) and it didn't matter what operating system you were using. If you weren't using a BBS, chances were that you were running DOS as an operating system, as was the computer to which you were speaking. It was a simpler time. Then, as computers got more complex, different operating systems arose. On one side of the dividing wall was the Unix empire, with its smaller kingdoms of Linux, Mac, and BSD. On the other side of the wall was the great Microsoft empire, beginning with the great King DOS and followed by his heirs, the Windows models from Windows 1.01 to today's Windows 8.1.

A relative peace existed between the kingdoms; in fact, the two sides rarely spoke, so there were no hostilities. As the Internet and other interconnected networks grew, however, it became necessary for the two sides to exchange files smoothly and without errors. The Unix empire, being the smaller of the two, adjusted all of its operating systems to easily become clients to a Windows server, as this was a common configuration in a network setup. The Windows side, however, refused to believe that it would ever stoop to receiving files from a *Unix server* and did nothing to make this easy—or even possible.

However, Unix and Linux servers have proliferated, even while the number of Windows desktop clients has increased, and thus it eventually became necessary for a Windows client to communicate and exchange files with a Unix-flavored server. While it could be done, it was not easy, and normally it required a super user with intimate knowledge of networking protocols and languages. Enter Samba—a program designed to allow these different computers to communicate easily with fewer headaches on the part of the user.

---

## Configuring Samba

Once Samba is installed, we need to configure it. It's a good idea to make a backup of the current configuration file before you edit it so that you can just restore it should you royally mess it up.

To do that, use Linux's cp command:

```
sudo cp /etc/samba/smb.conf /etc/samba/smb.conf.orig
```

This command copies the smb.conf file to the smb.conf.orig file in the same directory. It needs to be run as sudo, because the /etc folder can be edited only by the root user. When that's done, you can open the file for editing by typing

```
sudo nano /etc/samba/smb.conf
```

You'll be greeted by a rather large configuration file—don't let it scare you. We only need to change a few settings. The size of the configuration file is indicative of how adaptable Samba really is; because it's used all over the Internet, as both a web server and a file server, it's important that users can change it to suit their unique needs. Our needs are actually rather simple, and thus don't require us to change many things in the program's default settings.

The first setting we may need to edit is the workgroup. The workgroup is simply the domain that the Samba server (your Pi) will be a part of. As a home media server, the domain is what Windows calls a "workgroup"—your home network. Under the Global Settings, change

```
workgroup = WORKGROUP
```

to the name of your local workgroup, if you have one. If you don't have one set up, leave the workgroup setting as it is.

Then change server string to %h, uncomment the following line (by removing the hash tag):

```
#wins support = no
```

and change it to read

```
wins support = yes
```

Under the Networking settings, change the interfaces line to read

```
;    interfaces = eth0 wlan0 lo
```

Leave the following line as it is:

```
bind interfaces only = yes
```

A little farther down, if it's commented out, uncomment

```
security = user
```

The last part to change is the Share Definitions section. This section is where you list and configure the fields and folders you want Samba to share with others. Scroll down to the bottom of that section, and add the following lines:

```
[Media]
    comment = Media Drive
    path = /media/Media
    browseable = yes
    guest ok = yes
    writeable = yes
    public = yes
    available = yes
    create mask = 0666
    directory mask = 0777
```

This creates the sharing portion of your Samba installation to match the drive and folder we created earlier. It also makes the folder browse-able and creates the correct sharing permission for that folder.

## Setting Linux Permissions

Linux file permissions are an interesting beast, and they could use some illumination, because you're bound to come across them in some fashion in your travels through Raspberry Pi country in the land of Linux. Each file or folder has three permission groups associated with it: the *owner*, the *group*, and the *all users* group. Those permissions are either *r*, *w*, or *x*, for *read*, *write*, and *execute*.

When you list the files in a directory with

```
ls -l
```

you can see that each item in the directory is preceded by a line like this

```
-rwxrwxrwx
```

or

```
drwsr-xr-x
```

The first character is either a - (hyphen) or a d, which tells you that it's either a file or a directory. Next the permissions are listed in groups of three, in the order of owner, group, and all users. A file listed as -rwxrwxrwx means that the owner of the file, users belonging to the group that has been assigned to that directory, and all users all have read, write, and execute permissions to that file. If the file is listed as -rwxr-xr-x, on the other hand, it means that only the owner has write permissions (can write and save to it.) The other two groups may only read the file and execute it.

If you need to change a file's permissions, you use the chmod command, which can be done either explicitly or with a binary representation of those permissions. If you want to do it explicitly, the flags used for each group are u (owner), g (group), and o (all users.) For instance, if you wanted to change the -rwxrwxrwx file to be read only for all users, you would enter

```
chmod o-wx filename
```

which would change its directory listing to -rwxrwxr--. To do the reverse, you would enter

```
chmod o+wx filename
```

to restore write and execute permissions for all users.

If you'd prefer to use binary permissions, you can do that as well. Basically, each permission has a value; r = 4, w = 2, and x = 1. You add the integers for each group's permissions, and set them that way. So a group's rwx permissions would be a 7, and an r-x permission would be a 5. You need to set each group's permissions if you do it that way; if a file currently has -rwxrwxrwx permissions, and you want to take away write permissions for the group and all users, you would enter

```
chmod 755 filename
```

It can get a little confusing, but once you've worked a bit with permissions, it will all make perfect sense. In our Samba configuration file, you've set the mask and directory permissions to -r-xr-xr-x and -rwxrwxrwx, respectively, which is what we need in order to stream all files in that directory to clients.

## Fixing the Apostrophe Bug

There's one other thing you may need to edit in the default Samba configuration, and it's something that—in my opinion—you shouldn't have to do, but it's a bug and it can mess everything up if you miss it. Look through all of the uncommented lines in the file and make sure that there are no lone apostrophes (') used as possessives in the middle of a line. If there are, delete them. For instance, at the bottom of the file, there may be an apostrophe in the [cdrom] section:

```
;[cdrom]
;   comment = Samba server's CD-ROM
;   read only = yes
;   locking = no
;   path = /cdrom
;   guest ok = yes
```

See it there in the second line? The problem is that the configuration file treats everything after the apostrophe as a string literal, and it doesn't pay attention to anything contained therein until it comes across *another* single apostrophe (again, in an uncommented line) to close the string. So even if it's not in a section of the config file you think you'll use, it still screws up the configuration process. Just make the second line in this example look like this:

```
;   comment = Samba servers CD-ROM
```

and it should work fine after that. In my smb.conf file, there were three apostrophes that had to be deleted before the configuration worked correctly. If they're in a commented line (preceded by a "#") they're totally ignored by the computer, so those you can leave alone.

## Restarting the Samba Service

When you've finished editing the configuration file, restart your Samba service by typing

```
sudo service samba restart
```

When it's up and running again, go to a Windows machine on your home network and open a command prompt. At the prompt, type

```
net view \\192.168.xx.xxx
```

(substituting the IP address of your Pi, obviously). You should get something back like you see in Figure 7-2.

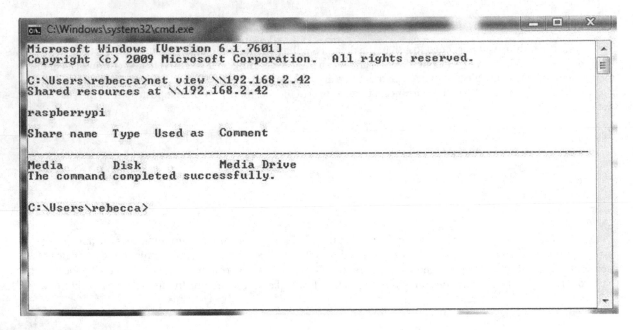

**Figure 7-2.** *Net view of a working Samba share*

Connecting to your Samba share as a shared (network) drive is, unfortunately, slightly different in every version of Windows. Because this book is about the Pi, not Windows, I can't go into all of the specifics for each version using a graphical interface. However, if you don't mind using a command-line interface, the command to mount the Media folder on a Samba share located at 192.168.2.42 on the same domain is actually very simple. It looks like this

```
net use z: \\192.168.2.42\Media * /USER:pi /P:Yes
```

If everything on the Pi is set correctly, you should see your Media folder mounted as a Z: drive. However, Windows 7 is notorious for not wanting to play nicely with Samba shared folders. If you're confident you have everything configured correctly but still can't see the contents of the folder (you're getting an "Access Denied" error, for example), try it with a different OS. Your Windows OS may be the problem.

## Connecting with Linux/OS X

"But wait!" I can hear some of you screaming weakly from the back of the room. "What if we want to connect to our server with a Linux or Mac box?"

Well, first of all, if you are running a Linux box somewhere else in your house, you probably don't need any help connecting to a Samba share. If, however, you're using a Mac, it's again pretty easy to connect. From your Finder, click "Go" and then "Connect to Server." (See Figure 7-3.)

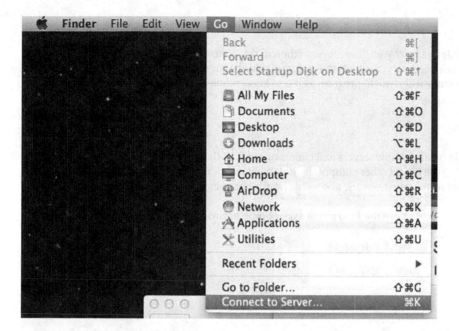

*Figure 7-3. Connection menu*

In the window that comes up, enter the address and shared folder and click Connect. (See Figure 7-4.) Enter the name and password you use to log in to the Pi in the next window, and the folder should mount as a shared drive, accessible from any Finder window. If you happen to be using Mac's Mavericks (OS 10.9), you may also have trouble connecting as "pi," but you may be able to connect as "Guest." This is an issue with Mavericks and, unfortunately, is not something I can easily solve here.

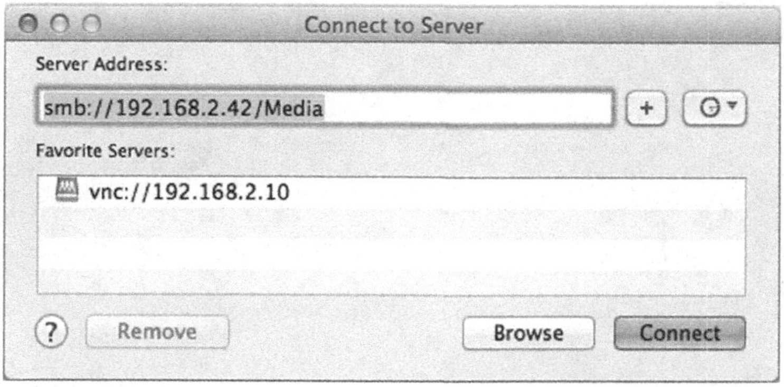

*Figure 7-4. "Connect to Server" dialog window on a Mac*

You now have a working Samba installation you can use to share anything you put into the folder, and because of the permissions you gave it, you don't have to worry about accidentally deleting a file in your Media folder from another device on the network. The only way to add to or subtract from the shared folder is from the Pi itself—a little security for your music and movies.

## Where's Python?

But wait! Where's the Python in this chapter? Well, there is no Python in this chapter. This is a good example of a situation where programming is not necessary; the tools that are available are good enough just as they are, and sometimes it's just as valuable to know when *not* to program as it is to know when *to* program.

## Summary

In this chapter, you learned a little bit about how servers and clients operate, both on the Internet and over your home network. You learned about getting the Pi and other computers (notably Windows) to play well together, and how to share all of your media files across your home network, accessible by any connected device, using a free file-sharing program.

In the next chapter, you'll learn how to use the Pi to protect your home network—not from hackers, but from physical intruders.

■ ■ ■

# CHAPTER 8

# The Home Security System

Living in modern times can be … well, let's face it. It can be a scary, stressful thing. Bad guys, and the crimes they commit, are everywhere. According to the FBI Crime Statistics web site, there were approximately 9 *million* property crimes committed in the United States in 2012—the most recent year for which statistics are available. The days of living on a peaceful street, where neighbors knew each other and you could leave your door unlocked while you went to work, are long gone.

Luckily, we're able to protect our homes and also to watch those homes with cameras—both still and video—that are mounted where we need them and capable of live-streaming that video to any of our always-connected devices, such as our laptops or phones. We can outfit our house with sensors, such as motion sensors and trip switches, and use the information gathered from those sensors as a trigger to perform certain actions. If you're willing to spend the money, you can install systems that do everything from protecting your home from fire and burglars to alerting you to carbon monoxide (CO) leaks.

As it happens, the Raspberry Pi is perfect for doing all those things for quite a bit cheaper than an entire network of closed-circuit cameras and the computer system to run them. Not a lot of computing power is necessary—it's small enough and power-miserly enough to actually be installed onsite, it can take pictures of important moments via its onboard camera, and because it's connected to a home network it can alert you when something is wrong. Perfect.

Yes, you could get a watchdog. In fact, that's what many people (some would say *normal* people) do. But let's take a moment to consider the pros and cons of owning a dog versus owning a Raspberry Pi. Then we can start building our home security system with the Raspberry Pi.

## Dogs as Security

Dogs (*Canis lupus familiaris*) are commonly known as man's best friend, and they have been used as watchdogs for nigh on 10,000 years. They are descended from the wolf and come in all shapes and sizes, from the pint-sized Chihuahua to the giant Great Dane.

One of the jobs of the dog has long been to protect the home from intruders. They are intensely loyal and protective of their human family members and their "den" and will bark at, and even attack, intruders. To keep up this behavior, they require food—sometimes quite a lot of it. And while they are often cute and cuddly, and great at keeping your feet warm on cold winter nights, the fact that they have to eat means, unfortunately, that they have to eliminate as well—a stinky undertaking for all concerned.

Dogs are also incapable of being upgraded. The last time I tried to plug a USB cable into my dog, she yelped. And even though dogs can be very cute when they stick their heads out of the window when you're driving down the road, you can't upgrade their drivers or use a package manager to download a more efficient gas-elimination program.

The upshot? Dogs are great for watching the house, but they have some serious shortcomings.

# Raspberry Pi as Security

The Raspberry Pi (*Rubus strigosus Pi*) is commonly known as the hobby-roboticist's best friend, and it has been used to make all kinds of off-the-wall projects for at *least* two whole years. These devices are descended from the Acorn RISC Machine in the early 1980s and, as mentioned previously, come in two versions: version A and version B.

The Raspberry Pi does not really have a specific job, but as a computer, it is well known that it will follow *all* instructions given it to a fault. If you program it to find all prime numbers between 1 and 10,000, it will do so; on the other hand, if you tell it to continue finding prime numbers until a pig flies overhead, it will continue computing until its processor burns out or until Porky grows wings. To do these amazing feats, the Pi does not have to eat, nor does it have to eliminate. The trade-off for the lack of metabolizing organic substances is that the Pi cannot keep your feet warm on cold winter nights.

You can upgrade a Pi, however, with judicious use of the *sudo apt-get install* command. The Pi welcomes a USB input, and it can be programmed to use sensors to watch your house and its surrounding grounds, and to alert you if those defenses are breached. Unfortunately—speaking from experience—people give you *very* strange looks if you drive down the street with your Pi hanging its head out of the window, but there's no malodorous gas problem, so there's that.

The upshot? The Raspberry Pi has some serious shortcomings, but those can be overcome to allow it to watch over your house. And since this *is* a book on the Pi, that's what we're going to use.

# Using a Sensor Network

The home security system (and the weather center in another chapter) is based on the concept of a *sensor network*. If a computer is like a brain, sensors are like the senses that allow it to gather information from and interact with the physical world. Cameras are like eyes, reed switches are like fingertips, and pressure switches are like toes that have been stepped on by a clumsy dog. Robots would be nothing without their sensors, and any robot brain, for example, is entirely dependent on that network of sensors.

This, as a matter of fact, is one of the coolest things about the Pi—its ability to easily interface with physical things like sensors. Most modern desktops and laptops have had all of their interesting ports—such as the parallel and the serial port—taken away, left with nothing but a few lonely USB ports and an Ethernet port. This leaves them crippled, unable to easily interact with the "real" world. Meanwhile, the Pi can be plugged directly into a motion sensor via its GPIO pins and let you know, with a few lines of code, whether Slenderman is creeping about in the bushes behind your bedroom.

In our security system, we're going to use several sensors: an infrared motion sensor, a pressure switch, a magnetic sensor, and a reed, or limit switch. The motion sensor can be placed anywhere on the grounds. The pressure switch might be useful placed inside a doorway, where an intruder is likely to step. The magnetic sensor can be used to detect if a window is opened, and the reed switch can be used to determine if someone touches a trip wire. We can use the Pi's onboard camera to take pictures if any sensors are tripped and access those pics any time. Last, we can use our home network to have the Pi send us a text message and/or email message should something interesting be happening in our security network—kind of like the security company calling you if they detect an alarm.

This is the sensor network we'll be working with. It's kind of basic, but it's also infinitely expandable. And although we'll just be using one of each kind of sensor, you can easily add more if you want to (one magnetic sensor for each window in your house, for example).

## Understanding a Pulldown Resistor

One important concept to know and remember any time you use an input with almost *any* circuit is that of the floating input and the pulldown (or pullup) resistor. Basically, whenever a pin (such as a GPIO pin on the Pi) is set to read input from a voltage source, such as a sensor, it is what's called a *floating input* until some voltage is read at the pin. Before a voltage signal is sent from the sensor, the level at the pin could be almost anything. This unspecified, floating voltage could seriously screw with your program: if you've programmed the self-destruct sequence to activate when the pin reads a 2.3V value, and the floating value *happens* to be at 2.3V, *BOOM!* We need a way to set the pin to a known value (such as a logical HIGH or a logical LOW) when nothing is being read from it.

The way to solve this problem is to use a *pullup* or *pulldown* resistor. This resistor connects the input pin to either Vcc or GND (pullup or pulldown, respectively). That way, if there is no input coming in, the pin will read either Vcc or 0, and we know that value. This is often done with a physical resistor (10KΩ or 100KΩ, normally), but many development boards (including the Pi) will let you do it via software—a huge advantage when you're working with limited space. Using the GPIO library, you can declare a pin as INPUT *and* at the same time, 'pull it down' as if with a pulldown resistor with the following syntax:

```
GPIO.setup(11, GPIO.IN, pull_up_down=GPIO.PUD_DOWN)
```

This defines the value read at pin #11 as LOW until it receives voltage from the sensor; at that point, that voltage is pulled HIGH, and the program can act. When the HIGH value disappears, the pin is again pulled LOW until the process repeats. A pullup resistor does almost the same thing, except the pin is pulled HIGH (to Vcc) until an input appears.

## A Shopping List of Parts

In order to build a functioning home security system, there are a few parts you're going to need:

- A Raspberry Pi (obviously) and power adapter
- A wireless USB dongle if you want to go wireless with your Pi
- Raspberry Pi camera module
- Pressure switch (such as http://bit.ly/0wc8aN, for example)
- Magnetic sensor (such as http://bit.ly/1cis71c, for example)
- Motion sensor (such as http://bit.ly/1c35pQp, for example)
- Reed switch (such as http://bit.ly/1k6n2RM, for example)
- Large spool of Ethernet cable (crimped ends not required—buy in bulk to save money)
- Solder, soldering iron, and miscellaneous jumper wires and connectors

Some of these parts are optional, of course; it all depends on how thorough you want your security system to be. You can even add items to your list as your security system grows. Each sensor merely adds to your sensor network, expanding your system's reach.

## Connecting to Your Network Wirelessly

When you set up your Pi as the main controller of your security system, it will have to connect with your home's network in order to allow you to remotely log in and administer it, and to send you a text message to inform you of an infraction. When you connect to your network, you have the choice of going wired or wireless. Each option has its pros and cons, of course, but I highly suggest you use a wireless connection. This is mainly for two reasons: a wireless connection allows you to place the Pi anywhere without having to run Ethernet cable to its location, and a wireless connection is also more secure—a burglar can cut a wired connection to your Pi to render it useless, but not so with a wireless connection.

The first thing you'll need is a good wireless USB dongle. A popular one is the Edimax EW-7811UN (shown in Figure 8-1), available on Amazon for only a few dollars. It works well, is easy to configure, and doesn't require a powered USB hub to operate well on the Pi.

*Figure 8-1. The Edimax wireless adapter*

Next, you'll want to set up your Pi to have a static IP address. This will allow you to log in to your Pi remotely from anywhere, regardless of whether it has been powered off since your last remote login. If you leave the Pi to receive its IP address dynamically from your home router, it's possible the IP address will change if the Pi has to reboot, meaning you'll be unable to log in (because you won't know what the new address is).

Luckily, setting up a static IP for your Pi's wireless connection is not difficult. You'll need to know your network's netmask (normally, either 255.255.255.0 or 255.255.0.0) and your gateway address (normally, your router's address, such as 192.168.2.1). You'll also need your Bcast value, which you can find by typing ifconfig at the command line.

Open your /etc/network/interfaces file for editing by typing

```
sudo nano /etc/network/interfaces
```

You'll have to use sudo, because the file is editable only by the root user. You should see a line that reads

```
iface wlan0 inet dhcp
```

Change that to read

```
iface wlan0 inet static
```

and add the following below it:

```
address 192.168.2.50 (or whatever address you want, obviously)
netmask 255.255.255.0 (or your netmask)
network 192.168.2.0 (your network's location)
broadcast 192.168.2.255 (your Bcast value from earlier)
gateway 192.168.2.1 (your router's IP address)
```

Save the file and reboot your Pi. When it comes back online, it should have the address you specified—double-check by running an ifconfig command. You now have a static IP address. Write it down so you don't forget it. Now, no matter where you end up placing your Pi in your security network, you'll be able to log in remotely to administer it.

To use the static IP, you'll need an SSH server running on the Pi. Depending on how you first set up your Pi, you might have one running already. The easiest way to get your SSH server up and running is to run your raspi-config tool by typing

```
sudo raspi-config
```

at the command line. You'll be greeted with the raspi-config screen (as shown in Figure 8-2).

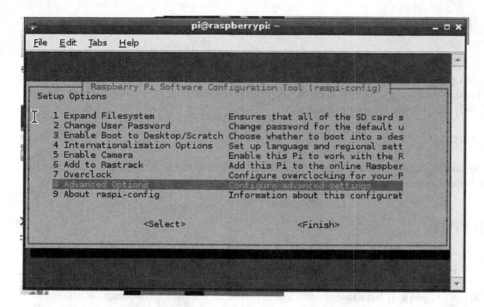

***Figure 8-2.*** *The raspi-config tool*

Cursor down to option #8, Advanced Options, press the right arrow key to highlight <Select>, and press Return. Then cursor down to #4 SSH, and again highlight <Select> and press Return. Make sure <Enable> is highlighted on the next screen (Figure 8-3), and press Return.

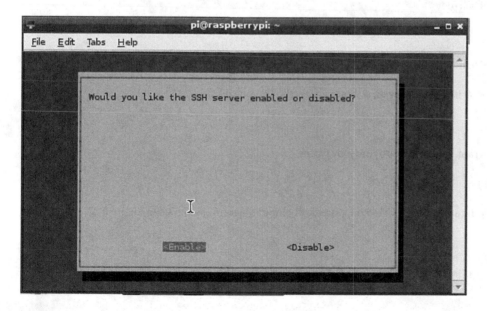

***Figure 8-3.*** *Enabling the SSH server*

Then back out of the raspi-config tool by selecting <Finish> and pressing Enter. Do a reboot by typing

```
sudo reboot
```

and your SSH server should be up and running. You can now remotely log in to your Pi from anywhere. If you're using a Windows machine, you'll need to download the free tool PuTTY in order to log into your Pi. If you're using a Mac or Linux box, ssh is enabled already. Just use the following command

```
ssh -l pi <your pi"s IP address>
```

and enter raspberry at the password prompt, and you're in! With PuTTY, enter your Pi's IP address in the box, add the username and password, and click Connect. You can now administer your Pi via the command line from anywhere.

## Accessing the GPIO Pins

As stated before, and as you've seen if you've read some of the other chapters in this book, the Pi's GPIO pins are the way we interface the Pi with the physical world, such as sensors, servos, motors, and lights. In order to do this, we use a Python library especially designed for this purpose: RPi.GPIO.

In order to work with the library, you may have to manually install two other libraries. (It depends on which version of Raspbian you're running.) First make sure your Pi is up to date by typing

```
sudo apt-get update
```

and then install the packages by typing

```
sudo apt-get install python-dev
```

and

```
sudo apt-get install python.rpi-gpio
```

which may (should) be already installed. Now, in order to access the Pi, you call

```
import RPi.GPIO as GPIO
```

in the first lines of your program, and then configure it by typing

```
GPIO.setmode(GPIO.BOARD)
```

which lets you identify the pins as they are labeled on a standard pinout diagram (as shown in Figure 8-4).

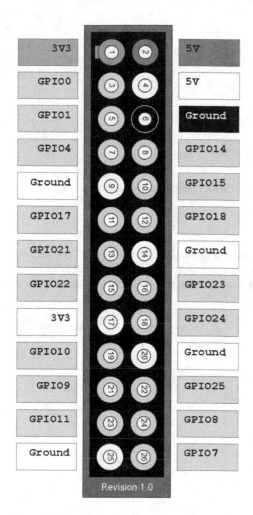

**Figure 8-4.** *The pinout diagram of the Pi's GPIO pins*

---

■ **Note**   Keep in mind that with GPIO.setmode(BOARD), when you refer to *pin 11*, you're actually referring to the physical pin #11 (which translates to GPIO17 in the diagram in Figure 8-4), *not* GPIO11, which translates to the physical pin #23.

---

Once you've set the mode, you can then set each pin to be either an input or an output. Users of the Arduino will probably recognize the concept here:

```
GPIO.setup (11, GPIO.OUT)
GPIO.setup (13, GPIO.IN)
```

and so forth. Once you've set a pin as an output, you can then send voltage to it (turn it on) by using

```
GPIO.output (11, 1)
```

or

```
GPIO.output (11, True)
```

and subsequently turn it off by using

```
GPIO.output (11, 0)
```

or

```
GPIO.output (11, False)
```

When you configure a pin as an input, remember to set a pullup or pulldown resistor as discussed earlier.

## Setting Up the Motion Sensor

One of the most important parts of a home security network is likely the motion sensor (shown in Figure 8-5)—with a few caveats. You can't rely solely on your motion sensor, because the moment you do, it'll be set off by a neighborhood cat, or possibly a Yeti (not necessarily a bad thing.) If, however, you use it in addition to all other sensors, you may have good luck with its results.

**Figure 8-5.**  *The motion sensor*

The sensor we're using, by Parallax or a close clone, detects motion by detecting changes in the infrared (heat) levels emitted by objects in the surrounding environment. Like most sensors, it then signals that a change has been detected by outputting a "HIGH" or "1" signal on its output pin. It has three pins: Vcc, Gnd, and Output.

The pins are (from the left in Figure 8-5) OUT, +, and -. A nice feature of this particular sensor is that it can use any voltage from 3V to 6V. To use and test it, connect the (-) pin to the Pi's ground pin (pin #6), connect the (+) pin to the Pi's 5V pin (pin #2), and connect the OUT pin to one of the GPIO pins.

To test the sensor and our coding prowess, we'll start by setting up the GPIO pins accordingly. We can use a simple setup to test our code—an LED on a breadboard that will light up when the sensor is tripped. Start a new Python script (let's call it *motion.py*) with nano motion.py and enter the following:

```
import RPi.GPIO as GPIO
import time

GPIO.setwarnings (False) #eliminates nagging from the library
GPIO.setmode (GPIO.BOARD)
```

```
GPIO.setup (11, GPIO.IN, pull_up_down=GPIO.PUD_UP)
GPIO.setup (13, GPIO.OUT)

while True:
    if GPIO.input (11):
        GPIO.output (13, 1)
    else:
        GPIO.output (13, 0)
```

That's it for the test code! In order to test it, first connect the (+) pin on the sensor to pin #2 on the Pi. Connect the OUT pin to pin #11 on the Pi. Connect the (–) pin to a common ground line on your breadboard. Finally, connect pin #13 on the Pi to the positive leg of your LED (through a resistor), and connect the negative leg of the LED to the common ground line. You should end up with something like you see in Figure 8-6.

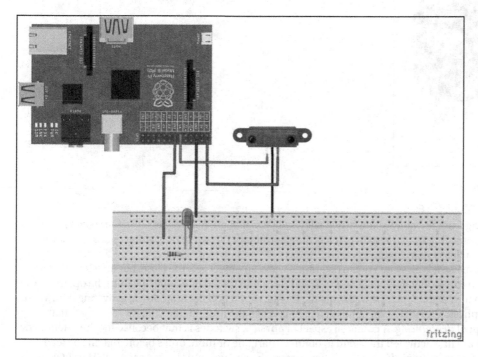

***Figure 8-6.*** *Testing the motion sensor*

When you run the preceding script (remembering to use sudo because you're accessing the GPIO pins), the LED should light up when you move your hand around the sensor, and then it should go out again after a few seconds of nonmovement. If it doesn't work, check your connections and your parts—a burned-out LED can cause all *sorts* of troubleshooting headaches, believe me!

Leave the sensor attached as it is, as we'll be using it in our system, and let's move on to the reed switch.

# Setting Up the Reed Switch

The reed, or limit, switch is a useful tool in many situations, not the least of which being our security system. It's often used by robots to determine the limits of movement, whether it's driving into a wall or closing a gripper around an object. Its concept is simple: the switch is normally open, letting no voltage through, and it has an armature protruding from the body of the switch, like a long lever. When an outside object presses on the lever, it closes the switch, sending voltage through the circuit—in our case, to the INPUT pin on the Pi that's listening for a signal. The limit switch we're using is also called a "sub-miniature snap-action switch." (See Figure 8-7.)

***Figure 8-7.*** *The limit switch*

The long arm protruding from the body of the switch allows objects that are far away to close the switch's contact—the small hump protruding from the switch. It has three terminals, but we're only going to use two because we're interested only in when the switch closes.

In our case, we're going to use a limit switch not to determine when an object gets too close, but to determine if a trip wire has been pulled. You can mount the switch on a wall and run a thin thread or fishing line from the opposite wall to the switch's lever. Position it so that if someone walks into the thread, they'll pull the lever down, activating the switch.

Because we're using a physical switch here, rather than a sensor like the motion detector, it's important that I introduce you to the concept of *debouncing*. A common aspect of physical switches is that because they're often made of spring metals, when they are first activated they tend to bounce apart one or more times before making a steady contact. The result is a very fast on-off-on-off-on-off "chatter" before the voltage settles at a steady HIGH or LOW. To combat this, we *debounce* the switch by reading from it only when it's no longer bouncing back and forth, like so:

```
import time
prev_input = 0
while True:
        #take a reading
        input = GPIO.input(11)
        #if the last reading was low and this one high, print
        if ((not prev_input) and input):
                print("Button pressed")
                #update previous input
        prev_input = input
        #slight pause to debounce
        time.sleep(0.05)
```

This little script illustrates the concept quite nicely. It ignores a button press if it occurs less than 0.05 seconds after the last one.

So to test our switch, let's hook it up to some GPIO pins and make sure we can read the input when its state changes. Just using the switch, connect your Pi's power pin (#2) to the switch's leftmost pin as shown in Figure 8-7. Then connect the *middle* pin to your Pi's pin #11. Try the following code by typing

```
import time
import RPi.GPIO as GPIO
GPIO.setwarnings (False)
GPIO.setmode (GPIO.BOARD)
GPIO.setup (11, GPIO.IN, pull_up_down = GPIO.PUD_DOWN)
prev_input = 0
while True:
    input = GPIO.input (11)
    if ((not prev_input) and input):
        print "Button pressed"

    prev_input = input
    time.sleep (0.05)
```

When you run this script (remembering to use sudo), pressing the switch will send voltage directly through it from pin #2 to pin #11, thus registering as HIGH at pin #11. It's a debounced signal, and the Pi should print "Button pressed" when you press the button. Congratulations! You're able to read when a switch is pressed!

Let's move to the next switch.

## Setting Up the Pressure Switch

The pressure switch is very similar to the limit switch, though it looks much different. (See Figure 8-8.)

**Figure 8-8.** *The pressure switch*

Rather than a physical lever and button, a square pad is used that simply registers pressure as a change in voltage. For this reason, it's even easier to connect than the limit switch. Connect your Pi's pin #2 to one of the leads, and connect the other lead to pin #11. Then run the same script as you did for the limit switch, and test it by pressing down on the pad with your finger. Voilá! You're now reading a value from a pressure switch! This is perfect for reading a footstep from underneath a welcome mat, for instance.

# Connecting the Magnetic Sensor

The magnetic sensor (shown in Figure 8-9) is a little device that, while not commonly used outside of certain specific applications, can come in handy for applications like ours. It measures the surrounding magnetic field and sends a signal when that field changes. For that reason, it is very good at determining when the relative position of two pieces of metal have changed, for instance.

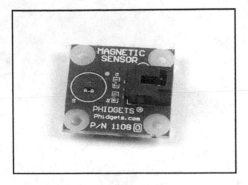

**Figure 8-9.** *The magnetic sensor*

In order to make sure we don't get any false readings, we can use some small external magnets to influence the sensor; the one we're using comes with two small neodymium magnets for just that purpose.

To test our magnetic sensor, we can again use our `switch.py` code we've been using. Connect the jumper wires that came with the sensor to the connector block on the sensor, and then connect them to your Pi: red to pin #2, black to pin #6, and white to pin #11. Now just change the code to read

```
import time
import RPi.GPIO as GPIO
GPIO.setwarnings (False)
GPIO.setmode (GPIO.BOARD)
GPIO.setup (11, GPIO.IN, pull_up_down = GPIO.PUD_DOWN)
prev_input = 0
while True:
    input = GPIO.input (11)
    if ((not prev_input) and input):
        print "Field changed"

    prev_input = input
    time.sleep (0.05)
```

and run the script. Your terminal will remain blank until you wave the magnet past the sensor. (You might have to experiment with different distances and speeds. My experience is that the magnets have to pass pretty closely to register.) At that point, it will tell you "field changed." After a little experimentation, you'll know just where you'll have to mount the magnet in order for the change in field readings to influence your security system. Now you can mount the sensor on one pane of a sliding window, for instance, and a magnet on the other pane, and should the window slide open, the magnetic sensor will register the movement of the magnet.

# Setting Up Pi's Camera

Finally, one of the features that makes the Pi attractive as a security system lynchpin is its ability to take pictures from a small, built-in camera. While this means that the Pi must be positioned in a strategic location in order to pick up anything interesting, the Pi is so small that finding a good place for it shouldn't be a problem.

In order to take pictures, you'll have to have two components working on your Pi: the wireless and the camera. I discussed the wireless setup earlier; the camera can be configured with the raspi-config tool, if you haven't configured it already.

Once you've enabled the camera, you have two commands you can use: raspistill (to capture pictures) and raspivid (to capture video). Each can be used with various flags and options to change the frame size, capture rate, and other configurations.

We're interested in taking still pictures, however; streaming the video via live feed, while possible, requires a few extra software tools that can be difficult to set up. Taking a picture is a simple call to raspistill from the command line. And while there is no Python library or module available as of this writing to use the camera, we can use the library call from subprocess import call to do the same thing. When you need to take a picture in your script, use these two simple lines:

```
from subprocess import call
call (["raspistill -o image.jpg"], shell=True)
```

A still image, labeled "image.jpg", will be stored in the current directory. We can put this picture-taking line in a take_pic() function and call it whenever a sensor is tripped. We then have evidence, should we need it for corroboration!

# Sending a Text Message from the Pi

In my opinion, having your Pi send you a text message when something unusual happens is one of the coolest parts of the project, and it's particularly useful if you're going out of town. A notification from your Pi can let you know that you need to call your neighbor (or the police) and have them check on your house. It's really pretty simple: the Pi uses the local network to send an email message, which is then translated by your mobile carrier into an SMS, or text message.

You'll need an email account that's web-accessible; most of us have a gmail or yahoo account, for instance. You'll also need to know how to send a text via email with your mobile carrier. Each carrier is slightly different, but the basic concept is the same—sending an email to a certain number (<mobile_number>@txt.carrier.net, for example) has that email delivered as a text. I use AT&T, and if you send an email to 19075551212@txt.att.net, it will be delivered as a text. So using Python's smtplib library, you can send an email to your phone.

It's probably easiest if I just show you with the following code:

```
def send_text(str):
HOST = "smtp.gmail.com"
SUBJECT = "Break-in!"
TO = "xxxxxxxxxx@txt.att.net"
FROM = "python@example.com"
text = str
BODY = string.join(("From: %s" % FROM, "To: %s" % TO, "Subject: %s" % SUBJECT, "", text), "\r\n")
s = smtplib.SMTP("smtp.gmail.com",587)
s.set_debuglevel(1)
s.ehlo()
s.starttls()
s.login("username@gmail.com", "mypassword")
s.sendmail(FROM, [TO], BODY)
s.quit()
```

Calling the send_text() function with a string such as "OMG I'm being robbed!" will send you a text message. Obviously, this code is designed to work with AT&T, and uses a gmail account. You'll need to modify it as necessary for your carrier and email provider. gmail's smtp access is through port 587, as you can see in line 9 in the preceding code; this may differ for Yahoo or MSN. You can call this function when you detect an input at any of your sensors, and you can even adjust the string sent according to which sensor is tripped.

## Implementing the Callback

There's one significant idea left to explore in this project, and that is the concept of the *callback*. You may have noticed that there's no easy way to check each switch; you have to continue to "poll" each switch and hope that nothing unusual happens while you're doing something else. Not a big deal if you have only three or four switches and sensors, but should you start adding to your network, the delay between something happening and being notified about it can get unwieldy quickly; limit switch #2 could get tripped while you're checking magnetic sensor #16, and you won't know about it for another two seconds. By that time, of course, the robber could have snuck by the trip wire and be well on his way to killing your entire family or stealing your *Star Wars* memorabilia.

Luckily, Python (and the Raspberry Pi) have an answer to that switch-checking problem. It's embedded in the RPi.GPIO library: the *threaded callback interrupt*. What this allows us to do is to start a different program thread for each switch. Each thread will go into a "waiting" mode, doing nothing, while the rest of the program (and the rest of the threads) go on about their business. If and when the switch gets tripped, it immediately issues a callback, or interrupt, to the main program to let it know ("Hey! I've been tripped over here!") and performs whatever function we want it to. In this way, we can be sure we won't miss an important button press or switch trip. Meanwhile, all of the other threads continue their holding pattern. At the bottom of this pattern, one switch functions as a base; if that one switch is tripped, you can end the program. Otherwise, it continues inside a while loop.

This callback feature is accomplished using either one of two functions: GPIO.wait_for_edge() or GPIO.add_event_detect(). GPIO.wait_for_edge() does just that—waits for a rising or falling edge on any particular pin and then acts when it detects that edge. GPIO.add_event_detect(), on the other hand, waits for a rising or falling edge on a particular pin and then calls the function declared in its parameters. You can see them both in use in the final code later in this chapter. Just be aware that for each sensor or switch, we have a unique callback function—one that is unique to that sensor so that we know exactly which switch has been tripped.

# Connecting All of the Bits

Now that we've determined how to use all of the pieces of this puzzle, let's quickly go over how to connect everything.

You'll need to use the Ethernet cable to make all of your connections; it's strong, easy to work with, and (mostly) waterproof. Strip the outer casing to reach the wires inside, and chop all but the two or three wires you need to connect each sensor to your Pi. You'll need a small breadboard to place next to the Pi, because everything should share a ground.

Find a good place to mount your Pi, where you can plug it in (no worrying about batteries) and where you can mount the camera so that it can take good pictures of the action. Once you've found a place, you can use poster putty to hold everything in place.

Finally, find good places for all of your sensors. Remember, they don't need to be in sight of the Pi: as long as you can run Ethernet cable to them, it's a good spot. Attach the cables securely and in such a way that nobody trips over them. Connect all of the negative wires to your common ground row on your breadboard, and connect each positive wire to a GPIO pin. At this stage, it'd probably be a good idea to write down what sensor is attached to which pin so that you can reference it in your code.

# The Final Code

So that completes all the individual parts of this project. All that's left is to put them all together in your final code, like so (you can download the final code file, called home_security.py at apress.com):

```python
import time
import RPi.GPIO as GPIO
from subprocess import call
import string
import smtplib

GPIO.setwarnings (False)
GPIO.setmode (GPIO.BOARD)
time_stamp = time.time() #for debouncing

#set pins
#pin 11 = motion sensor
GPIO.setup (11, GPIO.IN, pull_up_down=GPIO.PUD_DOWN)

#pin 13 = magnetic sensor
GPIO.setup (13, GPIO.IN, pull_up_down=GPIO.PUD_DOWN)

#pin 15 = limit switch
GPIO.setup (15, GPIO.IN, pull_up_down=GPIO.PUD_DOWN)

#pin 19 = pressure switch
GPIO.setup (19, GPIO.IN, pull_up_down=GPIO.PUD_DOWN)

def take_pic(sensor):
    call(["raspistill -o image" + sensor + ".jpg"], shell=True)
    time.sleep(0.5) #wait 1/2 second for pic to be taken before continuing

def send_text(details):
        HOST = "smtp.gmail.com"
        SUBJECT = "Break-in!"
        TO = "xxxxxxxxxx@txt.att.net"
        FROM = "python@mydomain.com"
        text = details
        BODY = string.join(("From: %s" % FROM, "To: %s" % TO, "Subject: %s" % SUBJECT, "", text), "\r\n")
        s = smtplib.SMTP("smtp.gmail.com",587)
        s.set_debuglevel(1)
        s.ehlo()
        s.starttls()
        s.login("username@gmail.com", "mypassword")
        s.sendmail(FROM, [TO], BODY)
        s.quit()

def motion_callback(channel):
    global time_stamp
    time_now = time.time()
```

```
        if (time_now - time_stamp) >= 0.3: #check for debouncing
                print "Motion detector detected."
                send_text("Motion detector")
                take_pic("motion")
        time_stamp = time_now

def limit_callback(channel):
    global time_stamp
    time_now = time.time()
    if (time_now - time_stamp) >= 0.3: #check for debouncing
        print "Limit switch pressed."
        send_text("Limit switch")
        take_pic("limit")
    time_stamp = time_now

def magnet_callback(channel):
    global time_stamp
    time_now = time.time()
    if (time_now - time_stamp) >= 0.3: #check for debouncing
        print "Magnetic sensor tripped."
        send_text("Magnetic sensor")
        take_pic("magnet")
    time_stamp = time_now

#main body
raw_input("Press enter to start program\n")

GPIO.add_event_detect(11, GPIO.RISING, callback=motion_callback)
GPIO.add_event_detect(13, GPIO.RISING, callback=magnet_callback)
GPIO.add_event_detect(15, GPIO.RISING, callback=limit_callback)

# pressure switch ends the program
# you could easily add a unique callback for the pressure switch
# and add another switch just to turn off the network
try:
    print "Waiting for sensors..."
    GPIO.wait_for_edge(19, GPIO.RISING)
except KeyboardInterrupt:
    GPIO.cleanup()

GPIO.cleanup()
```

# Summary

In this chapter, you learned about what sensors are, the concept of a sensor network, and how to hook different sensors to your Pi's GPIO pins. You set up the limit switch, pressure switch, magnetic sensor, and motion sensor (which we also use in the Pi-powered cat toy in the next chapter). With the knowledge you've gained here, you now have the ability to create a full-sized security system, with its breadth limited only by the amount of sensors you have and how much wire you've got to put them all together.

# CHAPTER 9

■ ■ ■

# The Cat Toy

Most people are pretty familiar with the "cat chasing the little red dot" paradigm. It's so popular it even had a short scene in one of the *Shrek* movies. Some cats will chase the laser spot until they drop. Some will only chase it for a little while. In any event, anyone who has a cat has probably played with a laser pointer with their feline friend at some point.

But wouldn't it be nice if you could entertain your cat when you're not there? A laser pointer, contrary to what you might think, does *not* have to be held and controlled by a human. A little programming and mechanical engineering magic, and you have yourself an autonomous cat toy.

However, in the cat-toy project we'll build in this chapter, we won't leave it at that. We just *can't*. After all, it wouldn't make sense to have the toy always moving, whether or not your cat is around to play with it, would it? So we'll add something special—an infrared sensor. That way, it'll turn on only when your cat's around, and it will turn off when the cat leaves the room.

Are you ready? Let's start by getting the parts we'll need to create our cat toy.

## A Shopping List of Parts

A nice feature of the cat toy, aside from being simple and homemade, is that the parts are actually pretty inexpensive. You will need the following:

- A Raspberry Pi.

- Two standard (*not* continuous) servos—I recommend the Parallax 900-00005 (http://www.parallax.com/product/900-00005), but any model will work.

- A cheap laser pointer, which you can purchase at a pet store for around $10 US. (See Figure 9-1.)

*Figure 9-1. An ordinary laser pointer used with the cat toy*

- A PIR motion sensor (http://parallax.com/product/910-28027).

- Glue/epoxy.

- Miscellaneous wires (red, black, and so forth).

- Flat-headed screw.

- Electrical tape.

- Popsicle stick.

- 9V battery.

- A container on which to mount everything—I used a short length of PVC pipe.

## The Concept Behind the Toy

The key to making this toy work is *random motion*. If you program the toy to make a series of concentric circles, one after another, and then repeat the pattern, it won't take long for your cat to recognize the pattern and get bored. However, by using Python's *random* or *randint* functions, you can randomize the patterns and keep your cat (and possibly your toddler) entertained.

Another thing to keep in mind is that you will be randomizing the motion on two axes—the x-axis and the y-axis—while keeping the motion within certain bounds (which is where the parameters of the randomizing functions and the movement extremes of the servos come in). You will be using two servos, but they'll be joined together so as to control the motion of one laser pointer. To control the servos, like several other projects in this book, we'll use the Pi's GPIO pins and Python's GPIO library. Another nice thing about this project is that the servos end up drawing so little power that they can be sourced with a simple 9V battery. You still need to power them separately from the Pi (*always* a good idea, regardless of the project), but you don't need a fancy battery setup as you do with many other projects.

# Creating and Using Random Numbers

You'd think creating and using random numbers would be simple. Just call a function, get a random integer, and proceed. While that may be how it works in practice and is all that most of us think of, the actual process of randomizing output is fascinating—it's actually the subject of intense study by many computer scientists and mathematicians. (See the sidebar "Oh, the Randomness.") To get a random number in Python, you can use several built-in functions. The first is, appropriately enough, the random() function. The random function returns a float (a *floating point*, decimal number). It takes no parameters, returning instead a random number between 0.0 and 1.0. This is often very useful, but for our purposes we're going to need somewhat larger numbers—preferably, in an integer format, which can be done with the randint() function.

---

## OH, THE RANDOMNESS

Since ancient times, humans have had many methods for generating "random" numbers, from flipping a coin, to rolling a die, to shuffling a deck of cards. And for most applications, any of these would be fine for generating a random number or set of numbers. If you need to decide who kicks the ball first, you can flip a coin; choosing one card out of a deck of 52 is random enough to make it very impressive when a magician successfully guesses its identity.

However, there are two main issues with using these methods to generate random numbers for any true mathematical or statistical endeavor. First of all, they are all based on physical systems—the flip of a round coin in air, the rolling of a more-or-less square die on a not-so-level patch of ground. Because they are physical systems, they can never be truly random. Given enough iterations, a pattern *will* eventually start to emerge based on imperfections in the system. A coin, for example, has a slight weight bias on one side, due to the patterns engraved on both faces. If you flip it enough times, that pattern will show itself in the collected results. It may take several million or several billion flips, but it will emerge. Likewise, a die will never be perfectly square or perfectly weighted, and will eventually show a bias toward one side after a sufficient amount of rolls.

The second issue with these methods of generating random numbers is simply that they take too much time. If you need a good batch of a million random numbers, you're going to be flipping a coin for a *long* time to get all those numbers. It's just impractical for large batches of data.

But computers are excellent at handling immense batches of numbers and data, and they can generate them incredibly fast. The average desktop computer can process at a theoretical speed of around 7 Gigaflops. (That's 7 billion floating-point operations per second.) At that speed, generating a million random numbers would take… well, let's see…carry the two…divide by yellow…um…about 7 milliseconds. Much faster than card shuffling.

However, computers, again, are physical systems. Yes, you're generating the numbers from within the "cyberspace" of the computer's central processor, but that processor is a physical silicon chip, with physical transistors and wires. No matter what program you use to generate those random numbers, they will eventually display a pattern that shows they are not truly random. Thus, you see the interest in random numbers by mathematicians and scientists. A truly random number generator would be incredibly useful in many areas of science, not the least of which is cryptography. Most ciphers are based on a random hash code; a truly random code would be infinitely more difficult to crack—which is one of the reasons for the intense interest.

Current random-number generators work by using algorithms that create long strings of pseudo-random numbers, often based on combinations of multiplications and modulus operations. Depending on the quality of the algorithm, the numbers thus generated may or may not be cryptographically sound, though they are most often random enough for applications such as video games. In other words, the algorithm you use to generate random numbers probably won't stop a concerted effort to crack the code by a supercomputer, but it's good enough to generate opponents when you play *Call of Duty: The Day We All Died At The Hands Of The Sixth-Grader Down The Block*.

This generation process is why, when you begin a program that will be using random numbers, you have to "seed" the random number generator with another number, such as today's date or the system time on your computer. The random seed is simply a number used to initialize the random number vector algorithm in the program. So long as the original seed is ignored, subsequent initializations should provide sufficiently random numbers. Yes, eventually a pattern will emerge—it's inevitable—but a randomly-seeded generator should be sufficiently random for most needs, particularly a random-motion cat toy. Schrödinger's cat might not be fooled, but your feline should be. (Sorry—just a little physics humor there.)

According to the Python docs, `randint(a, b)` returns a random number n, such that n is between a and b, inclusive. In other words, the following code

```
>>> import random
>>> x = random.randint(1, 10)
>>> print x
```

should return 1, 2, 3, 4, 5, 6, 7, 8, 9, or 10. We're going to use it to generate positions for the servos we use.

■ **Note**   The Python docs can be found at `http://docs.python.org`. I highly recommend that, as you learn the language, you get in the habit of consulting the docs. You can also type **help(*function*)** at the interactive Python prompt to get the same reading material.

# Using the GPIO Library

Now that you have an idea of how we're going to generate our random numbers, you need to know how to control the servos that will be attached to the Pi. Luckily, there is a Python library that is specifically designed for this purpose that comes preinstalled on the Pi. This library enables us to access the Pi's General Purpose Input Output (GPIO) pins and is called, simply, RPi.GPIO.

To work with the library, you may have to manually install two other libraries. First make sure your Pi is up to date by typing

```
sudo apt-get update
```

and then install the packages by typing

```
sudo apt-get install python-dev
```

and

```
sudo apt-get install python.rpi-gpio
```

We can start typing our final code for this project. Remember, it's available as cat-toy.py from Apress.com. Now, to access the Pi, you call the following in the first lines of your program:

```
import RPi.GPIO as GPIO
```

Then configure it by typing

```
GPIO.setmode(GPIO.BOARD)
```

which lets you identify the pins as they are labeled on a standard pinout diagram, shown in Figure 9-2.

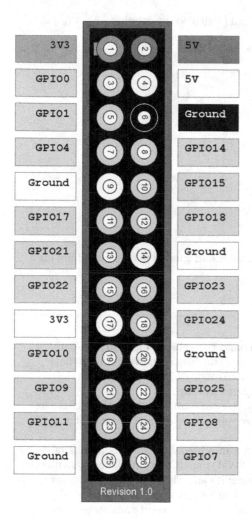

**Figure 9-2.** *Pinout of GPIO pins*

---

■ **Note**   Keep in mind that with GPIO.setmode(GPIO.BOARD), when you refer to pin 11, you're actually referring to the physical pin #11 (which translates to GPIO17 in the diagram in Figure 9-2), *not* GPIO11, which translates to the physical pin #23).

---

Once you set the mode, you can then set each pin to be either an input or an output. Users of the Arduino will probably recognize the concept here, but this is what you type for the Pi:

```
GPIO.setup (11, GPIO.OUT)
GPIO.setup (13, GPIO.IN)
```

and so forth. Once you set a pin as an output, you can then send voltage to it (turn it on) by entering

```
GPIO.output (11, 1)
```

or

```
GPIO.output (11, True)
```

Subsequently, you can turn it off by entering

```
GPIO.output (11, 0)
```

or

```
GPIO.output (11, False)
```

We'll use two pins to be servo controls: one pin to power the laser pointer, and another to read input from the IR sensor.

# Controlling the Servo

Servos are an important part of many, many different applications, from radio-controlled vehicles to high-end robotics. A servo is, at its heart, nothing more than a DC motor. However, with the help of software you can have *extremely* fine control over the motor's rotation. For example, if you need it to rotate 27.5 degrees and then stop (and assuming the servo is capable), you can send it that command programmatically.

So how do you do that using the GPIO pins on the Pi? Unfortunately, you can't just plug the servo's signal wire (the white one, usually) into a GPIO out pin, give it a positive and negative voltage, and expect it to work. It may, but then again it may not.

The answer lies in how to control servos. As analog pieces of hardware, they predate most of today's digital hardware, including the Pi. They operate using pulse width modulation (PWM) signals. To control them, you must be able to send PWM signals via whatever mechanism you're using, whether it's an Arduino pin, serial cable, or Raspberry Pi's GPIO pin. If you want to set a servo's position, you need to send it regular pulses of current—50 times a second is an average pulse speed—rather than one long pulse. That 50 times a second translates—if you're wondering—to one pulse every 20 milliseconds (ms).

The *length* of that pulse, moreover, is what determines the position of the servo. An *on* pulse of 1.5 ms, for example, sent every 20 milliseconds, will send the servo to the center position. Shorter pulses will turn it one direction, while longer pulses will send it the other. Thus, by precisely timing the length of the pulses you send to the servo, you can precisely position the servo head.

The graph in Figure 9-3 illustrates this best.

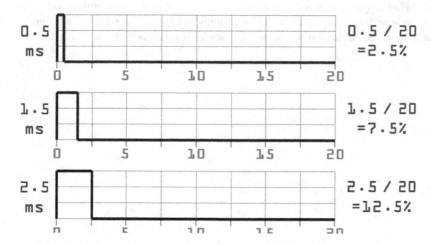

**Figure 9-3.** *Duty cycles of a servo*

If you want to send the servo to the neutral, "zero" position, you send it a 1.5-ms *on* pulse every 20 ms, which can be thought of as a *duty cycle* of 7.5%. Likewise, if you want to turn it counterclockwise with a 0.5-ms *on* pulse, it has a duty cycle of 2.5%, and a longer 2.5-ms *on* pulse translates to a 12.5% duty cycle. In other words, the servo is given a "high" pulse for 2.5%, 7.5%, or 12.5% of the time.

These directions are applicable to standard—*not* continuous—servos. The difference is that while standard servos use the length of the pulse to determine their final position (in degrees from center), continuous servos use the length of the pulse to determine the speed at which they should turn. A standard servo will move to its destination position and then stop until a new command is sent; a continuous servo is almost always moving, with the speed of the movement determined by the pulse lengths. And while you could conceivably use either type of servo for the cat toy, it makes more sense to use standard servos and thus have both the capability of exact positioning and the ability to stop completely, allowing the cat to—temporarily, at least—"catch" the little red dot.

The problem with this method of moving servos, however, is that it can be difficult to use the Pi and Python to send millisecond-length pulses to the GPIO pins. Like all other processes running on the Pi, Python is constantly being interrupted by system-level running processes, making precise timing of pulses by a Python program impractical, to say the least. However, once again the GPIO library has what we need: you can use the library to set a GPIO pin as a PWM pin, giving it the duty cycle necessary to send the correct-length pulses to the pin.

So while it is *theoretically* possible to script something like this:

```
while True:
    GPIO.output (11, 1)
    time.sleep (0.0015)
    GPIO.output (11, 0)
    time.sleep (0.0025)
```

the results would most likely be something completely unexpected, if it worked at all. Instead, what we can do is set the servo's signal pin (pin 11 in our example case here) to be a PWM output pin by entering

```
p = GPIO.PWM(11, 50)
```

The 50 in this case sets the pulses to 50 Hz (one pulse every 20 milliseconds), which is what the servo requires to work. We can then set the pin's duty cycle to 7.5% by typing

```
p.start (7.5)
```

If we put **p.start(7.5)** inside a while loop, the result is that the servo will move to the center position and then remain there. Changing the duty cycle with p.ChangeDutyCycle() will allow us to move the servo in different directions, which is what we're going for with the cat toy. So, for example, to see your servo move back and forth, try the following script:

```
import RPi.GPIO as GPIO
import time

GPIO.setmode (GPIO.BOARD)
GPIO.setup (11, GPIO.OUT)

p = GPIO.PWM (11, 50)
p.start (7.5)

while True:
    p.ChangeDutyCycle (7.5)
    time.sleep (1)
    p.ChangeDutyCycle (12.5)
    time.sleep (1)
    p.ChangeDutyCycle (2.5)
    time.sleep (1)
```

Running this script should make your servo sweep back and forth, pausing for a second between each direction change.

All that's left for our cat toy script is to implement some random numbers. Those numbers will determine which servo moves, in which direction, and for how long. The result should be a rather random path in two dimensions.

# Constructing the Servo Mechanism

Our cat toy is going to be sweeping a laser pointer in two directions, which means we need a servo capable of the same thing. While servos aren't generally capable of 2-dimensional motion, we can easily construct a pan-and-tilt servo mechanism using two normal servos attached to each other.

---

■ **Note**   This procedure will permanently bond your two servos, making them inseparable, so make sure you have others to use for other projects. However, remember that a pan-and-tilt setup like you're making here is a handy thing to have for projects where you need to move an item in two dimensions, and you'll probably use it again. So it's not like you're trashing the two servos completely.

---

All you need to do is mount the body of one servo to the horns of the other. To make a secure connection, you may need to remove the screw holding the servo horns of the base servo (let's call it the X-axis servo to keep the task simple) and file down the plastic a bit. You're trying to flatten out the top of the servo as much as possible to mate it tightly with the body of the other (Y-axis) servo.

When it's as flat as it's going to get, use a strong epoxy or adhesive to glue the Y-axis servo body to the horns of the X-axis servo. I used Gorilla Glue and got the result in Figure 9-4.

***Figure 9-4.*** *Bonded X and Y servos*

The laser pointer can now (after some not-so-minor modifications) be mounted to the top (Y-axis) servo.

# Constructing the Laser Mechanism

We're going to use a standard laser pointer, but we're going to modify it in a few important ways. The most important way is that instead of using batteries, we'll power it using the Pi's GPIO pins. This is important because it enables us to turn the laser on and off programmatically rather than fussing with the push-button switch.

To modify the laser pointer, you'll need some electrical tape and a flat-headed screw about two inches long and with a head just a tad smaller than the inside diameter of the laser pointer. Wrap the screw with the electrical tape so that it fits snugly inside the pointer. If necessary, when you're done, cut the end of the tape (as shown in Figure 9-5) so that the screw's point is exposed.

***Figure 9-5.*** *Screw mechanism for laser pointer*

Remove the laser pointer's base, and take out the batteries. Push the screw, head first, into the body of the pointer so that the screw head is pushing down the inner spring that is normally held down by the batteries. You may have to play with the amount of tape you use to wrap the screw; you want it to be a tight-enough fit to press down the spring and stay in place without danger of moving.

We also need to tape the laser pointer's power button down so that it's always on. As I said, we'll be taking care of powering the pointer from the Pi. Wrap a piece of tape around the pointer to hold down the button.

At this point, you should have something that resembles the image in Figure 9-6.

***Figure 9-6.*** *Completed laser pointer mechanism*

If you want to test your work, use a few alligator clips to connect the screw's point to pin #6 (the ground pin) on the Pi, and connect the body of the pointer to pin #1 (3.5V). The laser should light, showing you are powering it directly from the Pi's power pin. If nothing happens, make sure the screw head is pressing on the spring, the power button is securely taped down, and all your connections are solid. Once the connections are solid, you're ready to mount the laser to your two-dimensional servo contraption.

# Connecting the Laser to the Servo

Connecting the laser to the servo is probably the easiest part of the project. If you're like me, you don't want to permanently attach the laser to the pan-and-tilt servo setup you've got, because that setup can come in handy with other projects as well. So we need to find a way to *temporarily* attach the laser to the servo horns.

I used a popsicle stick to pull this off. We can glue the laser to the popsicle stick, and then screw the stick to the servo horns. This can be done with either the screws that came with the servo (you still have them, don't you?) or the smallest screws you can find in your workshop. Trust me—those are *really tiny* holes in the servo horn.

Using a strong glue (again, I like Gorilla Glue), affix the laser assembly to the popsicle stick. When the area is dry, use the small screws to attach the popsicle stick to the servo horns. When you're done, you should have a device that looks like Figure 9-7.

***Figure 9-7.*** *Laser mounted to servos*

A word of caution here: take some time and position the laser pointer and its associated servo so that the laser can spin freely no matter where in the cycle the two servos are. Obviously, the easiest way to do this is to remove the screws holding the servo horns to the servos, and reposition the horns based on the servos' travel arcs. Then run the two servos through all possible positions and make sure that your mechanism doesn't bind at any point in its motion. Since standard servos only travel through an arc of around 180 degrees, you *should* be able to find a suitable position for all the parts.

The last integral part of this project is connecting the motion sensor.

# Connecting the Motion Sensor

Not only does the motion sensor (shown in Figure 9-8) save your batteries, but it also seriously contributes to the *cool* factor: your toy turns on only when your cat (or a dog, or a roommate, or a Sasquatch) comes near it.

***Figure 9-8.*** *Parallax IR sensor*

Hooking up the IR sensor is simple: the positive and negative pins are connected to power, and the third pin (the leftmost pin in Figure 9-8) is connected to one of the Pi's GPIO pins configured as an INPUT. When the sensor detects motion, it outputs a HIGH signal on the output pin, which then travels to the Pi's INPUT pin. With the GPIO pin configured as an INPUT, we can read that signal and execute the Python script controlling the toy only when that signal is present.

Before we continue, I need to discuss the important concept of a *pullup or pulldown resistor*. Whenever you have an input in electronics, if that input is not directly reading anything, it is referred to as a *floating input*. That means the value read from that input could be absolutely anything. We need to define that input's "empty" state so that we'll know when that input changes.

To define an input's "empty" state, we normally connect a resistor (10K or 100K are common values) between the input and either a positive pin (thus creating a *pullup* resistor) or a ground (thus creating a *pulldown* resistor). Which one you use is not important—it's just important that the input is pulled up or down. Thus, if nothing is being read on the pin, and it's connected to a ground via a pulldown resistor, it will read "0." When it no longer reads "0," we'll know that it's receiving input.

In the case of our IR sensor, we need to define the value read at the pin when no motion is detected as "LOW," so we'll use a pulldown resistor. Luckily, to keep this process simple, the GPIO library allows us to do that in code, when we define a pin as an input like this:

```
GPIO.setup(11, GPIO.IN, pull_up_down=GPIO.PUD_UP)
```

If we connect our IR sensor's OUT pin to pin 11 on the Pi and initialize that pin with the preceding line of code, everything read on pin 11 will be "LOW" until movement is detected. At that point, the pin will read "HIGH" and we can call the function that turns on the laser and moves it around.

To test the sensor and our coding prowess, we'll start by setting up the GPIO pins accordingly. We can use a simple setup to test our code; an LED on a breadboard that will light up when the sensor is tripped. In a Python script, enter and save the following code:

```
import RPi.GPIO as GPIO
import time

GPIO.setwarnings (False) #eliminates nagging from the library
GPIO.setmode (GPIO.BOARD)
GPIO.setup (11, GPIO.IN, pull_up_down=GPIO.PUD_UP)
GPIO.setup (13, GPIO.OUT)
```

```
while True:
    if GPIO.input (11):
        GPIO.output (13, 1)
    else:
        GPIO.output (13, 0)
```

That's it for the test code! To test the code and the sensor setup, first connect the (+) pin on the sensor to pin #2 on the Pi. Connect the OUT pin to pin #11 on the Pi. Connect the (–) pin to a common ground line on your breadboard. Finally, connect pin #13 on the Pi to the positive leg of your LED, and connect the negative leg of the LED (through a resistor) to the common ground line. You should end up with something like the configuration you see in Figure 9-9.

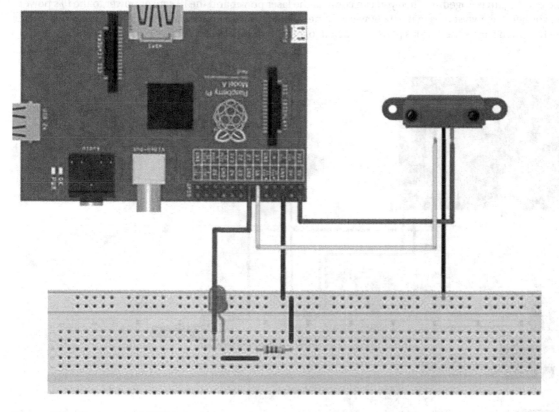

***Figure 9-9.*** *IR sensor and LED test setup*

■ **Note**    The image in Figure 9-9 was created with Fritzing (http://www.fritzing.org), a great open-source breadboarding/design tool. It's cross-platform, very easy to use and learn, and highly recommended.

When you run the script (remembering to execute the code as the superuser, or *sudo*, since you're accessing the GPIO pins), the LED should light when you move your hand around the sensor, and then go out again after a few seconds of nonmovement. If it doesn't work, check your connections and your parts—a burned-out LED can cause all *sorts* of troubleshooting headaches, believe me!

If everything works as planned, we can now wire the toy and complete all the connections.

# Connecting All the Bits

After you successfully test the infrared sensor, the code needed to operate it, and the code used to work the servos, and when everything is attached to everything else, it's time to wire everything up and make all the connections. This is where a small breadboard comes in handy, because you can connect all your grounds together (an *absolute* necessity) and run power to everything as needed. I used a 9V battery for the two servos, but feel free to try different batteries as you prefer. It's not necessary to use a rechargeable RC battery in this case, as we do in some other projects, because weight isn't really an issue and the servos don't run the battery down too fast, as they're not constantly running—thanks to the sensor. However, you *do* need to power the servos with a separate source from that which you're using to power the Pi; otherwise, you'll get constant freezes and crashes. With a breadboard that has two power channels, you can run the +9V down one positive channel, connect pin #2 on the Pi to the other positive channel, and then wire the two negatives together. Then you can connect the laser power and the IR sensor power to the Pi's power channel and connect the two servos to the 9V power channel, and all your grounds will be tied together.

See Figure 9-10, which shows the various parts connected together using a breadboard.

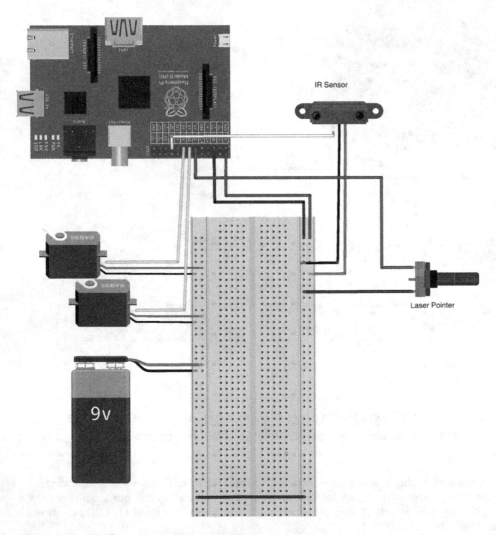

***Figure 9-10.*** *Final component interconnections*

Figure 9-10 is not completely accurate because the laser pointer is supposed to be attached to the servos, but you get the general idea. The pointer is powered with pin #11, the servos are powered with pins #13 and #15, and pin #19 is the sensor input. Then everything is given its respective voltage to make it work.

There are a few mechanical engineering tasks involved in the building of this toy, not the least of which is the best way to permanently attach the power and ground wires to the laser pointer. While alligator clips are fine for testing, as soon as the servos start jerking the pointer around in circles, they're going to come undone.

The best solution to this is to solder the wires to the pointer parts. If you can, use sandpaper to roughen the point of the screw and the pointer casing. If you have room, drill a small hole in the pointer casing to hold the positive wire. Then attach your wires and solder everything. Your results may vary, depending on your soldering abilities and the materials with which you're working. You can even use glue, as long as you don't get glue between the metal contacts of the wires and pointer parts. It's important that all the wires have a good, solid connection.

The last step is to mount the entire device in some sort of container to hold it all in place and to protect the guts of the machine from feline investigation. You can keep all the parts breadboarded, as long as it's protected from the end user (your cat.) I tend to use PVC pipes in cases like these, because a standard servo fits almost perfectly in a 2-inch I.D. PVC pipe. In this case, you can mount the lower servo to the edge of the pipe, and most of the wires and guts can be stowed securely inside of it, with a hole drilled in the side for the IR sensor. The Pi won't fit, but it can be safely stowed away in a separate box, connected to the pipe assembly via long jumper wires.

Hopefully, you end up with a cat toy that looks something like Figure 9-11.

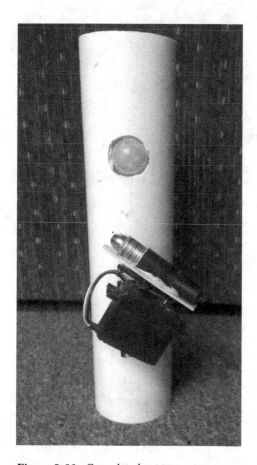

*Figure 9-11.* *Completed cat toy*

It's not pretty, but your cat won't care. It can be gussied up, of course, with a cap on the end of the pipe and a coat of paint. Probably the most important detail to remember (and it's not shown here) is to hide the guts and wires from prying eyes (and paws). The PVC pipe I've used here is too narrow, but a pipe with a larger cross-section could easily be fitted with the Pi and all the other guts inside of it, making a self-contained unit. Then you can add a power switch for the outside, and it's ready to go.

That should be it! Executing the cat_toy.py script should now keep your feline friend (and quite possibly your human ones) entertained for hours. It's worth noting that you now have the knowledge and capability to *aim and fire a laser* with your Raspberry Pi. Yes, it's a measly little laser pointer, but the concept can easily be applied to *any* laser, regardless of size or power. *Any* laser.

Have fun!

# The Final Code

This code, available on the Apress.com website as cat-toy.py, sets up the GPIO output pins, seeds the random-number generators, and then spins the servos and lights the laser in random motions.

```
import RPi.GPIO as GPIO
import time
import random
random.seed()

#set pins
GPIO.setmode (GPIO.BOARD)
GPIO.setwarnings (False)
GPIO.setup (11, GPIO.OUT) #laser power
GPIO.setup (13, GPIO.OUT) #X-servo
GPIO.setup (15, GPIO.OUT) #Y-servo
GPIO.setup (19, GPIO.IN, pull_up_down=GPIO.PUD_UP) #in from IR

#setup servo pwm
p = GPIO.PWM (13, 50)
q = GPIO.PWM (15, 50)

#set both servos to center to start
p.start (7.5)
q.start (7.5)

def moveServos():
    "Turns on laser and moves X- and Y-servos randomly"
    lightLaser ()

    p.ChangeDutyCycle (random.randint (8, 12))
    time.sleep (random.random())
    q.ChangeDutyCycle (random.randint (8, 12))
    time.sleep (random.random())

    p.ChangeDutyCycle (random.randint (3, 5))
    time.sleep (random.random())
    q.ChangeDutyCycle (random.randint (3, 5))
    time.sleep (random.random())

    dimLaser ()
```

```
def lightLaser():
    GPIO.output (11, 1)

def dimLaser():
    GPIO.output (11, 0)

#main loop
while True:
    #check for input from sensor
    if GPIO.input (19):
        moveServos()
        time.sleep (0.5) #wait a half sec before polling sensor
    else:
        dimLaser()
        time.sleep (0.5)
```

# Summary

In this chapter, you successfully constructed a two-axis servo mechanism, hacked a laser pointer to be fired by the Raspberry Pi, and used your programming skills to randomly point and fire the laser to entertain your cat.

In the next chapter, we're going to get your Pi out of the house and send it into the sky on a radio-controlled airplane.

■ ■ ■

# CHAPTER 10

# The Radio-Controlled Airplane

Many of us have long dreamed of flight—of soaring through the air, free as a bird. Or, as the pilot John Magee Jr. put it, slipping the "surly bonds of Earth. . .," dancing through the skies "on laughter-silvered wings," and topping "the wind-swept heights with easy grace."

Unfortunately, slipping the surly bonds of Earth often takes time and money that we don't have, and this may partly explain the advent of the radio-controlled (RC) airplane. While we may not be able to afford ground or flight school, a 1:12 scale Piper Cub can go a long way toward making us feel less grounded, and we get the chance to fly an actual airplane without having to step foot off *terra firma*.

The problem, however, is that while we can control the plane from the ground, it's not quite like actually being there. While there are complicated, expensive ways of attaching a small video camera to your RC plane, it'd be nice if you could do something similar with your Pi. And it'd be really cool if you could keep track of your flight, and then load the coordinates into Google Earth to see what your flight looked like.

Well, in this project you can do just that. The plan for this project is to put the Pi and a GPS receiver aboard an RC plane and then fly it. The Pi's camera will take pictures during the flight, and the GPS will log location data. Then, when you return home, you'll use a Python script to parse the location data into a KML file you can upload to Google Earth

---

■ **Note** This chapter contains some advanced programming concepts—perhaps more advanced than anything you've come across thus far, like threads and even a little bit of object-oriented programming (OOP). But they are not terribly complicated, and I'll explain the concepts as they arise.

---

## A Shopping List of Parts

Although this project does not require many parts, it might actually be the most expensive project to build in this book, because it requires a medium-sized, radio-controlled (RC) airplane. Here are a few additional parts you'll need:

- Raspberry Pi (with camera)

- GPS receiver (https://www.adafruit.com/products/746)

- Antenna for receiver (optional) (https://www.adafruit.com/products/851)

- Medium-sized RC airplane

- RC battery and 5V regulator to power the Pi

If you happen to already be an RC enthusiast, you'll most likely have a plane you can use, but if you're new to the sport, you'll need to purchase a good starter plane. As an amateur myself, I can recommend a good beginner's plane—the Switch, by Flyzone (shown in Figure 10-1).

*Figure 10-1.* *The Switch (Image ©Flyzone Planes at* http://www.flyzoneplanes.com)

This plane is sturdy enough to endure a few crashes while you learn to fly it, steady enough to be flown by an absolute beginner, and—most importantly—powerful enough to carry the extra weight of a Pi, GPS receiver, and the battery to power them both. Its name comes from the fact that as you become more adept at flying, you can remove the wings from the steady "top" configuration and switch them to a lower, "mid" configuration for more aerobatic maneuvers. As you'll see, the "top" configuration is perfect not just because it's easy for beginners, but because the Pi and GPS can sit comfortably atop the wing.

Ready? Let's start by creating a directory for our plane program:

```
mkdir plane
```

and then navigate into it by typing **cd**.

Now let's get the Pi to communicate with our GPS device.

# Connecting the GPS Receiver to the Pi

To get your Pi to talk to the GPS receiver, you first need to connect the two. To do this, we'll use the Python library called gpsd, and the Pi's UART (Universal Asynchronous Receiver/Transmitter) interface (pins 7 and 8). The Python gpsd module is part of a larger library of code designed to allow devices such as the Pi to monitor attached GPS and AIS receivers, with ports to C, C++, Java, and Python. It allows you to "read" the National Marine Electronics Association (NMEA)–formatted data transmitted by most GPS receivers.

The UART interface is an old one. It's basically a serial (RS-232) connection, but for our purposes it's all we need. It consists of a positive (+) and negative (-) connection for power, and transmit and receive pins. Start by typing the following line to install the software we'll need to read the GPS, gpsd and its associated programs:

```
sudo apt-get install gpsd gpsd-clients python-gps
```

Next we need to configure the Pi's UART interface. By default, it's set up to connect to a terminal window, but we need to communicate with the Tx and Rx (transmit and receive) pins. To do that, first make a copy of /boot/cmdline.txt by typing

```
sudo cp /boot/cmdline.txt /boot/cmdlinecopy.txt
```

and then edit it by typing **sudo nano /boot/cmdline.txt**. Delete the following portion

```
console=ttyAMA0,115200 kgdboc=ttyAMA0,115200
```

so that the file reads

```
dwc_otg.lpm_enable=0 console=tty1 root=/dev/mmcblk0p2 rootfstype=ext4 elevator=deadline rootwait
```

Save the file, and then edit the inittab file by typing

```
sudo nano /etc/inittab
```

Comment out the following line (the very last line), which tells the Pi to start a terminal connection, by adding a hashtag to the beginning of the line:

```
#T0:23:respawn:/sbin/getty -L ttyAMA0 115200 vt100
```

Now reboot by typing **sudo shutdown -r now**.

When you're back up and running, connect the GPS receiver to the Pi like so:

1. Connect the receiver's VIN to the Pi's 5V (pin #2).

2. Connect the GND to Pi pin #6.

3. Connect the Tx to Pi Rx (pin #10).

4. Connect the Rx to Pi Tx (pin #8).

When the receiver's LED starts to blink, you know you have power. Now you can test it by starting the gpsd program by typing

```
sudo gpsd /dev/ttyAMA0 -F /var/run/gpsd.sock
```

Then start the generic GPS client by typing

```
cgps -s
```

The cgps client is a generic viewer; it simply takes the data the gpsd program is receiving and displays it to the user.

It may take a moment for data to begin to stream, but when it does, you should see a screen like the one in Figure 10-2.

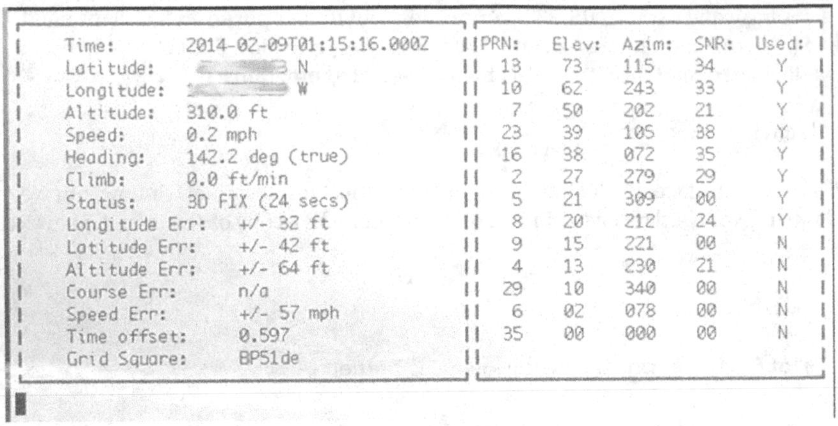

| Time: | 2014-02-09T01:15:16.000Z | | PRN: | Elev: | Azim: | SNR: | Used: |
|---|---|---|---|---|---|---|---|
| Latitude: | 3 N | | 13 | 73 | 115 | 34 | Y |
| Longitude: | W | | 10 | 62 | 243 | 33 | Y |
| Altitude: | 310.0 ft | | 7 | 50 | 202 | 21 | Y |
| Speed: | 0.2 mph | | 23 | 39 | 105 | 38 | Y |
| Heading: | 142.2 deg (true) | | 16 | 38 | 072 | 35 | Y |
| Climb: | 0.0 ft/min | | 2 | 27 | 279 | 29 | Y |
| Status: | 3D FIX (24 secs) | | 5 | 21 | 309 | 00 | Y |
| Longitude Err: | +/- 32 ft | | 8 | 20 | 212 | 24 | Y |
| Latitude Err: | +/- 42 ft | | 9 | 15 | 221 | 00 | N |
| Altitude Err: | +/- 64 ft | | 4 | 13 | 230 | 21 | N |
| Course Err: | n/a | | 29 | 10 | 340 | 00 | N |
| Speed Err: | +/- 57 mph | | 6 | 02 | 078 | 00 | N |
| Time offset: | 0.597 | | 35 | 00 | 000 | 00 | N |
| Grid Square: | BP51de | | | | | | |

*Figure 10-2. The cgps stream*

If you see nothing but zeros, it means the GPS can't find a satellite fix. You may have to wait a few minutes or even give the GPS a clear view of the sky. My experience is that this particular GPS board, even without the optional antenna, is very sensitive. When I added the antenna, I had no problem getting a GPS signal, even in my house.

Once you know that the GPS unit is working and communicating with the Pi, we need to put that information into a format we can use in a log file. Although the generic client, cgps, that we used here is useful for viewing coordinates, unfortunately it's really difficult to get usable information from it. For this reason, we'll use the Python gps module to interact with the receiver.

---

■ **Note**   The gps module allows you to communicate with many different GPS receivers, not just the one we're using in this project. There are a few receivers that generate proprietary data streams, but most of them output the same NMEA-formatted data as the chip we're using here.

---

# Setting Up a Log File

When we get the stream from the GPS, we need to have a place to store it for later use, as it won't do us much good if we're just printing it to a (nonconnected) screen during the flight. What we can do is set up a log file, using Python's logging module, and then when the Pi is back on the ground, we can parse the file and put it into a format we can use in Google Earth.

Setting up the log file is very simple. Start by typing

```
import logging
logging.basicConfig(filename='locations.log', level=logging.DEBUG, format='%(message)s')
```

These two lines import the module, declare the log's file name and what gets logged, and give the format of each line. We'll save each GPS call in three strings: the longitude, latitude, and altitude—the three coordinates used by Google Earth. (They're actually saved as floats, not strings, which means that we'll have to convert them to strings when we write them to the log file.) To write a line to the log file, the format is simply this:

```
logging.info("logged message or string or what-have-you")
```

It is not necessary to use the newline (\n) character, because each time you call the logging.info() function, it begins on a new line.

In case you're wondering, yes, we could simply write the GPS data to a regular file, but logging is an important, useful concept that many programmers either don't fully understand or skip over completely. In the case of Python's logging module, you can set log entries to be entered depending on the severity of the event being tracked. There are five severities possible: DEBUG, INFO, WARNING, ERROR and CRITICAL.

---

## THE FIVE SEVERITIES (LEVELS)

While I'm using the term 'severities,' to describe log entries perhaps "levels" might be a better term. When a program executes (no matter what language it's written in), it normally generates events that can be logged by the logging module. DEBUG events are detailed and are usually used only to diagnose problems. INFO events are confirmations that things are working correctly. WARNING events do just that—they warn that while things are still working, there may be a problem in the near future. ERROR and CRITICAL events happen only when something breaks, and CRITICAL normally means that the program can't continue working. The default level is WARNING, which means that unless you set your logging function differently, events given a DEBUG or INFO severity (because they are *below* WARNING) will not be logged.

---

To see the logging module in action, type **python** to start up a Python prompt and enter the following:

```
>>> import logging
>>> logging.warning("I am a warning.")
>>> logging.info("I am an info.")
```

The second line will output WARNING:root:I am a warning, while the third line, classified as an INFO level, will not be output to the console. If, on the other hand, you enter

```
>>> logging.basicConfig(level=logging.DEBUG)
```

it sets the default level to DEBUG, meaning that every event will be logged or output, regardless of severity. Entering the filename and format, as we did earlier, sets the log file and how events are written to it.

---

■ **Note**   Logging events is an important skill to know for any programmer; if you want to learn about Python's logging module in more depth, I highly recommend you read the Python documentation at http://docs.python.org/2/howto/logging.html.

---

# Formatting a KML File

A KML file is a special kind of XML (eXtensible Markup Language) used by Google Earth to delineate landmarks, objects, and even paths. It looks similar to an HTML file, with opening and closing < > tags for different levels of information, such as <Document> and </Document>, and <coordinates> and </coordinates>. Once we've got the log file from the GPS, we need to format the included coordinates in a KML file that Google Earth can recognize. Luckily, this is very easy, since we formatted the log file to just have longitude, latitude, and altitude, separated by spaces—with format='%(message)s' and the logging.info() line. Now we can parse each line in the log file, separate it by spaces with string.split, and write it into a preformatted .kml file. By using the write() function, we can write each line to the new file, called 'kml' in the script, like so:

```
kml.write('<Document>blah blah blah</Document>\n')
```

Since we know how the final KML file needs to look for Google Earth to use it, we can actually write the program that parses the file before our plane ever leaves the ground. That way, all we need to do is get the data to input from the actual log file, which we'll get when the plane lands. The other parts of the file that don't require actual coordinates can be formatted ahead of time. For instance, every Google Earth–compatible KML file begins with the line

```
<?xml version="1.0" encoding="UTF-8" ?>
```

which is then followed by

```
<kml xmlns="http://www.opengis.net/kml/2.2">
<Document>
<name>
```

and so on. So we can write our script to add those lines to our final plane.kml file.

We'll write our on-the-plane code to both take a picture and log the current GPS position every 30 seconds or so. Because we're taking data points at specified times along a certain route, we can use KML's path function to create a visual record of exactly what our plane did. The path will end up looking something like what you see in Figure 10-3.

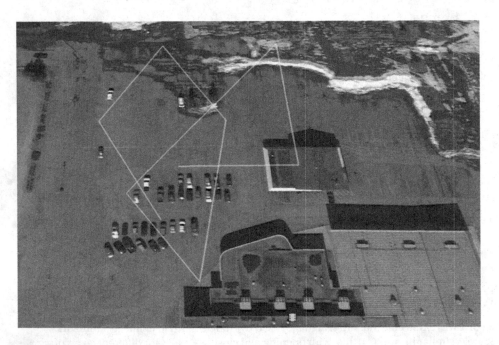

***Figure 10-3.*** *KML file in Google Earth*

Remember that because we're only polling the GPS unit every 30 seconds, we won't have a nice curved line. Instead, the path will connect the places where the plane was at those intervals, and the connections will be straight lines. As you can see in Figure 10-3, I used a parking lot for my test flights—my advice to a beginning flyer is to use a grassy field if you can, as crash landings in grass are likely to be easier on your plane! Everything in Alaska was covered by snow during my test flights, so it didn't really matter where I tested things.

# Using Threading and Objects

An important programming feature we'll be using in this program is *threads*. You may have seen them before; I even use them in one or two of the other projects in this book. Threads are important because they allow your program and processor to do several tasks at once, and they don't tie up all the memory and processing power doing one simple task. A simple call to import threading gives you the full power of threads and all they can do for you.

---

## WHAT DO THREADS ACTUALLY DO?

Threads allow your computer to (seemingly) execute several tasks at once. I say "seemingly" because the processor can still execute only one process at a time, but threads allow it to switch back and forth between processes so fast it seems to be executing them simultaneously. As an example, say you're working on your computer, with a word processor open in one window and an Internet browser open in another. While the word processor runs in one thread, another thread (executed between your key strokes) keeps your browser updated, still another one checks your email client for new messages, and so on.

---

What we'll do with them in this program is use them to poll the GPS receiver. By using a thread, our main buffer won't fill up with data as we continue to get data, yet we can still log the data in our log file for later use. To use threads in the most efficient way possible, we'll create an object called a *Poller* that will request information from the GPS receiver every so often (let's say every three seconds) using the gps module. Every time we get a position reading, we'll update the log and take a picture.

---

## OBJECTS, CLASSES, AND FUNCTIONS, OH MY!

Right about now, you're probably starting to freak out a bit: "Objects? Classes? What's he talking about?" To quote Douglas Adams, "Don't Panic." Consider this an easy, *non-stressful* introduction to object-oriented programming (OOP).

Think of a *class* as a set of similar objects that share certain characteristics. For instance, squares, triangles, and pentagons are all members of the shape class—they have sides, a calculable perimeter, and a calculable area. An *object* is one particular member, or *instance*, of that class: myRectangle, for example, is a certain instance of the shape class.

When you define a class, you define its characteristics, such as the fact that a shape has sides and is a closed object. You can also define functions that are unique to that class. To illustrate, every member of the shape class can have a function defined that specifies how to calculate its perimeter. That calculation may vary according to the individual shape object, so it is unique to that object, but every shape object has a defineArea() function.

The thread we create in our final program will contain one object—a member of the Thread class—with a set of variables and functions unique to it. So when we start our thread, it will have an associated GPS polling function that will handle the location retrieval and picture taking.

---

Our thread object will be defined like so:

```
class myObject(threading.Thread):
    def __init__(self):
        #function used to initiate the class and thread
        threading.Thread.__init__(self)        #necessary to start the thread
    def run(self):
        #function performed while thread is running
```

From the main portion of the program, we can start the thread by declaring a new myObject object (a new thread):

```
newObject = myObject()
```

and then starting it with

```
newObject.start()
```

The thread is now running with its own instance of the myObject, called newObject. Our thread (as shown in the final code at the end of the chapter) will be initiated with threading.Thread.__init__(self). Once it has been started, it will continue to execute its function (in our case, collecting GPS data and taking pictures) until we quit the program.

# Setting Up Automatic Startup

Because it's likely that we won't have a monitor or keyboard plugged in when we power up the Pi before we strap it to the plane, we'll need to make sure that our GPS logging script starts automatically. The easiest way to do that is to add an entry to the /etc/rc.local file (as explained in the sidebar "What Is the rc.local File?"). In our case, if our GPS logging code is called getGPS.py, and it's stored in our Documents/plane folder, we can add the line

```
/home/pi/Documents/plane/getGPS.py
```

to the rc.local file. Open it with sudo

```
sudo nano /etc/rc.local
```

and add the line

```
python /home/pi/Documents/plane/getGPS.py
```

to the file, before the last exit 0 line in the file.

---

## WHAT IS THE RC.LOCAL FILE?

The `rc.local` file is a standard part of the Linux kernel. It is one of the system startup `rc` files and resides in the `/etc/` directory. After the kernel initializes all devices at startup, it goes through the `rc` files one by one, running the scripts contained in each. The `rc.local` file is the last one to run and contains scripts that don't fit in any of the other files. For this reason, this file is editable by the system administrator and is often used (as it is here) to keep scripts that need to be run whenever the computer starts.

An important detail to remember about adding scripts in this file is that because it is not executed as any particular user, you must give the script's *complete* path, not merely `~/Documents/myscript.py`, for example.

---

However, that's not all we need to do. Before the GPS program will even work, we need to turn on the GPS feed again, as we did when we were testing the generic GPS client (earlier in "Connecting the GPS Receiver to the Pi"). So we need to put that line into `/etc/rc.local`:

```
sudo gpsd /dev/ttyAMA0 -F /var/run/gpsd.sock
```

Finally, we need to wait for the GPS unit to get a fix on some satellites before we start logging, otherwise, we'll be logging a whole lot of `0.0,0.0,nan` coordinates. (The nan stands for *not a number*.) My experience is that it takes about 30 seconds for the unit to get a fix and start returning real data, so waiting 45 seconds before starting the script is probably safe. To do that, just put

```
sleep 45
```

after the `sudo gpsd` line you just added, and the system will wait 45 seconds before starting the Python script in the next line. When you're done, your `/etc/rc.local` file should end like this:

```
sudo gpsd /dev/ttyAMA0 -F /var/run/gpsd.sock
sleep 45
python /home/pi/Documents/plane/gpstest.py
```

Save and exit, and the script will now run on startup.

# Connecting the Bits

Once you have the plane, building this project is relatively easy. You'll need a battery for the Pi and a regulator to make sure you're not giving it too much juice. I'm particularly fond of the Li-Po batteries (shown in Figure 10-4) that RC enthusiasts use, because they're light and pack a lot of power in a small package. The ones I use give me 1.3A for an hour—much longer than I need.

*Figure 10-4.* *Lithium Polymer (li-po) batteries*

For the voltage regulator, I hacked a USB car charger, as shown in Figure 10-5.

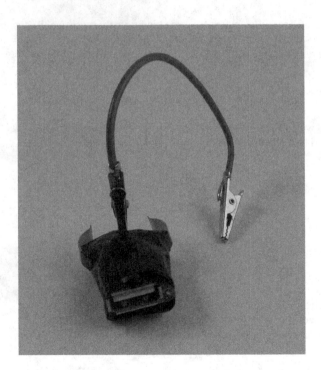

*Figure 10-5.* *Hacked car charger*

The middle terminal goes to the battery's (+) lead, and one of the outer terminals goes to GND. Then a simple USB cable gets plugged into the Pi, and you have power.

When it comes to putting everything on the plane, it's kind of a hodge-podge. The important details to remember are to keep the plane balanced, and to not disrupt airflow over the wings. I put the GPS on the nose, and taped the Pi to the wings. It's kind of hard to see in the picture in Figure 10-6, but the camera is taped to the port wing, pointed at the ground. Just behind the wing you can see the USB plug that will be plugged into the Pi. The whole setup looks ungainly, but it flies pretty well.

***Figure 10-6.*** *An overview of the setup*

Figure 10-7 shows how I attached the GPS unit to the nose of the plane.

***Figure 10-7.*** *A closeup of the GPS unit on the plane's nose*

Figure 10-8 shows how I attached the Pi to the plane's wing.

***Figure 10-8.*** *A closeup of Pi on the plane's wing*

When you're ready to go and have done all your pre-flight checks, plug in the Pi and wait 45 seconds for the plane.py script to start and for the GPS unit to acquire some satellites. Then take off and get some great pictures!

When you're back home with the Pi, log in to it and run the .kml conversion script, called kml.py here. That script will open the locations.log file created by the plane.py script, parse its text, and write all of its included locations into a valid .kml file, called plane.kml.

You can then transfer that file to any computer with Google Earth installed. When it's loaded onto your computer, right-click on the file and open the "Open with. . ." menu. Find "Google Earth" in the program options, and click Open (as shown in Figure 10-9).

***Figure 10-9.*** *Opening* plane.kml *with Google Earth on a Mac*

When the file is loaded, you'll get an image like the one of the parking lot in Figure 10-3 earlier in the chapter. The pictures taken by your camera, meanwhile, will be located in the same folder as your gpstest.py file or wherever you specify in your script. (See the final code at the end of this chapter for an example.)

Here's a final hint: Because you put the gps script in your /etc/rc.local file, it will continue to start every time you power up until you remove that line from the file. If you want to kill the gps script so that it's not running in the background and using processor resources, but you haven't gotten around to deleting its line from rc.local, type

```
top
```

into a terminal. This command shows you all processes currently running on the Pi. To stop the Python script, look for a process titled "python" and note the PID (Process ID) in the first column. Press "Q" to quit top, and then type

```
sudo kill xxxx
```

where *xxxx* is the PID you noted earlier. That will kill the Python script until you remove its line from rc.local and reboot.

# The Final Code

The final code consists of two parts: the plane program and the KML conversion program.

# The Plane Program

This portion of the program is what runs while the plane is in the air, taking pictures and logging GPS coordinates. It's available as plane.py from Apress.com:

```python
import os
from gps import *
from time import *
import time
import threading
import logging
from subprocess import call

#set up logfile
logging.basicConfig(filename='locations.log', level=logging.DEBUG,
format='%(message)s')


picnum = 0
gpsd = None

class GpsPoller(threading.Thread):
    def __init__(self):        #initializes thread
        threading.Thread.__init__(self)
        global gpsd
        gpsd = gps(mode=WATCH_ENABLE)
        self.current_value = None
        self.running = True

    def run(self):              #actions taken by thread
        global gpsd
        while gpsp.running:
            gpsd.next()

if __name__ == '__main__':    #if in the main program section,
    gpsp = GpsPoller()          #start a thread and start logging
    try:                        #and taking pictures
        gpsp.start()
        while True:
            #log location from GPS
            logging.info(str(gpsd.fix.longitude) + " " + str(gpsd.fix.latitude) + " " +
str(gpsd.fix.altitude))

            #save numbered image in correct directory
            call(["raspistill -o /home/pi/Documents/plane/image" + str(picnum) +
".jpg"], shell=True)
            picnum = picnum + 1  #increment picture number
            time.sleep(3)
    except (KeyboardInterrupt, SystemExit):
        gpsp.running = False
        gpsp.join()
```

# KML Conversion Program

This program is run when the Pi is back on the ground. It takes the GPS logging file and converts it to a KML file. It's available as kml.py from Apress.com:

```
import string

#open files for reading and writing
gps = open('locations.log', 'r')
kml = open('plane.kml', 'w')

kml.write('<?xml version="1.0" encoding="UTF-8" ?>\n')
kml.write('<kml xmlns="http://www.opengis.net/kml/2.2">\n')
kml.write('<Document>\n')
kml.write('<name>Plane Path</name>\n')
kml.write('<description>Path taken by plane</description>\n')
kml.write('<Style id="yellowLineGreenPoly">\n')
kml.write('<LineStyle<color>7f00ffff</color><width>4</width></LineStyle>\n')
kml.write('<PolyStyle><color>7f00ff00</color></PolyStyle>\n')
kml.write('</Style>\n')
kml.write('Placemark><name>Plane Path</name>\n')
kml.write('<styleUrl>#yellowLineGreenPoly</styleUrl>\n')
kml.write('<LineString>\n')
kml.write('<extrude>1</extrude><tesselate>1</tesselate>\n')
kml.write('<altitudeMode>relative</altitudeMode>\n')
kml.write('<coordinates>\n')

for line in gps:
    #separate string by spaces
    coordinate = string.split(line)
    longitude = coordinate[0]
    latitude = coordinate[1]
    altitude = coordinate[2]
    kml.write(longitude + "," + latitude + "," + altitude + "\n")

kml.write('<\coordinates>\n')
kml.write('</LineString>\n')
kml.write('</Placemark>\n')
kml.write('</Document>\n')
kml.write('</kml>\n')
```

# Summary

In this chapter, we connected a GPS to the Pi and read its input via the Pi's UART connections. We then put that information into a Python log file. We strapped the Pi and the GPS to a radio-controlled airplane and logged our flight, taking pictures every few seconds as we flew. Then, after landing the plane, we transcoded our GPS log file to a KML file and put that file into Google Earth to see a satellite display of our final flight path. This chapter demonstrated the true portability of the Raspberry Pi.

In the next chapter, we'll take the Pi even higher by sending it in a weather balloon to the upper atmosphere.

# CHAPTER 11

■ ■ ■

# The Weather Balloon

You may be familiar with weather balloons. Sometimes up to 20-feet in diameter, they can be filled with helium, given a small scientific payload, and ascend to the upper limits of the atmosphere, taking and recording various sensor readings as they go. Then, when the outside pressure becomes significantly less than the interior pressure of the balloon, they burst, and the payload falls back to earth with the assistance of a small parachute. The group that launched the balloon tracks down the fallen package and retrieves the data. In this way, scientists and hobbyists can learn a great deal about the upper reaches of the atmosphere.

Although operating the radio-controlled airplane with a Raspberry Pi in the previous chapter was cool, it was also somewhat tame in that we logged its position and uploaded its path data to Google Earth. The concept behind *this* project, building a weather balloon, is very simple but more advanced. We'll inflate and launch a small weather balloon capable of sending the Raspberry Pi to at least 30,000 feet. We'll then program the Pi to take a picture every so often, giving us a pictorial record of our flight and use a small GPS unit to log our Pi's trip.

But we won't stop there because that's kind of boring, and it's been done by many different hobbyists and professionals. In addition, we'll get an update, in real time, as to what the balloon is doing—its latitude, longitude, and even altitude—by programming the Pi to record itself speaking its coordinates every 15 seconds or so. Then we'll broadcast that recording to a radio on the ground. All we need to do is tune our small FM radio to a pre-assigned frequency, and we'll be able to hear our balloon talking to us, giving us live updates on its condition.

Let's go shopping for parts!

---

■ **Caution**   In the United States, FAA regulations require you to notify the agency 6 to 24 hours before your launch with relevant information, such as the time and place of the launch, predicted altitude, balloon description, and forecast of the landing location. The FAA also requires you to keep track of the balloon's location and have the ability to update the FAA with that information should it be required. Regulations differ for moored versus free balloons; for more information, see the full regulations at http://www.gpo.gov/fdsys/pkg/CFR-2012-title14-vol2/pdf/CFR-2012-title14-vol2-part101.pdf.

---

## A Shopping List of Parts

Like the RC plane, this is one of the more expensive projects in the book, if only because weather balloons can be sort of expensive, and you'll need to purchase or rent a tank of helium from a party supply store or welding supply house. Here's what you'll need:

- Raspberry Pi with camera board
- LiPo battery and 5V regulator to power the Pi
- Latex weather balloon 6-7 foot diameter
- GPS receiver—(https://www.adafruit.com/products/746)

- Antenna for GPS (optional)—(https://www.adafruit.com/products/851)

- Handheld AM/FM radio

- 10-foot length of wire

- Small Styrofoam cooler

- Model rocket parachute

- Hand warmers

- Fishing line—at least 5000 yards

- 1-foot surgical tubing, about 1-inch I.D.

- Helium—about 250 feet[3]

- Duct tape, electrical tape, rubber bands, zip ties

# Setting Up the GPS Receiver

As with the RC plane project in Chapter 10, an integral part of this project is to get the GPS unit up and running with your Pi. To do this, you're going to install the Python gpsd module, and use the Pi's Universal Asynchronous Receiver/Transmitter (UART) pins, #7 and #8. The Python gpsd module is part of a larger library of code designed to allow devices such as the Pi to monitor attached GPS and Automatic Identification System (AIS) receivers, with ports to C, C++, Java, and Python. It allows you to "read" the National Marine Electronics Association-formatted data transmitted by most GPS receivers.

The UART interface is an old one; it's basically a serial (RS-232) connection, but for our purposes it's all we need. It consists of a positive (+) and negative (–) connection for power, and transmit and receive pins. Start by typing the following line to install the software we'll need to read the GPS, gpsd, and its associated programs:

```
sudo apt-get install gpsd gpsd-clients python-gps
```

This will install gpsd and all of its dependencies and associated programs. Next, you'll need to set up the Pi to communicate over its UART Tx (transmit) and Rx (receive) pins, because their default configuration is to communicate with a terminal window. To do that, first make a copy of /boot/cmdline.txt:

```
sudo cp /boot/cmdline.txt /boot/cmdlinecopy.txt
```

and then edit it by typing **sudo nano /boot/cmdline.txt**. Delete the following line:

```
console=ttyAMA0,115200 kgdboc=ttyAMA0,115200
```

so that the file reads

```
dwc_otg.lpm_enable=0 console=tty1 root=/dev/mmcblk0p2 rootfstype=ext4 elevator=deadline rootwait
```

The /boot/cmdline.txt file passes arguments to the Linux kernel as the Pi boots.
After you save it, edit the inittab file by typing

```
sudo nano /etc/inittab
```

and comment out the line that tells the Pi to start a terminal connection (the very last line):

```
#T0:23:respawn:/sbin/getty -L ttyAMA0 115200 vt100
```

Now reboot by typing **sudo reboot**.

While the Pi reboots, solder the headers that came with it onto your GPS board. You won't need to use all the connections for this project (you'll only need four of them, in fact), but you may need the other pins later, so make sure you connect those as well.

When the Pi comes back online, connect your GPS receiver to it. Using jumpers, follow these steps:

1. Connect the board's VIN to the Pi's 5V pin (#2).

2. Connect the GND pin to the Pi's ground (#6).

3. Connect the Tx and Rx pins to the Pi's Rx and Tx pins, respectively (#10 and #12).

You should immediately get a blinking red light on the GPS unit, letting you know the board is powered. If you purchased the optional external antenna for your GPS (never a bad idea), connect it to the small connector on the board. It may take a while for your unit to "see" any satellites, particularly if you're indoors. However, you'll know when it does: the red light that was previously blinking once per second will slow down, blinking once every 15 seconds, indicating that the GPS has a fix on satellites.

To use the gpsd program, you need to start it, by typing

```
sudo gpsd /dev/ttyAMA0 -F /var/run/gpsd.sock
```

in your terminal. Then, to see the current GPS information, start the generic GPS client by typing

```
cgps -s
```

It may take just a moment for data to begin to stream to the display, but when it does you should see a screen like Figure 11-1.

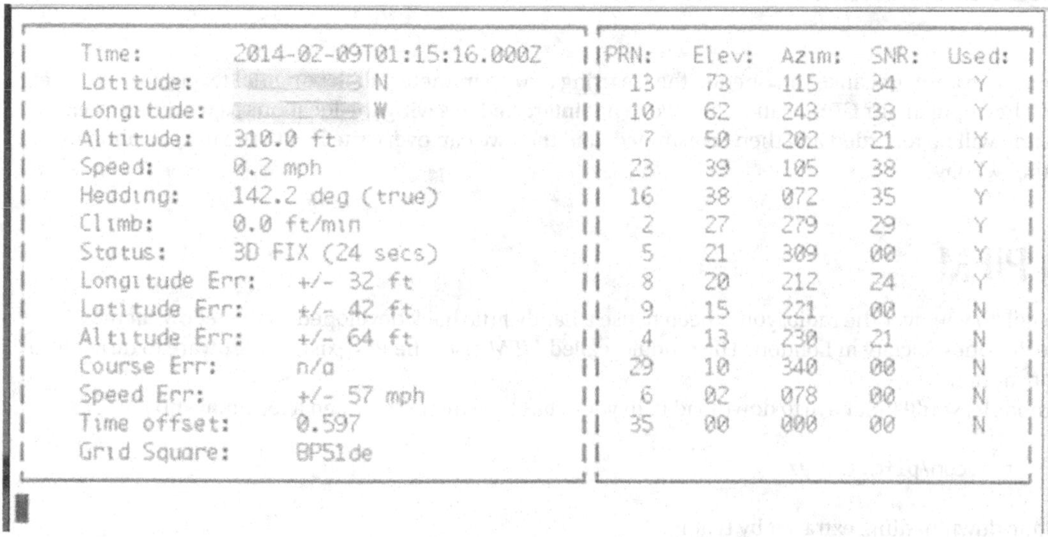

```
┌─────────────────────────────────────────┐┌──────────────────────────────────────┐
│  Time:        2014-02-09T01:15:16.000Z   ││PRN:    Elev:   Azim:   SNR:   Used:  │
│  Latitude:                      N        ││ 13      73      115     34      Y     │
│  Longitude:                     W        ││ 10      62      243     33      Y     │
│  Altitude:    310.0 ft                   ││  7      50      202     21      Y     │
│  Speed:       0.2 mph                    ││ 23      39      105     38      Y     │
│  Heading:     142.2 deg (true)           ││ 16      38      072     35      Y     │
│  Climb:       0.0 ft/min                 ││  2      27      279     29      Y     │
│  Status:      3D FIX (24 secs)           ││  5      21      309     00      Y     │
│  Longitude Err:    +/- 32 ft             ││  8      20      212     24      Y     │
│  Latitude Err:     +/- 42 ft             ││  9      15      221     00      N     │
│  Altitude Err:     +/- 64 ft             ││  4      13      230     21      N     │
│  Course Err:       n/a                   ││ 29      10      340     00      N     │
│  Speed Err:        +/- 57 mph            ││  6      02      078     00      N     │
│  Time offset:      0.597                 ││ 35      00      000     00      N     │
│  Grid Square:      BP51de                ││                                      │
└─────────────────────────────────────────┘└──────────────────────────────────────┘
```

***Figure 11-1.*** *The cgps display*

The cgps client is a generic viewer; it simply takes the data the gpsd program is receiving and displays it to the user. We won't be using the cgps display—it's just a handy way of making sure the GPS unit is hooked up correctly and is working. We'll use Python's gps module to communicate with the GPS board.

# Storing the GPS Data

For this project, you'll be writing the GPS data into a file, to be read, recorded, and transmitted later. We could use a logging file for this, as we did for the RC plane project, but it's also important that you learn to use Python to read from and write to normal files. In your terminal, start a Python prompt and type

```
f = open('testfile.txt', 'w')
```

This opens a file—in this case, testfile.txt. The second parameter can be one of the following four values:

- **'r'**   The file is read-only.
- **'w'**   The file is only for writing. (Previous data will be erased each time the file is opened.)
- **'a'**   The file will be appended to.
- **'r+'**   The file is open for both reading and writing.

To continue, type

```
f.write('This is a test of my file-writing')
f.close()
```

If you now exit your Python prompt by pressing Ctrl+d and list your directory contents, you'll see testfile.txt listed, and viewing its contents will show you the line you just entered. Now, try it again: start another Python prompt and type

```
f = open('testfile.txt', 'w')
f.write('This text should overwrite the first text')
f.close()
```

and exit your Python prompt. Because you opened the file using a 'w' parameter, all the original text was overwritten. This is what you'll be doing in our GPS location file. We're not interested in saving the locations as we did before; rather, each location will be recorded and then transmitted, and then we can overwrite it with the next location by opening it with the 'w' flag.

# Installing PiFM

To get your Pi to talk to you over the radio, you'll need to use a handy little hack developed by the fellows at the Imperial College Robotics Society in London. The module, called *PiFM*, uses the Pi's existing hardware to turn it into a nice little FM transmitter.

To use the module, you'll first have to download it. In your /balloon directory, open a terminal and type

```
wget http://omattos.com/pifm.tar.gz
```

When it's done downloading, extract it by typing

```
tar -xvzf pifm.tar.gz
```

This will place a compiled binary, as well as the source code and a few sound files, in your directory. You're now ready to use the PiFM package. To try it out, attach a foot-long wire to your Pi's pin #7 (GPIO pin #4). Now, in your terminal, type

```
sudo ./pifm sound.wav 100.0
```

and tune your radio to 100.0 FM. You should be rewarded with a familiar tune. If by chance you don't hear anything, try adding **'22050'** to the end of the command, because that extra parameter (the sample rate of the sound file) may be necessary to state explicitly, depending on the version of software you have.

Congratulations! You've turned your Pi into a radio transmitter. Now, let's make it a DJ.

# Installing festival

I'm pretty sure most of us would love it if our computers would talk to us. Luckily, since we're using Linux, we have a few options when it comes to a good speech synthesizer program. The one we'll be using, festival, is free and very easy to use. It also comes with a handy text-to-speech recording function that we'll be using.

festival is available from your standard Pi repositories, which means that to use it, you only need to type

```
sudo apt-get install festival
```

in your terminal, and it will download and install. Once the download and installation process is complete, try it out. Plug a pair of headphones into your Pi's 3.5-mm audio out jack. Then, in your terminal, type the following:

```
echo "I'm sorry Dave, I'm afraid I can't do that." | festival --tts
```

and your Pi will proceed to speak to you. (In case you don't know, that line is spoken by the computer, HAL, in the classic movie *2001: A Space Odyssey*. If you haven't seen it, put this book down and go watch it. Now. I'll wait.)

Okay, so now you can make your Pi speak whatever line you tell it to in the command line. While that's pretty cool, we need to have it read a line from a text file: something like "Current altitude 10,000 feet, current position 92 degrees latitude, 164 degrees latitude." The easiest way to do that is to use festival's very handy text2wave function. This function reads from a file—position.txt, for example—and makes a recording of it. Its syntax is

```
text2wave position.txt -o position.wav
```

Now, knowing that we'll be updating the position.txt file every 15 seconds, we can just use the text2wave function to re-record its contents before broadcasting that recording using PiFM.

There's one small snag, however: text2wave encodes its recordings using a sample rate of 44100 kHz, and PiFM needs a recording with a sample rate of 22050 kHz. This requires another program for our toolkit—ffmpeg.

# Installing FFMPEG

In the world of audio and video encoders, decoders, and transcoders, ffmpeg is definitely one of the most popular and powerful programs available. It can transcode movie files from MPG to AVI format, separate an AVI file into its individual frames, and even separate the audio from a film, run it through successive filters, and re-attach it to the video.

However, while all those feats are impressive, all we need to use it for is to change our audio from 44100 kHz to 22050 kHz. Start installing it by typing

```
sudo apt-get install ffmpeg
```

into your terminal. There are many different installation and configuration options, but this is the easiest and most straightforward. Now, to convert our position.wav file, we use the following syntax, so type

```
ffmpeg -i "position.wav" -y -ar 22050 "position.wav"
```

Depending on when you're reading this chapter, you may get the following deprecation warning: "This program is only provided for compatibility and will be removed in a future release." The command should still work, but if you prefer, you can use the replacement's command, avconv, like so:

```
avconv -i "position.wav" -y -ar 22050 "position.wav"
```

That's it—position.wav has now been re-encoded with a 22050 kHz sample rate and is ready to be broadcast. If we want to broadcast the contents of position.wav, we would type in a terminal

```
sudo ./pifm position.wav 103.5 22050
```

(103.5 FM is the frequency it will be broadcast to. Adjust for your local stations, of course.)

# Preparing the Pi

If you're reading this chapter after the RC plane chapter, you may recognize much of the setup here, as many of the parts of this project are very similar. The first thing you need to do is to make sure that the gpsd module will be running every time you start the Pi. To do that, open your rc.local file by typing

```
sudo nano /etc/rc.local
```

and add the following line to the end:

```
sudo gpsd /dev/ttyAMA0 -F /var/run/gpsd.sock
```

---

■ **Note**    For more information about the rc.local file, see the sidebar in Chapter 10.

---

Now the gpsd module will run every time we start the Pi.

However, we're not done in the rc.local file. It's likely that when you launch the balloon, you'll want to just power the Pi and launch, without having to worry about logging in and starting up the program you've written. Luckily, you can do that with the rc.local file too. Upon startup, after the gpsd module launches, you'll want to give your GPS board a few seconds to get a fix on some satellites before it starts logging data. To do that, after the gpsd line just shown, add the line

```
sleep(45)
```

to make the Pi pause for 45 seconds, and then add the line

```
sudo python /home/pi/Documents/balloon/balloon.py
```

(Make sure this line matches wherever you're storing your balloon program, of course.) Your balloon program will now start automatically, 45 seconds after your GPS module begins to read data from its satellite fixes.

# Using Threading and Objects

An important programming feature we'll be using in this project is *threads*. If you already built the RC plane project in Chapter 10, this will be old hat to you. If you haven't, however, here's a quick rundown.

Threads are important because they allow your program and processor to do several tasks at once, and they don't tie up all the memory and processing power doing one simple task. A simple call to import threading gives you the full power of threads and all they can do for you.

What do threads actually do? Threads allow your computer to (seemingly) execute several tasks at once. I say "seemingly" because the processor can still execute only one process at a time, but threads allow it to switch back and forth between processes so fast it seems to be executing them simultaneously. For more of an introduction to threads, see the sidebar in Chapter 10.

What we'll do with them in this program is use them to poll the GPS receiver. By using a thread, our main buffer won't fill up with data as we continue to get data, yet we can still log the data in our position.txt file for later use. To use threads in the most efficient way possible, we'll create an object called a *Poller* that will request information from the GPS receiver every 15 seconds using the gps module. Every time we get a position reading, we'll update the text file and take a picture.

---

■ **Note**    For a refresher on objects, classes, and object-oriented programming, see the sidebar in Chapter 10.

---

Our thread object will be defined like so:

```
class myObject(threading.Thread):
       def __init__(self):
       #function used to initiate the class and thread
       threading.Thread.__init__(self)        #necessary to start the thread
       def run(self):
       #function performed while thread is running
```

From the main portion of the program, we can start the thread by declaring a new myObject object (a new thread):

```
newObject = myObject()
```

and then start it with

```
newObject.start()
```

The thread is now running with its own instance of the myObject, called newObject. Our thread (as shown in the final code at the end of the chapter) will be initiated with threading.Thread.__init__(self). Once it has been started, it will continue to execute its function (in our case, collecting GPS data, transmitting it, and taking pictures) until we quit the program or power off the Pi.

# Connecting the Bits

The construction of this weather balloon project can be rather involved, so set aside a few hours to get everything ready.

The first thing to do is set up the helium tank. When you rent the tank, it should come with a regulator and a tilt-nipple used to fill balloons. This can be used to fill your balloon, with one small modification. Slip the surgical tubing over the regulator and tape it securely. The tubing can then be inserted into the neck of your balloon to fill it (as shown in Figure 11-2) and secured with a zip tie.

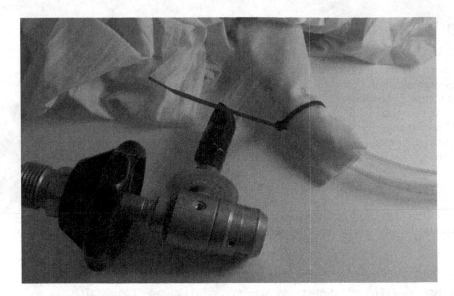

*Figure 11-2.* *Regulator-to-balloon neck setup*

With the regulator-to-balloon connection secured, you can put together your payload. Cut a small hole in the bottom of your Styrofoam cooler large enough to fit the Pi's camera board. Fit the camera into the hole, securing it with tape if necessary. (See Figure 11-3.) On the bottom of the cooler, install the Pi and its battery pack, ready to connect upon mission launch.

*Figure 11-3.* *Camera positioned in the cooler*

Poke a small hole in the bottom of the cooler. This is where the GPS antenna, FM antenna, and balloon tether will go. Slip them through the hole and connect the FM antenna to the Pi's pin #7. Attach your GPS board to the Pi if it isn't already (see the section "Setting Up the GPS Receiver" earlier in the chapter), and connect the antenna to the GPS. The two antennas should be hanging freely out of the bottom, and the tether should be connected to your fishing-line spool. Fasten the free end of the tether to your cooler in a way that won't tear the cooler; I cut a length of PVC pipe the length of the cooler and tied the tether to it. (See Figure 11-4.)

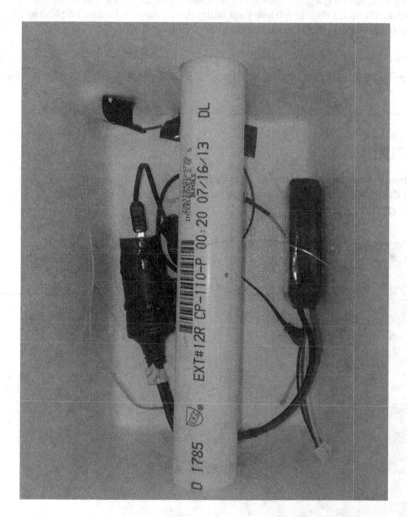

**Figure 11-4.** *Interior of the cooler showing the tether attached to a PVC pipe*

Now break open the hand warmers and activate them by shaking and mixing the contents. Lay them on the bottom of the cooler, and put your Pi and battery pack on top of them. The hand warmers are important because it gets pretty cold in the upper atmosphere—cold enough to cause your electronics to stop working. The warmers should keep the interior of the cooler warm enough to allow your Pi to continue working at the apex of its flight.

You'll need to attach the parachute to the lid of your cooler as a way to save your Pi in case the balloon bursts. I found that the best way to do this is to poke a hole in the lid, thread the parachute strings through the hole, and secure them to the lid with hot glue. Then *loosely* tie a string around the chute—tightly enough to keep the parachute closed upon ascent, but loosely enough to allow the chute to break free and open if the cooler begins tumbling in free fall.

The last things to do are power up the Pi, tape the lid tightly onto the cooler, and attach it to the filled balloon. When the balloon is at its desired volume (and this will vary with the weight of your payload, so some experimentation is necessary), remove it from the tank and tie off the end with either zip ties or rubber bands. Then attach the neck of the balloon to your cooler, again using zip ties, and release it. The balloon will float into the atmosphere, taking pictures as it goes. Meanwhile, tune your radio to 103.5 FM (or whatever station you set in your final code) and listen to the live updates as your balloon tells you exactly how high it is. Unless it bursts (always a distinct possibility), the balloon should travel to the end of the attached fishing line, which is a good reason to get as much line as you can, in order to allow your balloon to ascend as high as possible. When it's time to retrieve your balloon, use the attached fishing line to reel it back in. To save your arm muscles, you may want to attach the fishing-line spool to an electric drill.

---

■ **Note**  Check with your local branch of the FAA or its equivalent before flying your balloon to determine the best time and place to launch.

---

# Reviewing the Photo Results

Unfortunately, I can't show you any actual results from the PiBalloon yet; as it happens, during my maiden voyage, the camera on my Pi got twisted and was facing the Styrofoam and recorded no pictures whatsoever. However, Figure 11-5 shows the sort of image you should be able to record.

***Figure 11-5.*** *Alaskan mountain range (photo ©2013 by NASA)*

My version of the PiBalloon will be flying again soon; check the website for this book for further details and hopefully some better pictures.

# The Final Code

This code (available as balloon.py from Apress.com) will query the GPS board, record and transmit its coordinates, and take a picture periodically with the onboard camera:

```python
import os
from gps import *
import time
import threading
import subprocess

#set up variables
picnum = 0
gpsd = None

class GpsPoller(threading.Thread):
    def __init__(self):
        threading.Thread.__init__(self)
        global gpsd
        global picnum
        gpsd = gps(mode=WATCH_ENABLE)
        self.current_value = None
        self.running = True
    def run(self):
        global gpsd
        while gpsp.running:
            gpsd.next()

if __name__ == '__main__':
    gpsp = GpsPoller()
    try:
        gpsp.start()
        while True:
            f = open('position.txt', 'w')
            curAlt = gpsd.fix.altitude
            curLong = gpsd.fix.longitude
            curLat = gpsd.fix.latitude
            f.write( str(curAlt) + " feet altitude, " + str(curLong) + " degrees longitude, " +
            str(curLat) +
 " degrees latitude")
            f.close()
            subprocess.call(["text2wave position.txt -o position.wav"], shell = True)
            subprocess.call(['ffmpeg -i "position.wav" -y -ar 22050 "position.wav"'], shell = True)
            subprocess.call(["sudo ./pifm position.wav 103.5 22050"], shell = True)
            subprocess.call(["raspistill -o /home/pi/Documents/balloon/image" + str(picnum) +
            ".jpg"], shell=True)
```

```
        picnum = picnum + 1
        time.sleep(15)
except (KeyboardInterrupt, SystemExit):
    gpsp.running = False
    gpsp.join()
```

# Summary

In this chapter, you programmed your Pi to get its location from a GPS module and transmit its location to you so that you could stay on the ground and send it into the upper atmosphere to take pictures. You worked with threads again, as well as a bit more with object-oriented code, and got a few good pictures from on high, I hope.

In the next chapter, we'll go in the opposite direction and send the Pi underwater.

■ ■ ■

# CHAPTER 12

# The Submersible

Submersibles, both remotely operated and autonomous, have been used for both scientific research purposes and private enterprise for several decades. They have studied life on the barren intercontinental plains, have explored volcanic vents in the middle of the Atlantic Ocean, and have gone places impossible for humans to go. In the commercial world, they were thrust into the spotlight during the Deepwater Horizon oil disaster in 2010. A fleet of submersibles was used to cap the oil well and stop the spill in 5,000-foot depths—far below what human divers could reach. They are routinely used to conduct maintenance on deep-sea oil rigs and offshore wave farms.

There are basically two kinds of submersible: ROVs and AUVs. *ROV* stands for *Remote Operated Vehicle*, and describes a sub that is remotely controlled from a ship via a tether—a cable that provides both power to the sub and two-way communication with its onboard systems. Ordinarily, an onboard camera sends a video signal up the tether to a monitor in the control room, where a specially trained operator uses the video feed to control the sub with a high-tech version of an Xbox controller. The remote operator controls the sub's propulsion, steering, and depth, and that person is also able to work the vehicle's grippers and sample collectors, assuming it is so equipped.

*AUV*, on the other hand, stands for *Autonomous Underwater Vehicle* and describes a submersible that works without human intervention or control. It may or may not use an onboard camera; if it does, the video from the camera is often used only for data-gathering purposes, not for navigation. An AUV has an array of onboard sensors and a relatively sophisticated onboard computer that is programmed to perform a variety of tasks and movements, based on information from the sensors.

Using the Raspberry Pi, you can actually construct either an ROV or a full-scale AUV, but for our purposes we're going to make a (much simpler) remotely operated vehicle. We can use the Pi's onboard camera to take snapshots of our underwater explorations, and we can control the sub with a hacked Wii nunchuk. You won't be able to navigate via video, because sending a video signal through a cable to an external monitor is slightly beyond the scope of this book, but as long as you don't go too deep, you should be able to follow the sub with a raft or small boat and direct it from the surface. Again, to keep the project within the scope of a single book chapter, we're going to avoid depth control as well; instead, we're going to make the sub neutrally buoyant.

---

### PRECAUTIONS IN THE EVENT YOU FRY YOUR PI

This build involves both deep water and electronics—two things that historically go together about as well as water and cats. There is a **very** good chance of frying your Pi and/or its associated bits if the enclosure you create is not completely watertight. With that in mind, you should do one or both of the following:

- Buy an extra Pi to use in your submersible. It's relatively inexpensive, and should you happen to fry it, you'll still have your original Pi with all of its tweaks and added modules. If you duplicate your SD card (see the next bullet point) the submersible Pi will be exactly like your regular one.

- Back up your SD card regularly, just as do with your computer's hard drive. If you back up as you go, you won't lose too much hard work if something happens to the card.

---

# A Shopping List of Parts

For this build, you will need the following:

- Raspberry Pi

- Raspberry Pi camera kit—available from Adafruit, Amazon, and Sparkfun

- 1 Edimax EW7811UN USB wireless dongle

- Motor Driver—dual L298 H-bridge (http://www.sparkfun.com/products/9670)

- Nintendo Wii nunchuk controller

- 1 Wiichuck adapter (http://www.sparkfun.com/products/9281)

- Headers

- 2 DC motors

- Model propellers

- 2 battery packs (the Lithium-Polymer packs used by RC hobbyists are a good choice)

- 1 waterproof enclosure—think Tupperware or something similar

- 1 tube of 5200 marine waterproofing sealant

- PVC pipe and elbow joints

- Assorted zip ties

- Chicken wire or plastic mesh/netting

- Wire—red and black, 18 gauge

- Ethernet cable—25 feet (buy it in bulk if possible, as you won't need the plastic terminals, just the cable)

- Wax

- Caulk

# Accessing the Raspberry Pi's GPIO pins

One of the features that makes the Raspberry Pi so incredibly useful is its GPIO (General Purpose Input/Output) pins. Using a specific Python module that comes preinstalled on the Pi, the GPIO pins can be directly controlled, sending voltages to external devices and reading inputs that can then be used in programs.

---

### GPIO: WHAT'S THE BIG DEAL?

GPIO pins are like some of the ports on an old computer. An easy way to interface with the external world used to be either the serial port or the printer (parallel) port. Both could be accessed with the correct programming libraries, sending signals directly to each pin. But as technology progressed, both ports disappeared and were replaced with USB and Ethernet connectivity. As a result, it became much more difficult to control external devices from a programming standpoint, and this is why many people are excited by the possibilities offered by the Pi's GPIO pins.

---

To configure your Pi to access the GPIO pins programmatically, you may need to install the correct development kit and tools. Just enter

```
sudo apt-get install python-dev
```

and when that finishes, type

```
sudo apt-get install python.rpi-gpio
```

---

■ **Note**   `python-rpi.gpio` may already be installed, depending on your Raspian version. Depending on the date you're reading this chapter, it may also return an error of "Unable to locate package." No big deal—it's most likely already installed.

---

You're now ready to access the pins. The Python module used to access them is the `RPi.GPIO` module. It is normally called in the first lines of your program by typing

```
import RPi.GPIO as GPIO
```

and then configured by typing

```
GPIO.setmode(GPIO.BOARD)
```

which lets you identify the pins as they are labeled on a standard pinout diagram, as shown in Figure 12-1.

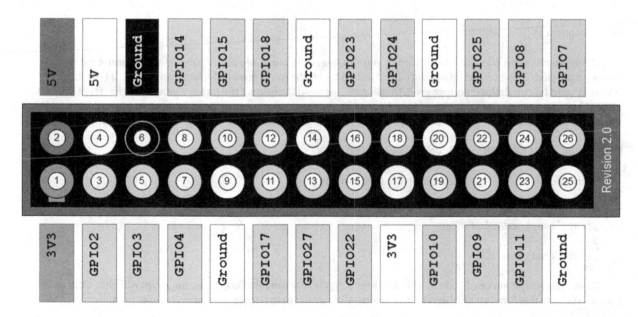

*Figure 12-1.*  *The GPIO pinout diagram*

175

---

■ **Note**    Keep in mind that with GPIO.setmode(GPIO.BOARD), when you refer to pin 11, you're actually referring to the physical pin #11 (which translates to GPIO17 in the diagram in Figure 12-1), *not* GPIO11, which translates to physical pin #23.

---

Once you've set the mode, you can then set each pin to be either an input or an output. Users of the Arduino will probably recognize the concept here. Type the following

```
GPIO.setup (11, GPIO.OUT)
GPIO.setup (13, GPIO.IN)
```

and so forth. Once you've set a pin as an output, you can then send voltage to it (turn it on) by typing

```
GPIO.output (11, 1)
```

or

```
GPIO.output (11, True)
```

and subsequently turn it off by typing

```
GPIO.output (11, 0)
```

or

```
GPIO.output (11, False)
```

If the pin has been configured as an input, you can query the pin to see if a button or switch connected to it has been pressed. However, an important caveat here is that if the pin is merely declared an INPUT, it is defined as "floating" and has no defined voltage level. In this case, we need to connect the pin to a ground so that it is always LOW (0) until we press a button. This is done by putting a resistor between the pin and a common ground. Luckily, the RPi.GPIO module allows us to do this in software by typing the following:

```
GPIO.setup (11, GPIO.IN, pull_up_down=GPIO.PUD_DOWN)
```

At this point, you can "poll" the pin at any time by typing

```
if GPIO.input(11):
    print "Input was HIGH"
else:
    print "Input was LOW"
```

Insert this simple piece of code in a loop in your script; every time the loop runs, the script will check the pin's status. We'll use this functionality in our final submersible program to trigger the camera to take pictures.

# Installing the Raspberry Pi Camera Board

The submersible we'll build will be equipped to take pictures, either at preset intervals or at the press of a button. Obviously, this means we need to install the camera module that interfaces with the Pi.

When you get the camera board, it will most likely come in a plain white box, inside of which is an anti-static gray bag containing the camera board. Make sure you have discharged any static electricity from your body (because the camera is very sensitive to static) by touching a good ground, and then remove the camera from the bag.

The camera connects to the strip connector located on the board between the HDMI output and the Ethernet port. Open the connector by pulling up on the sides—it'll "pop" up by a few millimeters, which is all you need. Position the end of the camera's ribbon cable so that the connectors (the silver side, not the blue side) are facing the HDMI port. Slide the cable into the connector until it bottoms out to make sure you have a good connection. Then, while holding the cable still, press down on both sides of the connector until they snap into place. (See Figure 12-2.)

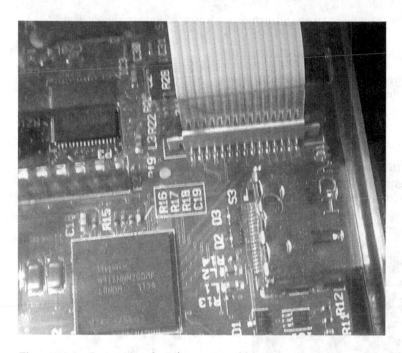

*Figure 12-2.* *Connecting the Pi's camera cable*

You should have enabled the camera support when you set up your Pi in Chapter 3; if you didn't, however, it's not difficult. From the terminal, type

```
sudo apt-get update
```

and

```
sudo apt-get upgrade
```

to make sure your Pi is running all the latest kernel fixes and software updates. When both of those finish, type

```
sudo raspi-config
```

to start the configuration program. Navigate to the "camera" selection and click "Enable." Then select "Finish" and reboot the Pi.

When the Pi comes back up, you can use its built-in camera functions, `raspistill` and `raspivid`, to experiment with the camera. For a full list of commands, simply enter

```
raspivid
```

or

```
raspistill
```

at the command prompt for instructions. For example, to take a still picture in a "cartoon" format, simply type

```
raspistill -o image.jpg -ifx cartoon
```

and the image will be saved in whichever directory you happen to be in. You can change the image resolution, height, width, effects, and delay, and even set up a time-lapse situation using the `-tl` flag (which we may use later).

# Controlling the Sub

To control the sub, we are going to use two DC motors, a motor driver chip (already placed on a printed circuit board), and a Wii nunchuk (as shown in Figure 12-3). Using a special adapter, you can access the nunchuk's wires and connect them directly to the Raspberry Pi without having to cut the connector from the end of the controller.

***Figure 12-3.*** *The Wii nunchuk*

The nunchuk communicates via a protocol known as I2C, or IIC, which stands for *Inter-Integrated Circuit*. If you're working your way through the projects in order, you may remember the I2C protocol from Chapter 6, "The Weather Station." I2C was created by Philips in the early 1980s as a way for different devices to communicate on a single *bus* (communication wire). It has since undergone several revisions, but the basic concept remains the same. On an I2C bus, one machine serves as a "master," and can be connected to a variety of different "slaves." Each machine can communicate on the same set of wires, using a clock signal transmitted by the master to synchronize the communication. Luckily, for our purposes, the Raspberry Pi can utilize the I2C protocol over some of its GPIO pins, and the communication is relatively simple, because there are only two devices communicating: the Pi, serving as the master, and the Wii nunchuk as the solitary slave.

## Attaching the Wiichuck Adapter

The first thing to do is to solder a set of four headers to your Wiichuck adapter. Using just a small amount of solder, connect the headers to the adapter (as shown in Figure 12-4). Like many commercially available boards, the adapter is covered with a solder-phobic coating, which prevents the solder from flowing between connections and shorting them out. This makes soldering headers to the connector a simple process even for inexperienced solderers.

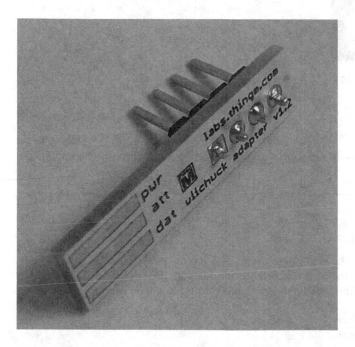

***Figure 12-4.*** *Headers soldered to the Wiichuck adapter*

You'll make four connections to the Wiichuck—positive, negative, SDA (the I2C data line), and SCL (the I2C clock line). You'll connect the positive wire to GPIO pin #1 and the negative wire to GPIO pin #6. Connect the SDA wire to pin #3 and the SCL wire to pin #5. You can see the Wiichuck correctly inserted into the controller in Figure 12-5.

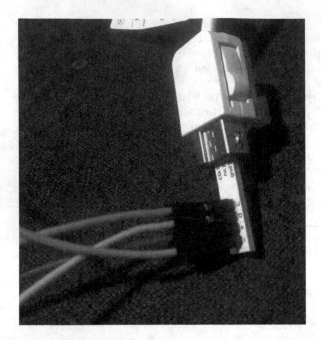

*Figure 12-5. Correct positioning of Wiichuck adapter*

---

■ **Caution**   You should connect the nunchuk to the Pi's #1 pin (3.3V), *not* the #2 pin (which is 5V). The reason is that the Wii's nunchuk is designed to run on 3.3V, not 5V. Although it will work with 5V, it can severely shorten the life of the controller.

---

## Activating the Pi's I2C

To use the controller with the Pi, we need to activate the Pi's I2C capability, which is not enabled by default. To enable it, you need to edit the Pi's blacklist-configuration file, which lists modules the Pi does not need to load on startup. Modules are normally listed here because although they are available, they are not often used. Open the blacklist-configuration file by typing

```
sudo emacs /etc/modprobe.d/raspi-blacklist.conf
```

Comment out the last two lines to remove their blacklisted status. When you're done, the file should look like this:

```
# blacklist spi and i2c by default (many users don't need them)

#blacklist spi-bcm2708
#blacklist i2c-bcm2708
```

Save the file and exit. You must also add the I2C drivers to the kernel. To do this, open the /etc/modules file by typing

```
sudo emacs /etc/modules
```

and then type

```
i2c-bcm2708
i2c-dev
```

to the end of the file. Save and exit. Lastly, to use the I2C tools, you'll need to use sudo apt-get to add these few packages:

```
sudo apt-get install i2c-tools
sudo apt-get install python-smbus
```

When those packages are finished installing, reboot your Pi.

## Testing the Nunchuk

To see if the I2C configuration worked, connect your nunchuk to the correct pins (1, 3, 5, and 6). Start your terminal, and enter the following:

```
sudo i2cdetect -y 0
```

This queries the I2C bus for the address of all connected devices. You should receive a response like this:

```
     0  1  2  3  4  5  6  7  8  9  a  b  c  d  e  f
00:          03 04 05 06 07 -- -- -- -- -- -- -- --
10: -- -- -- -- -- -- -- -- -- -- -- -- -- -- -- --
20: -- -- -- -- -- -- -- -- -- -- -- -- -- -- -- --
30: -- -- -- -- -- -- -- -- -- -- -- -- -- -- -- --
40: -- -- -- -- -- -- -- -- -- -- -- -- -- -- -- --
50: -- -- 52 -- -- -- -- -- -- -- -- -- -- -- -- --
60: -- -- -- -- -- -- -- -- -- -- -- -- -- -- -- --
70: -- -- -- -- -- -- -- --
```

This shows that the nunchuk is connected at address #52.

If you don't see anything, and you're certain you've hooked up the nunchuk wires correctly, try running

```
sudo i2cdetect -y 1
```

instead. The "1" or "0" depends on which Pi model you have. Although it's most likely that the board you have uses the "0," try the "1" if you're having no luck reading the bus.

---

■ **Tip** If you have trouble getting results, and you're positive you hooked up all the wires and devices correctly, check that all your wires are intact. I have lost hours and hours troubleshooting a build, only to find that one or more of the cheap jumper wires I was using was broken inside the insulation, meaning I wasn't getting signals where I was supposed to. It happens more often than you think!

---

# Reading from the Nunchuk

You're now ready to read from the nunchuk. Eventually, of course, we're going to translate signals from the nunchuk into commands for the motors, but it might be instructional to see what signals we're getting to begin with. To do this, let's create a Python script that imports the correct modules, listens for signals from the nunchuk, and outputs them to the screen. There are seven signals sent over the wire: the X- and Y-position of the joystick, the state of the "Z" and "C" buttons on the front, and the X-, Y-, and Z-state of the nunchuk's built-in accelerometer. We won't use all of these for the sub, but we can still take a look at them.

Here's the full script for you to type in:

```
#import necessary modules
import smbus
import time

bus = smbus.SMBus(0)        # or smbus.SMBus(1) if you had to use -y 1 in the i2cdetect command

#initiate I2C communication by writing to the nunchuk
bus.write_byte_data(0x52,0x40,0x00)
time.sleep(0.1)

while True:
  try:
    bus.write_byte(0x52,0x00)
    time.sleep(0.1)
    data0 =  bus.read_byte(0x52)
    data1 =  bus.read_byte(0x52)
    data2 =  bus.read_byte(0x52)
    data3 =  bus.read_byte(0x52)
    data4 =  bus.read_byte(0x52)
    data5 =  bus.read_byte(0x52)
    joy_x = data0
    joy_y = data1
    accel_x = (data2 << 2) + ((data5 & 0x0c) >> 2)
    accel_y = (data3 << 2) + ((data5 & 0x30) >> 4)
    accel_z = (data4 << 2) + ((data5 & 0xc0) >> 6)
    buttons = data5 & 0x03

    button_c = (buttons == 1) #button_c is True if buttons = 1
    button_z = (buttons == 2) #button_z is True if buttons = 2

    print 'Jx: %s Jy: %s Ax: %s Ay: %s Az: %s Bc: %s Bz: %s' % (joy_x, joy_y, accel_x, accel_y,
accel_z, button_c, button_z)
  except IOError as e:
    print e
```

If you haven't already, create a folder for your submersible program, save this script in that folder, and run it. After importing the necessary modules, the script creates a "bus" over which all communications will be made with the nunchuk. It then begins communication by writing to the nunchuk's I2C address (bus.write_byte_data()). It then enters a loop where it continuously reads the 5-byte strings coming from the nunchuk (data0, data1, and so on) and categorizes them as joystick directions, accelerometer readings, and button presses, in that order. Then it prints those values to the screen and repeats the process.

Because it involves reading and writing to the I2C bus, you'll have to run it as root, so type the following:

```
sudo python nunchuktest.py
```

As soon as the script starts, it will show you a running status report of all the nunchuk's sensors, updated in real time and formatted like so:

```
Jx: 130 Jy: 131 Ax: 519 Ay: 558 Az: 713 Bc: False Bz: False
```

With the script running, try moving the joystick, pressing the buttons, and shaking the nunchuk to watch the values change. You now know how to read values from the nunchuk, which we're going to use to drive the motors.

## The Nunchuk and LED Test Side Project

As a little side project (and as a test for my nunchuk-reading ability), I hooked up six LEDs to a small breadboard and some GPIO pins so that they would light up depending on which way I moved the joystick or pressed the buttons. This might be a worthwhile test to conduct to make sure that not only are you reading the values, but that you are able to do something with those values. In this case, choose four GPIO pins and set them as outputs. Connect those pins to a resistor and the positive leg of your LEDs connected in parallel (as shown in Figure 12-6), tie all the grounds together, and run the following script:

```python
import smbus
import time
import RPi.GPIO as GPIO
GPIO.setwarnings(False)
GPIO.setmode(GPIO.BOARD)

#set pins
GPIO.setup (11, GPIO.OUT)
GPIO.setup (13, GPIO.OUT)
GPIO.setup (15, GPIO.OUT)
GPIO.setup (19, GPIO.OUT)
GPIO.setup (21, GPIO.OUT)
GPIO.setup (23, GPIO.OUT)

bus = smbus.SMBus(0)

bus.write_byte_data (0x52, 0x40, 0x00)
time.sleep (0.1)
while True:
    try:
        bus.write_byte (0x52, 0x00)
        time.sleep (0.1)
        data0 = bus.read_byte (0x52)
        data1 = bus.read_byte (0x52)
        data2 = bus.read_byte (0x52)
        data3 = bus.read_byte (0x52)
        data4 = bus.read_byte (0x52)
        data5 = bus.read_byte (0x52)
        joy_x = data0
        joy_y = data1
```

```
# the following lines add the necessary values to make the received 5-byte
# strings easier to decode and print
        accel_x = (data2 << 2) + ((data5 & 0x0c) >> 2)
        accel_y = (data3 << 2) + ((data5 & 0x30) >> 4)
        accel_z = (data4 << 2) + ((data5 & 0xc0) >> 6)
        buttons = data5 & 0x03
        button_c = (buttons == 1)
        button_z = (buttons == 2)
        print 'Jx: %s Jy: %s Ax: %s Ay: %s Az: %s Bc: %s Bz:
%s' % (joy_x, joy_y, accel_x, accel_y, accel_z, button_c, button_z)
        if joy_x > 200:
            GPIO.output (11, 1)
            GPIO.output (13, 0)
            GPIO.output (15, 0)
            GPIO.output (19, 0)
            GPIO.output (21, 0)
            GPIO.output (23, 0)
        elif joy_x < 35:
            GPIO.output (11, 0)
            GPIO.output (13, 1)
            GPIO.output (15, 0)
            GPIO.output (19, 0)
            GPIO.output (21, 0)
            GPIO.output (23, 0)
        elif joy_y > 200:
            GPIO.output (11, 0)
            GPIO.output (13, 0)
            GPIO.output (15, 1)
            GPIO.output (19, 0)
            GPIO.output (21, 0)
            GPIO.output (23, 0)
        elif joy_y < 35:
            GPIO.output (11, 0)
            GPIO.output (13, 0)
            GPIO.output (15, 0)
            GPIO.output (19, 1)
            GPIO.output (21, 0)
            GPIO.output (23, 0)
        elif button_c == True:
            GPIO.output (11, 0)
            GPIO.output (13, 0)
            GPIO.output (15, 0)
            GPIO.output (19, 0)
            GPIO.output (21, 1)
            GPIO.output (23, 0)
        elif button_z == True:
            GPIO.output (11, 0)
            GPIO.output (13, 0)
            GPIO.output (15, 0)
            GPIO.output (19, 0)
            GPIO.output (21, 0)
            GPIO.output (23, 1)
```

```
    else:
        GPIO.output (11, 0)
        GPIO.output (13, 0)
        GPIO.output (15, 0)
        GPIO.output (19, 0)
        GPIO.output (21, 0)
        GPIO.output (23, 0)
except IOError as e:
    print e
```

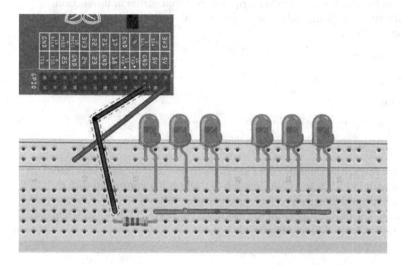

***Figure 12-6.*** *LED test setup*

As mentioned earlier, the code first creates a "bus" over which all communications will be made with the nunchuk. It then begins communication by writing to the nunchuk's I2C address (bus.write_byte_data()). It then enters a loop where it continuously reads the 5-byte strings coming from the nunchuk (data0, data1, and so on) and categorizes them as joystick directions, accelerometer readings, and button presses, in that order. The value of those strings indicate what each component of the nunchuk is doing: if buttonZ is True, for example, the button has been pressed. Likewise, the joystick's Y-direction value indicates whether the joystick is being pushed forward or pulled back. The long sequence of if-elif statements simply iterates through the received values and lights the corresponding LED.

Running it (again, using sudo) should result in different LEDs lighting depending on what you're doing with the nunchuk.

As you can see, hooking the LEDs in parallel means that they all share a common ground, and a common high voltage line. In contrast, if you were to connect them in series, the positive leg of each LED would hook to the negative leg of the next LED, with a resistor between the last LED and either the positive or negative pin of the Pi.

## Controlling the Sub Motors and Camera with the Nunchuk

Now that you've got the nunchuk working, we need to use it to control the motors of the sub, which involves using the L298 motor controller chip. Ordinarily, we can't drive very powerful motors or servos with the Pi, because the Pi can't source (supply) enough current to drive them. To get around this limitation, we use a motor controller chip such as the L298. Chips like this, called *H-bridges*, allow you to hook an external power source to your motors and use the Pi to turn the motors on and off as needed. The L298 chip costs only a few dollars and can be used to drive incredible amounts of current and voltage—up to 4 amps and 46 volts. It's commonly used with hobby robots and is perfect for this type of application.

However, though the chip is cheap, connecting it to your Pi and the motors can be complicated because you need to use several 10nF capacitors and some flyback diodes to protect the Pi from voltage spikes coming from the motors. For that reason, I highly recommend getting the L298 motor driver board from Sparkfun, as mentioned in the "A Shopping List of Parts" section. It makes the connections much simpler: you plug in the external source, input signals from the Pi, and output wires to the motors, and you're done. For the rest of the chapter, I'm going to assume you're using the Sparkfun board. If you decide to breadboard the chip yourself, some good schematics can be found online.

To control the sub and the motors, we can modify the LED-driving script I introduced earlier in the section "The Nunchuk and LED Test," but instead of turning LEDs on and off, we're going to turn motors on and off, and activate the camera. Control will basically be as follows:

- Joystick forward = both motors spinning

- Joystick left = right motor spinning

- Joystick right = left motor spinning

- C button pressed = take still picture with camera

- Z button pressed = take video with camera

To power the motors with the L298 board, seven wires connect the Pi to the board—three for each connected motor, and the ground. Motor A is controlled with IN1, IN2, and ENA ("enable A"). Motor B is controlled with IN3, IN4, and ENB. To control motor A, you set ENA to high, and then send voltages down either IN1 or IN2 (or neither, to brake the motor). Motor B is controlled the same way. The power supply for the motors is connected to the board, bypassing the Pi entirely. To see an illustration, take a look at Table 12-1 and Figure 12-7.

*Table 12-1.* *Motor values and settings*

| ENA Value | ENA = 1 | ENA = 1 | ENA = 1 | ENA = 0 |
|---|---|---|---|---|
| **IN1 Value** | IN1 = 1 | IN1 = 0 | IN1 = 0 | - |
| **IN2 Value** | IN2 = 0 | IN2 = 1 | IN2 = 0 | - |
| **Result** | Motor A spins clockwise | Motor A spins counter-clockwise | Motor A brakes | Motor A stops |

***Figure 12-7.*** *Motors and the motor controller connected to the Pi*

Obviously, all we need to do is set up three GPIO pins for each motor. At the same time, we read the GPIO pins set as I2C inputs, and set the motor pins high or low, depending on the signals we're getting from the nunchuk. We'll also check for button presses in order to activate the camera. (Figure 12-7 shows the connections for one motor, not both.)

There are no Python libraries available yet to directly interface with the Pi's camera module. However, fear not: we can use Python's subprocess module to make system commands as if we were in the command line. If you wanted to take a still picture using the camera from within a Python script, you would type

```
from subprocess import call
call (["raspistill -o image.jpg"], shell=True)
```

The video command is almost the same:

```
from subprocess import call
call (["raspivid -o video.mp4"], shell=True)
```

We can set each command within its own function and call that function when the appropriate button is pressed on the nunchuk. Similarly, we can set up functions to run the motors and call those functions according to the position of the joystick. All of this happens within a while loop and continues until we kill the program or the batteries die.

# Starting the Program Remotely

There are several ways to get the Python program running once you power up your submersible, as you won't have a keyboard, mouse, or monitor connected to the Pi. It would seem that the easiest way would be to set up a static IP address, remotely log in to the Pi from a laptop, and then start the program from there. However, this will only work if you are logged on to a wireless network, and chances are that there won't be any networks available out on the middle of a lake (or ocean, or wherever you happen to be using your submersible).

You could set up an *ad hoc* network, which is where the Pi and your laptop create a small, exclusive network, and then log in to the Pi from your laptop. However, setting up an ad hoc network can be problematic, and if it doesn't work for some reason, you'll be unable to access your Pi, rendering your submersible useless.

After some thought, I decided that the best way to proceed would be to simply start the sub control program automatically, when you start up your Pi. That way you can turn it on, send power to the motors, and proceed to work with your sub.

To do this, all we need to do is to edit one file—your Cron scheduler. The Cron scheduler is a job scheduler you can edit. It enables you to schedule tasks and scripts at specified times and intervals. To edit it, you open the file called the crontab by typing

```
sudo crontab -e
```

Each user has its own crontab, but by using sudo we'll be editing the root user's Cron, which is the user we need to run our Python script. You'll see something like Figure 12-8.

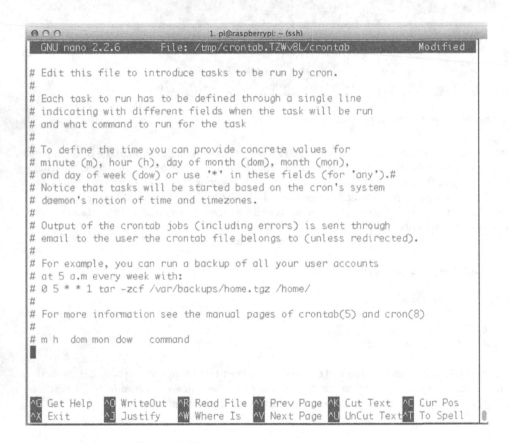

***Figure 12-8.*** *The user's crontab file*

Scroll down to the end of the file, and enter the following:

```
@reboot python /home/pi/Desktop/submersible/sub.py &
```

This is the specific path to your Python script (assuming you've saved sub.py in the "submersible" folder on your Desktop), and the "&" tells Cron to run the job in the background, so as not to interfere with the normal startup routine. Save the file by typing **Ctrl+X, Y** and then press Return. The next time you reboot the Pi, sub.py will be running—test it if you like!

# The Final Control Program

We now have all the different Python pieces programmed; all that remains is to combine them into one script. We've determined the movement parameters, so let's write some functions that will be called from the main program loop to react to joystick movements and button presses. The easiest will be the camera functions. To take a still picture, type

```
def takeStillPic(picNum):
    "Take still picture when C button is pressed"
    call (["raspistill -o image" + str(picNum) + ".jpg"], shell=True)
```

And for a video, type:

```
def takeVideo():
    "Take video when Z button is pressed"
    call (["raspivid -o video.mp4"], shell=True)
```

The first function, takeStillPic(picNum), takes a picture, using the system call raspistill, with the name of the parameter, picNum. The second function, takeVideo(), takes a video with the .mp4 extension, using the raspivid system call.

We'll do a from subprocess import call early in the program, with all of our other imports. It's a good programming practice to import all of your modules when you first start the program, even though it's technically possible to import a needed module anywhere in the script. Keeping your imports in one place can make it easier to debug the script later. You'll also notice that takeStillPic takes an integer as a parameter; if we keep a counter of each time we press the C button and send that count to the function, we'll get a different image name ("image4.jpg", "image5.jpg", and so on) each time we press the button. If we don't do that, each time we call the function it will create another "image.jpg", overwriting the previous image of the same name. Also, note that the parameter needs to be cast as a string with str() in order to be inserted into the filename string given.

To keep things simple, we're not going to use the camera's video capabilities in this program. Rather, we can take a picture with the nunchuk button, wait until the camera process is finished, and then continue with the program's main loop until the button is pressed again.

# The Final Code

Save the following code on your Pi, preferably in its own folder. It's also available as sub.py on the Apress web site.

```
from subprocess import call
import time
import smbus
import RPi.GPIO as GPIO
GPIO.setwarnings (False)
GPIO.setmode (GPIO.BOARD)

def take_stillpic(num):
    call (["raspistill -o image" + str(num) + "jpg"], shell=True)

def go_forward():
    GPIO.output (19, 1) #IN1 on
    GPIO.output (23, 0) #IN2 off
    GPIO.output (11, 1) #IN3 on
    GPIO.output (15, 0) #IN4 off
```

```python
def go_backward():
    GPIO.output (19, 0) #IN1 off
    GPIO.output (23, 1) #IN2 on
    GPIO.output (11, 0) #IN3 off
    GPIO.output (15, 1) #IN4 on

def go_right():
    GPIO.output (19, 1) #IN1 on
    GPIO.output (23, 0) #IN2 off
    GPIO.output (11, 0) #IN3 off
    GPIO.output (15, 1) #IN4 on

def go_left():
    GPIO.output (19, 0) #IN1 off
    GPIO.output (23, 1) #IN2 on
    GPIO.output (11, 1) #IN3 on
    GPIO.output (15, 0) #IN4 off

#set motor control pins
#left motor
# 11 = IN3
# 13 = enableB
# 15 = IN4
GPIO.setup (11, GPIO.OUT)
GPIO.setup (13, GPIO.OUT)
GPIO.setup (15, GPIO.OUT)

#right motor
# 19 = IN1
# 21 = enableA
# 23 = IN2
GPIO.setup (19, GPIO.OUT)
GPIO.setup (21, GPIO.OUT)
GPIO.setup (23, GPIO.OUT)

#enable both motors
GPIO.output (13, 1)
GPIO.output (21, 1)

#setup nunchuk read
bus = smbus.SMBus(0)  # or a (1) if you needed used y -1 in the i2cdetect command
bus.write_byte_data (0x52, 0x40, 0x00)
time.sleep (0.5)

x = 1

while True:
    try:
        bus.write_byte (0x52, 0x00)
        time.sleep (0.1)
        data0 = bus.read_byte (0x52)
```

```
data1 = bus.read_byte (0x52)
data2 = bus.read_byte (0x52)
data3 = bus.read_byte (0x52)
data4 = bus.read_byte (0x52)
data5 = bus.read_byte (0x52)
joy_x = data0
joy_y = data1
accel_x = (data2 << 2) + ((data5 & 0x0c) >> 2)
accel_y = (data3 << 2) + ((data5 & 0x30) >> 4)
accel_z = (data4 << 2) + ((data5 & 0xc0) >> 6)
buttons = data5 & 0x03
button_c = (buttons == 1) or (buttons == 2)
button_z = (buttons == 0) or (buttons == 2)

if joy_x > 200: #joystick right
    go_right()
elif joy_x < 35: #joystick left
    go_left()
elif joy_y > 200: #joystick forward
    go_forward()
elif joy_y < 35: #joystick back
    go_backward()
elif button_c == True:
    x = x+1
    take_stillpic(x)
elif button_z == True:
    print "button z! \n"
else: #joystick at neutral, no buttons
    GPIO.output (19, 0)
    GPIO.output (23, 0)
    GPIO.output (11, 0)
    GPIO.output (15, 0)

except IOError as e:
    print e
```

# Constructing the Sub

At this point, we're ready to start building the actual submersible. Gather your parts together: the PVC pipes and elbows, waterproof container, glues, screws, and the rest. Remember that the design I illustrate in the following sections is just that—an illustration, *not* a step-by-step instruction sheet. As long as you end up with a frame of some sort, upon which you can mount your waterproofed Pi enclosure and waterproofed motors and propellers, you will have succeeded in this task.

---

■ **Note**   Construction plans, particularly motor-waterproofing procedures have been influenced heavily by the Seaperch program (http://www.seaperch.org), a program designed to teach students of all ages about building a remote-controlled submersible and that encourages involvement in engineering and mathematical fields. It is a valuable program, and I highly endorse its goals.

---

## Building the Frame

Using the PVC pipe and 90° elbows, construct a roughly square frame large enough to hold your Pi enclosure. After using PVC glue or screws to fasten everything in place, cut the plastic netting to fit the square and use the zip ties to fasten it to the frame. You should end up with a plastic "tray" like the one in Figure 12-9.

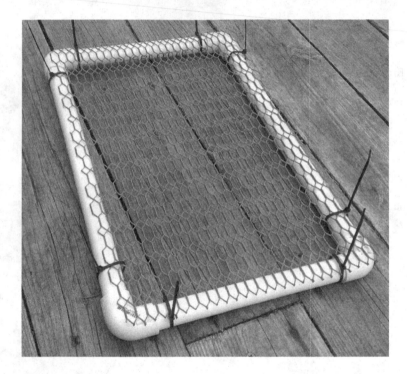

***Figure 12-9.***  *The sub platform*

This is your sub's body. I've left it large enough to add strips of Styrofoam on the sides if I need to change the buoyancy—though I shouldn't have to, seeing as how the Pi's enclosure is filled with air.

## Creating the Pi's Enclosure

You need a *clear* plastic container large to hold all your electronics. I specify "clear" because your camera will be looking through it and needs to be able to see. When you've selected your container, drill three small holes in it—two for the wires to the motors, and one for the wire to the nunchuk—as you see in Figure 12-10.

*Figure 12-10.* *Waterproof Pi enclosure*

## Waterproofing the Motor Enclosures

Perhaps the hardest part of this project is waterproofing the motors, as they'll be outside the enclosure. I used prescription pill bottles to hold mine. First, wrap the motor entirely with electrical tape to seal the large holes in the casing. (See Figure 12-11.)

*Figure 12-11.* *Motor wrapped in electrical tape*

Then strip the ends from a short length of Ethernet cable and solder two of the enclosed wires to the wires from the motor. When it's totally wrapped and the wires are connected, drill two holes in the pill bottle—one in the lid for the propeller, and one in the base for the control wires. Slide the wires through the bottle and make sure everything fits snugly in the bottle, as shown in Figure 12-12 and Figure 12-13.

***Figure 12-12.*** *Motor ready to insert in the pill bottle*

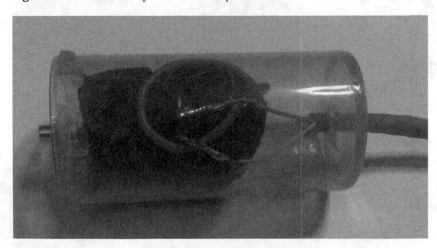

***Figure 12-13.*** *Motor snugly fitted in the bottle*

Now (and here's the waterproofing key) stand your pill bottle upright and fill it with wax, surrounding the motor and the wires, as shown in Figure 12-14. Paraffin wax, available from your supermarket, works well for this. You'll probably have the best luck if you add a small layer of wax, let it harden, and then continue until the bottle is full.

***Figure 12-14.*** *Motor surrounded by wax*

When it's securely surrounded by wax, make sure your motor shaft can still turn and then slide on the cap, fitting the motor shaft through your pre-drilled hole. Then slide your propeller onto the exposed shaft, and you should have a waterproofed motor that resembles Figure 12-15. Repeat for the other motor for the other side of the sub, and then fasten the two motors to your sub's frame with zip ties.

***Figure 12-15.*** *Waterproofed motor, ready for mounting*

## Connecting the Nunchuck

Since we're going to be running Ethernet cable from the sub to your nunchuck (which will be kept onboard your boat), you'll need to use another length of Ethernet cable. Strip the ends, grab four wires and solder them to your wiichuck controller. Slide the other end of the cable through the top hole in your sub's body, and connect the other ends of those four wires to your Pi's GPIO pins.

## Assembling the Final Product

Once your motors are waterproofed, you can assemble the final product. Run the wires from each motor through the holes in your container, and connect them to the motor controller board the same way you did for testing. When all the wires have been fed through the holes, use the marine epoxy to seal the holes.

---

■ **Warning**   The 5200 sealant is **extremely** sticky and messy, and if you get it on your skin it won't come off. Wear gloves, and do all your work outside if you can. Also, don't be stingy with the sealant—you're trying to protect all your electronics, so make sure there's no way water's getting into your enclosure.

---

When the holes are sealed, make sure all your electronic connections are sound and put the Pi and the motor controller into the enclosure. Use a small piece of tape or poster putty (which is what I used) to press the camera against the front "wall" of the enclosure, and to hold the various boards in place. Use a small breadboard to connect your grounds, and add your two batteries—one for the Pi, and one for the motor controller.

When you power your Pi with a battery, you *must* use a 5V supply because the Pi does not have an onboard voltage regulator. You can experiment with different battery combinations, or you can use a voltage regulator to do the work for you. For all of my portable Pi work, I have hacked a USB car charger, seen in Figure 12-16, for that purpose, because it delivers 5V and about 1 amp perfectly.

*Figure 12-16.*  *USB car charger*

Crack the casing open, and use a USB-to-micro-USB cord to attach the USB power out to your Pi's power in. Then attach your battery's power to the charger's power inputs, and voila! You have 5V powering your Pi!

Once you've got your power issues sorted, you can place everything in the enclosure, power on your Pi, and seal it up. Hopefully, you've got something that looks similar to Figure 12-17.

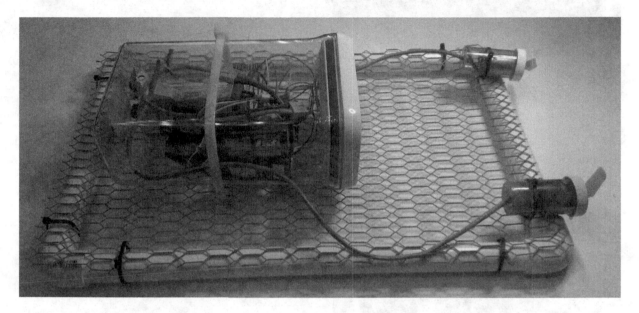

***Figure 12-17.*** *Completed submersible*

Obviously, the version of the product shown in Figure 12-17 is unfinished—I haven't connected the nunchuk yet—but you can see the placement of the motors and the enclosure itself. As a final construction photo, Figure 12-18 shows the placement of the Pi's camera against the front wall of the enclosure, held in place with poster putty.

*Figure 12-18.* *Pi camera placement in enclosure*

If you've followed all the instructions carefully, you should now have a Pi-powered submersible that you can control from onshore or your boat, using a Wii nunchuk. Pressing the button on the nunchuk will let you take pictures, and you can transfer these to your home computer when you bring the Pi back onboard.

And what sort of pictures can you take? Well, if you live in Australia, you could take something like you see in Figure 12-19.

***Figure 12-19.*** *Underwater photography*

(Full disclosure here: this picture was *not* taken with a Pi sub. But it *could* have been.)

If, however, you live in Alaska, the pictures you get may end up looking more like Figure 12-20 and Figure 12-21.

*Figure 12-20.* *Alaskan underwater photography*

*Figure 12-21.* *More Alaskan underwater photography*

These were taken in a lake not far from my house. Yes, it's pretty boring—not much going on in Alaskan lakes in late autumn. I'll probably try again in the spring or summer.

Enjoy your submarine!

# Summary

In this chapter, you learned about using the I2C protocol to connect a Wii nunchuk to your Pi and use it to control a few different functions on your Pi. You then constructed a watertight, mobile enclosure for your Pi, connected some motors and your camera, and were able to remotely pilot your sub and take some (hopefully) impressive underwater pictures.

In the next chapter, you'll learn how to connect a microcontroller—the Arduino—to your Pi to increase its capabilities.

# CHAPTER 13

■ ■ ■

# The Gertboard

While the Raspberry Pi is an impressive piece of hardware, with audio and video interfaces, Ethernet, USB, and GPIO pins, it's not all-powerful. For example, it doesn't have an onboard voltage regulator, making it possible to easily fry your Pi by giving it too much voltage. Nor does it have an easy way to control other circuits, such as motors that require more current than the Pi can conveniently source.

Enter the Gertboard. An add-on circuit board, it's about the size of an index card and significantly extends the functionality of your Raspberry Pi. While you most definitely don't need one to work with your Pi, having one makes it much easier to do things you couldn't do otherwise. For example, you can add more sensors, drive external motors, and much, much more.

It owes its existence (and its name) to its designer, Gert Van Loo. Gert was one of the original volunteer engineers who donated great portions of his time to the Raspberry Pi project and helped with the design that eventually became the Raspberry Pi model B. Because he wanted to further expand the capabilities of the Pi, he designed the Gertboard, which was first available only as a kit; you had to solder the board together before you could use it. However, you can now buy a fully assembled board from several online retailers.

Development continues on the Gertboard, so there's a good chance that your board may differ from the one in the pictures in this chapter, but the overall placement of parts and sections hasn't changed. ICs (integrated circuits) may differ, but the headers used to plug into them won't. There is even another version of the Gertboard called the *Multiface board*, put out by Tandy. The Multiface version is designed with all through-hole parts, which means that it can be sold as a kit and requires no surface-mount soldering.

In this chapter, I'll give you a quick tour of the Gertboard and its parts, and even walk you through some of the programs available for you to use. This will give you a working understanding of what the different components do and show you how to interface with them—and, in turn, give your Pi another interface to the physical world.

## Examining the Board

The Gertboard is an impressive PCB (printed circuit board). It measures 13.2 by 8.4 cm. (5.1 by 3.3 inches, for you American folks) and about 1.4 cm. (1/2 inch) high when it's sitting on its included plastic supports. Those supports are designed to allow it to "sit" on top of the Raspberry Pi with its female GPIO headers interfacing precisely with the Pi's male pins (as shown in Figure 13-1).

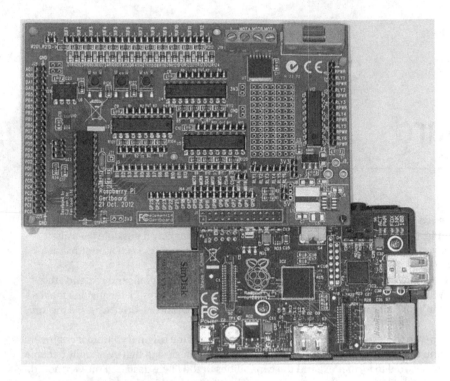

**Figure 13-1.** *The Gertboard connected to the Pi*

Starting from where it interfaces with the Pi, and moving clockwise, let's take a short tour around the board to identify what all of those pins and buttons are for, shall we?

## The GPIO Pins

As a quick reminder, the Pi's GPIO pins (the row of pins next to the SD card on the Pi) are the easiest way to allow it to interact with the world, with ground pins, both 3.3V and 5V pins, and assorted pins that can be configured as either inputs or outputs to read switches and drive motors, for instance. (See Figure 13-2.)

**Figure 13-2.** *The GPIO pins*

Since plugging the board into the Pi covers the Pi's GPIO pins, those pins obviously need to be made accessible, and they are, as you can see in Figure 13-2. If you look closely at the pin numberings, you'll notice that *only* the GPIO pins are in that row; the 3.3V, 5V, and GND pins are elsewhere on the board.

## Atmega Chip

An interesting (and helpful) addition to the Gertboard is the Atmega 328P chip (shown in Figure 13-3)—the same chip used in most Arduinos. It's a very useful microcontroller, and in one of its other incarnations on the Arduino line of boards (which I'll talk about in Chapter 14), it's used by many, many hobbyists. Having it available in an easily accessible form like this is something that many users on the Raspberry Pi online forums had been asking for.

**Figure 13-3.** *The Atmega chip*

Although the Atmega chip on the Gertboard is not bootloaded with the Arduino software, it is definitely possible to add that software to the chip. The pins circled in Figure 13-3 are the connections to the Atmega chip.

## A-to-D and D-to-A Converters

An important part of any board like the Gertboard is conversion—analog-to-digital and digital-to-analog. The four pins highlighted in Figure 13-4 and their associated IC manage those conversions for us.

**Figure 13-4.** *The converters*

A digital-to-analog converter is useful for converting digital signals to a form used by analog devices; for example, many modern audio signals are stored as digital MP3 files and must be converted to an analog form in order to be played through speakers. Digital video signals must be converted in order to be played on an analog monitor. An enterprising Pi user might want to output his or her digital signals to an analog device, and these pins make it possible.

On the other hand, analog-to-digital conversion is also very handy when interfacing a digital computer to an analog world, and the converter on the Gertboard can be used for that as well. For example, you may want to read the values from an analog pressure sensor hooked to a hydraulic pressure line. Those values are analog values, but the Pi's GPIO pins read only digital input. You must use a chip to convert those analog values to a digital HIGH or digital LOW so that the Pi can understand them.

## I/O Section

The I/O section of the board is entirely used for buffered inputs and outputs, including switches, buttons, and LEDs. (See Figure 13-5.) In addition to the top row of headers, it consists of a row of 12 small, surface-mounted LEDs, three push-button switches, and three SN74HC244N chips. These chips are buffers, and they're used to prevent damage to your Pi from the weird things you're probably going to be plugging into the pins. There are series resistors in place to protect the Pi's processor if you mistakenly program the GPIO as an output but leave the input jumper in place. Likewise, sending 9V to a GPIO pin configured as an input could damage the processor if it weren't for those buffered chips.

***Figure 13-5.*** *The I/O section*

An important detail to remember about the pins on the board is that while they can be configured as "inputs" or "outputs," the Gertboard is attached to the Pi and is not an extension of it. In other words, if you call a pin on the Gertboard an "input," that means it will take as input a Pi output. Likewise, an "output" pin on the Gertboard is output to an "input" pin on the Pi.

# The Motor Controller

The motor controller section of the board (shown in Figure 13-6) is especially useful for robotics and other power-intensive projects. It allows you to control high-powered items, such as large motors, with an external power source. While we won't be using this in any of the projects in this book, Chapter 12, "The Submersible," uses an external motor controller. If you have a Gertboard, it's perfectly acceptable to use it rather than the external controller.

*Figure 13-6.* *The motor controller*

The two middle screw terminals are where you attach the motor, and the outer terminals allow you to attach a power source capable of delivering more current than the Gertboard (or the Pi) can safely deliver. The direction and speed of the motor is controlled by two headers located just above the GPIO pins labeled—appropriately—MOTA and MOTB.

## Open Collector Driver

On the right side of the board is a ULN2803 chip that is used as an open collector driver. The six ports are used to turn on and off external devices that require different voltage, higher current, or separate power from that used on the Pi or Gertboard. (See Figure 13-7.) In a nutshell, the open collector connects the ground of an external circuit to the ground on the board, and it gives the circuit power. Each port can take up to 50V and put out 500mA.

***Figure 13-7.*** *The open collector*

As mentioned earlier, your board may look slightly different from these pictures, because there have been considerable modifications and improvements to the design since the board was first released, but the general design is the same. As you can probably now see, the Gertboard *greatly* increases the Pi's capabilities when it comes to interfacing with the physical world. With the Gertboard's onboard motor controller and its collector drivers that allow it to turn external circuits on and off, your Pi now has the ability to truly become an electronic mastermind over whatever collection of circuits you decide to connect to it—whether it's your home automation system or your personal 200W CO2, laser-powered death ray.

## Jumpers

When you purchase a Gertboard, it comes with a selection of plastic jumpers (shown in Figure 13-8). These are used to make connections between adjacent pins without having to use very short jumper wires—a situation that would quickly lead to a chaotic mess on the board, given the amount of jumpers that are commonly used. Very often their placement determines whether a particular pin is going to function as an "input" or an "output." Don't lose these jumpers. Most kits sold also come with a few longer jumpers as well. If yours didn't, don't fret; standard female-female jumpers work just fine on the board.

***Figure 13-8.*** *The Gertboard jumpers*

There is one jumper that must in place at all times—the power jumper (shown in Figure 13-9). Located on the lower right of the board, it connects the 3.3V input from the Pi to all the other parts of the board that need power.

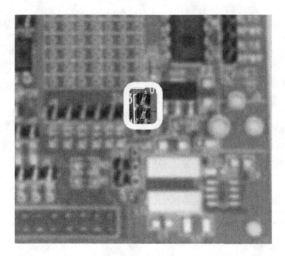

***Figure 13-9.*** *The top two pins in this block must be connected by a jumper*

Now that we've had a look around the Gertboard, let's set up some preliminary jumpers and then do a few simple wiring projects to help you get the hang of using the board and its connections.

# Some Example Projects

The Gertboard manual has a selection of scripts to experiment with, written in both C and Python. So we'll do that now. You'll notice that many of the scripts are almost duplicates, with names like `leds-rg.py` and `leds-wp.py`. The reason is that there are two different libraries you can use to access the Pi's GPIO pins: RPi.GPIO, which you're familiar with from this book, and WiringPi—a library written and released by Gordon Henderson. While the WiringPi library is effective, and even addresses some issues with the Pi that RPi.GPIO does not (such as an easy way of controlling outputs with PWM), I chose to use RPi.GPIO for the projects in this book, so we'll concentrate on that version of the scripts here. If you're interested, however, I recommend you check out the WiringPi library, because it's intended to make the interface to the Pi resemble the Arduino's Wiring library.

## Configuring the Preliminary Jumper Setup

Before we use the board for a few simple projects, we need to install some jumpers. The first one, of course, was illustrated in Figure 13-9: it sends power to the rest of the board from its 3.3V input.

The second batch of jumpers need to be installed on the "output" side of every IC in the buffered I/O section. There are three chips (shown in Figure 13-5), each with eight output pins directly above it. Using four jumpers per chip, connect each pair of pins together. (See Figure 13-10.)

**Figure 13-10.** *Jumpers in an "output" position*

This setup is necessary for the buffered outputs to function as outputs rather than inputs. If you want to use the pins as inputs, the jumpers need to be connected on the bottom row of pins for each IC. Once you've got the pins connected as illustrated, you can continue. Plug the Pi into your board (as shown in Figure 13-1); once you do so, various LEDs in the top row should light up, showing that everything has power. You can now commence with your first program!

## Making Some LEDs Blink

Perhaps the easiest introduction to the Gertboard is to do something impressive with the LEDs. After all, aren't blinking lights one of the reasons you're playing around with electronics in the first place? The Python code in the Gertboard user manual was written by Alex Eames of http://raspi.tv and is basically a translation of the C code. To download the Python code for the board to experiment with, first make a new directory on your Pi by typing

```
mkdir gertboard
```

and then **cd** into that directory. Once you're there, download the zipped programs by typing

```
wget http://raspi.tv/download/GB_Python.zip
```

Then unzip the folder by typing

```
unzip GB_Python.zip
```

and **cd** into the resulting folder.

The first simple script we'll use is the aforementioned leds-rg.py. I'll walk you through this script, so open it to follow along and see what it does. The first three lines should be familiar to you; you're importing time, RPi.GPIO, and sys. The next line, board_type = sys.argv[-1], uses a system call to determine what type of board you have—the regular Gertboard or the Tandy multiface version. This information is then used to print the correct wiring instructions for your board.

```
import RPi.GPIO as GPIO
from time import sleep
import sys
board_type = sys.argv[-1]
```

---

■ **Note**  Because you will be following along in the code you just downloaded, the entire script is not reprinted here.

---

The next section of code checks the Pi's revision number to set the output ports correctly; the first revision of the Pi uses port 21, while the second revision uses port 27. The script then creates a list of the ports—ports = [25, 24, 23, .... 7]. After the list is created, we then copy it to ports_rev and then reverse it with a call to the reverse() method. Now we have two lists of ports—one numbered sequentially forwards, and one numbered backwards. The next line simply sets the GPIO mode to BCM.

The next two lines are an excellent example of Python's for loop syntax. They simply run through the list of ports and set them all to outputs:

```
for port_num in ports:
GPIO.setup(port_num, GPIO.out)
```

The variable after the for can be named whatever you like; the variable after in is the list or dictionary or range or whatever item it is that you're iterating through. In this case, ports has already been declared as a list and is therefore iterable.

We then define a method to turn the LEDs on and off—led_drive(), which takes as parameters the number of repetitions (reps), whether we're lighting single or multiple LEDs at a time (multiple), and direction. We can then use these parameters to do nifty things with the LEDs.

Back in the main function, we then simply go through a predefined list of calls to the led_drive() function. That's the whole script.

To set up the board, make sure the output jumpers are set as described earlier. Then, depending on which Pi revision and Gertboard design you have, connect jumper wires from the GPIO header section (section J) to the row of output headers (section B). When you're done, the board should look similar to Figure 13-11.

**Figure 13-11.** *Jumper positions for the LED script*

Now you can simply run the script by typing

```
sudo python leds-rg.py
```

and you'll be rewarded with some fancy light sequences.

No, we didn't write any elaborate Python here, but that's sort of the point. Simply by connecting a few wires, we were able to get some pretty impressive results with just a few lines of code—no external LEDs or resistors required. The output pins can be connected to any number of external devices; for example, a batch of tone generators, perhaps. You could write a script that activated the generators in certain sequences, and thus play a tune.

## Experimenting with Motor Controllers

The next section of the board we can play with is the motor controller section. It has two pins, MOTA and MOTB, which are connected to the two wires coming from a standard DC motor. The two pins can handle a maximum of 18V DC and 2A. Each of them can be set high or low, including with a pulsed width modulation (PWM) signal to control the motor speed, and the result of different combinations of HIGHs and LOWs are shown in Table 13-1.

**Table 13-1.** *Motor Speeds and Directions*

| MOTA | MOTB | Motor Direction |
|------|------|-----------------|
| LOW | LOW | STOP |
| LOW | HIGH | CLOCKWISE |
| HIGH | LOW | COUNTERCLOCKWISE |
| HIGH | HIGH | STOP |

So, for example, if you needed your motor to turn clockwise, you'd send a 0 to MOTA and a 1 to MOTB.

Again, the Python code that comes with the examples is an excellent way of seeing what the motor driver can do. Open motor-rg.py, and take a look at it. Again, you should recognize the first few imports, and then a few variables are declared, as are some functions designed to run the motor. Some wiring instructions are printed, depending on your board model, and then the main program starts.

To run it, connect one wire of your motor to MOTA and another to MOTB, and then the (+) and (-) leads of your power to the MOT+ and MOT- pins. Then run two jumper wires from GP17 to MOTB and GP18 to MOTA, and type sudo python motor-rg.py at the prompt. The motor will go through its paces, going from zero to full-speed and back to zero in one direction, and then repeating the process in the other direction. As you can tell from the code, it uses GPIO pins 17 and 18 as outputs; obviously, if you choose to use the motor controller, you can set whatever pins you like to be the motor outputs.

## Using the Open Collector Drivers

The open collector drivers on the Gertboard are perhaps one of the most overlooked, yet most useful, parts of the board. That's because they can be used to turn an external circuit on or off using the Pi, whatever that circuit may be and whatever voltage or amperage it needs (within reason, of course). In this way, they are similar to the motor controller, but much more adaptable—the motor controller can be used only for motors, after all!

There are six drivers available, making it possible to drive six external circuits. A good test circuit is simply an LED and a resistor in series.

---

■ **Caution** You *do* know to *always* wire a resistor in line with your LEDs, right? Resistors limit current flow, thus preventing an excess of current from burning out an LED.

---

Take a small breadboard, hook a power source like a 9V battery to it, and then connect your LED circuit to a completely different row of inputs. Then run the open collector program by typing sudo python ocol-rg.py, select a driver, and follow the wiring instructions it prints. To test the first driver, for example, follow these steps:

1. Connect the (+) of your 9V to the RPWR pin in the J6 header (at the top right of the board).

2. Connect the (-) of your 9V to any available pin on the board marked GND. (They're all connected, after all.)

3. Connect the negative lead of your LED to the pin marked RLY1 in the J12 header (again, at the top right of the board).

4. Connect the positive lead (after a resistor in series) to any pin on the board marked RPWR.

Press Enter, and you'll see the LED blink on and off several times.

Impressive? No, not really. But it bears repeating: the ability to control an external circuit, completely independent of the Pi's power source, is an important one. It allows the Pi to act as a mastermind, or puppeteer, turning subsystems on or off as required.

## Using the Digital/Analogue Converters

The Gertboard is equipped with a digital-to-analogue converter chip from Microchip. It's either an 8-, 10-, or 12-bit chip, depending on what parts were available when the board was manufactured. To determine which one you have, closely inspect the chip in U10. (See Figure 13-12.)

*Figure 13-12. D/A converter by Microchip*

There is a number stamped on the chip—either 4802, 4812, or 4822. The third digit will tell you if your chip is an 8-, 10-, or 12-bit version. Regardless of which chip you have, the pinout is the same, and the results are the same: sending a digital input of HIGH, or all 1's (11111111, 1111111111, or 111111111111, depending on your chip version) results in a voltage out of 2.04V. According to the chip's datasheet, the output of the chip can be determined by the following equation:

$$V_{out} = (D_{in} \div 256) \times 2.048V$$

The analogue-to-digital converter on the board is also from Microchip, and is a 10-bit MPC3002. It returns a digital HIGH of 1111111111 when an analogue voltage of 3.3V is applied. If you apply a lower voltage, the 10-bit value will be adjusted accordingly. So if you're trying to read that pressure sensor I mentioned, and it's only reading 2.7V, the returned value from the MPC3002 will be lower, and your program can act on that lower value however you wish.

# Summary

That is a concise and useful overview of the Gertboard and its various components. You got a tour of the board, learned how to use jumpers to connect various components, and used some available Python programs to test some of the different uses for the board.

The one section we didn't cover in detail or experiment with is the Atmega chip, and there's a reason for this: I cover that in much more detail in the next chapter, on the Raspberry Pi and the Arduino.

# CHAPTER 14

■ ■ ■

# The Raspberry Pi and the Arduino

Peanut butter and jelly. Batman and Robin. Dr. Jekyll and Mr. Hyde. Some things are just meant to go together, and we know it from the moment we first lay eyes on the combination. Such is the case with the Raspberry Pi and the Arduino. Many hobbyists and engineers (including me) had been using the Arduino for projects, but were wishing there was a device similar in size with just a *bit* more power. Well, our wishes were granted with the introduction of the Pi. It has more power than the Arduino (the Arduino is only a microcontroller), and it has a full ARM processor.

Of course, other options are in the consumer microprocessor board market. A popular choice is the Beagleboard, an ARM-processor-based board that also runs different versions of Linux, including Angstrom and even Ubuntu. Its main drawback is its $100 price tag. Parallax puts out a few prosumer-grade boards as well, such as the eight-processor Propeller with a built-in breadboard, but again—it's more similar to the Pi than the Arduino, and as of this writing costs $129. Intel's newest entry into the microprocessor market is the Galileo, an Arduino-compatible development board, which also goes for around $100.

None of these boards, however, have gained anywhere near the following of the Arduino. An entire culture has sprung up around this popular little board and the incredible things the average person can do with it. There are many books, web sites, forums, and groups dedicated to its projects, so I won't rehash those sources here. However, information on interfacing the Arduino with the Raspberry Pi is a bit more scarce. The Pi *is* a Linux-based computer, and as such is perfectly capable of running the Arduino software. In this chapter, I'll walk you through installing that software and creating one or two simple projects that run solely on the Pi and the Arduino—no desktop machine is required.

## Exploring the Arduino

For those of you unfamiliar with it, the Arduino is a popular implementation of microcontroller technology, packaged to make it easy for the layperson to program and do complex, interesting tasks with some complex electronics. For people who just want to *make* stuff, it's a boon; the Integrated Development Environment (IDE) used to program the Arduino runs on almost any computer, the programming language is very much like C, and—perhaps best of all—the board is inexpensive, with most Arduino versions costing less than $30 US.

There are several versions of the Arduino, ranging from the tiny Arduino Nano to the much larger Arduino Duemilanove (shown in Figure 14-1) and the Mega. All of the boards have an Atmega168 or 328 chip as their central processor, and they have a serial-to-USB chip onboard to enable them to communicate with your computer. They have a selection of jumpers, similar to the GPIO pins on the Pi, but most of them are female sockets rather than male pins.

***Figure 14-1.*** *The Arduino Duemilanove*

Using the Arduino on a regular computer is a simple process, beginning with downloading the IDE version appropriate for your computer from the project's main web site, `www.arduino.cc`. Once it is installed, you can open a new Arduino program, called a "sketch," and immediately start to interface with hardware connected to the board. (See Figure 14-2.)

```
head_turn | Arduino 1.0.5

head_turn
#include <Servo.h>

void setup()
{
  randomSeed(analogRead(0));
  myservo.attach(9);  // attaches the servo on pin 9 to the servo object
}

void loop()
{
  long firstStopInterval = random(500, 4000);
  long secondStopInterval = random(500, 4000);

  long rightInterval = random(500, 4000);
  long leftInterval = random(500, 4000);

  //95 = stop
  //94 = veeeeery slow CW
  //96 = veeeeery slow CCW
  myservo.write(95);
  delay(firstStopInterval);
  myservo.write(94);
  delay(rightInterval);
  myservo.write(95);
  delay(secondStopInterval);
  myservo.write(96);
  delay(leftInterval);
}

1                              Arduino Duemilanove w/ ATmega328 on /dev/tty.usbserial-A400fO1M
```

*Figure 14-2. A typical Arduino sketch*

In the figure, you can see the code used to interface with a servo; you include the Servo.h library, create a servo object called myservo, and then write values to that object in order to move it. Similarly, to light an LED, for example, you simply set a particular pin to be an output, and then send values of "1" or "0" to it to turn a connected LED on or off, respectively. As I mentioned before, you can see that it's not Python code. Lines are terminated with semicolons, and blocks of codes are delineated with brackets, not indentations.

Another nice feature of the Arduino's setup is that you can pull the Atmega chip off of the board and use it in a standalone breadboarded project. In other words, let's say you want to design a circuit on the Arduino that will use servos and motors to open and close a pet door in your house. You can write and test the program on your Arduino board, but then you can pull the chip and place it in your standalone circuit. Then you can replace the chip on the board with another one from Atmega (costing about $3), burn the Arduino bootloader onto the chip, and go on programming. You don't have to use an entire Arduino every time you design a new circuit.

# Installing the Arduino IDE on the Pi

Installing the Arduino IDE on the Pi is a simple matter of opening a command line and typing

```
sudo apt-get install arduino
```

You'll be prompted to accept all of the necessary dependencies, and then the IDE will download and install.

When it finishes, you'll need to install pyserial—a Python library that makes it easy to communicate with the Arduino through a serial interface. Open Midori (your Pi's Internet browser), and browse to http://sourceforge. net/projects/pyserial/. Click the "Download" button, and save the file. It's a gzipped tar file, which means you'll have to unzip and untar it. Back in your terminal window, browse to the file's location and unzip/untar it by typing

```
gunzip pyserial-2.7.tar.gz
tar -xvf pyserial-2.7.tar
```

You'll have a new folder called pyserial-2.7. Navigate into that folder by typing **cd**, and install the library by typing

```
sudo python setup.py install
```

---

■ **Note**    The process described in this section is routine when installing a Python-based library. setup.py is a common script used to install a Python library like this, and it requires the install parameter to run. If you're installing a module that is system-wide (in other words, one that doesn't require you to be in the same directory to run it), inside its unpacked folder you'll most often find a folder called "build" and a file called "setup.py." You don't need to do anything with the build folder, because the setup.py script does everything for you. Using sudo (you'll be changing system-level files, so you need to execute the script as the root user) type sudo python setup.py install into your terminal, and the script will install the module.

---

The library is now available for your use in any Python script.

To test it, we'll have to write some Arduino code. Bear with me, and I'll walk you through it, since it may be new to you. Open your Arduino IDE (shown in Figure 14-3), and in the sketch window that appears, type the following code:

```
int ledPin = 13;
void setup()
{
    pinMode(ledPin, OUTPUT);
    Serial.begin(9600);
}

void loop()
{
    Serial.println("Hello, Raspberry Pi!");
    delay(1000);
}
```

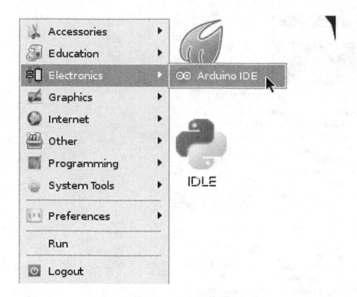

*Figure 14-3.* *Opening the Arduino IDE on the Pi*

The first line of this script sets the variable ledPin to a number, 13. The following setup() function sets pin 13 to be an OUTPUT, and then opens communication with the serial port. Finally, the loop() function (which is every Arduino sketch's main program loop) prints the string "Hello, Raspberry Pi!" to the serial port every 1000 milliseconds (one second). Save the sketch and name it pi_test.

Now connect your Arduino to your Pi with the Arduino's USB cable. Remember—though it's a USB cable, the Pi will actually be communicating via the serial protocol, because the Arduino has an onboard USB-to-serial converter. When the Arduino's green power light comes on, you'll need to select it from the available boards in the "Tools" menu in your Arduino IDE. (See Figure 14-4.)

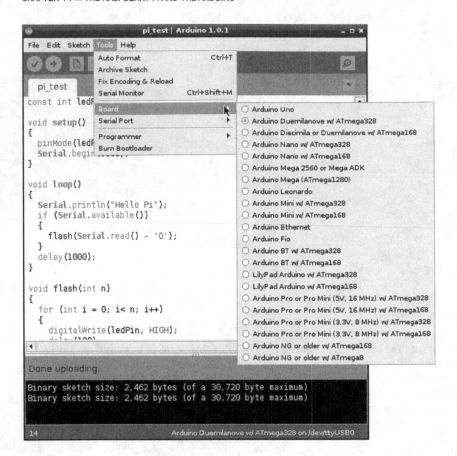

*Figure 14-4.* *Selecting your Arduino board*

Before you upload the `pi-test` script you just wrote, it's a good idea to make sure that your board is connected properly and that you can upload a sketch to it. To do that, let's run the "Blink" sketch that comes with the Arduino IDE. From the File menu, select Examples > 01. Basics > Blink. (See Figure 14-5.) The Blink sketch will open in a new window so that you don't lose your work for the `pi-test` sketch. The Blink sketch simply blinks the Arduino's embedded LED on and off, and it's often used to make sure everything in your setup is correctly configured.

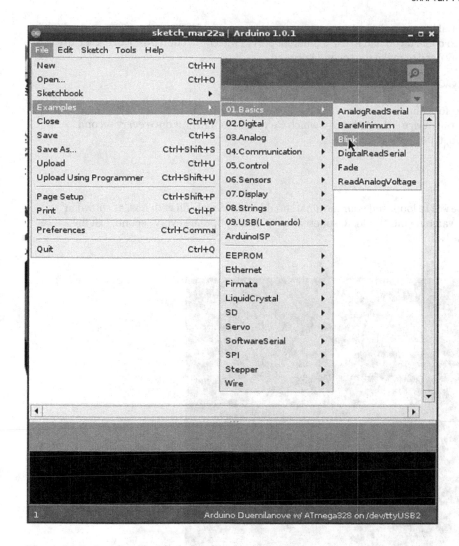

**Figure 14-5.** *Loading the Blink sketch*

When the Blink sketch is loaded, select Upload from the File menu, and wait for the IDE to compile the Blink sketch and upload it to your board. When the Arduino window displays "Done uploading," the red LED on your Arduino should be blinking slowly. If not, double-check your connections and try uploading again. You may get an error message stating that the COM port you selected can't be found and asking if you want to choose another one. Take note of the suggested port (you'll use that information later), select it, and upload your sketch.

Once you know that your connection is correct, switch to the pi_test sketch and upload it to the Arduino by choosing "Upload" from the File menu.

When it's compiled and uploaded in a terminal window, start a Python session and type the following:

```
import serial
ser = serial.Serial('/dev/ttyUSB0', 9600)
```

Here you're importing the serial library and starting a communication over the USB0 port at 9600 baud, which is the value we placed in our Arduino code. If you had to use a different port in the connection protocol earlier, use that port instead. For example, you may need to make the second line read

```
ser = serial.Serial('/dev/ttyACM0', 9600)
```

if you had to use the ttyACM0 port for your connection.

Now we can read from the serial device—the Arduino—which we've told to transmit once every second. Continuing in your Python session, type

```
while True:
    ser.readline()
```

Press Enter twice to finish the while loop, and your terminal should immediately fill with text, as shown in Figure 14-6. When you get bored watching the "Hello, Raspberry Pi\r\n" lines populate every second, exit the while loop that's running by pressing Ctrl+C.

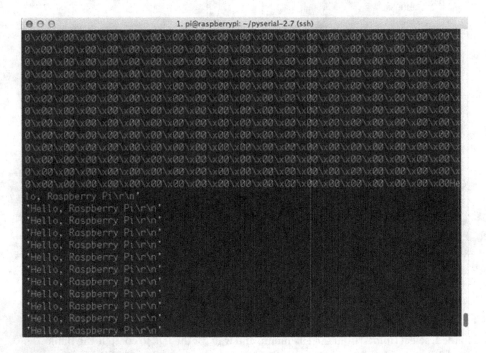

**Figure 14-6.** *Reading from the Arduino's serial port*

So we've now established that we can *read* from the Arduino over the serial connection. Let's establish that we can *write* to it, as well. Go back to your Arduino pi-test sketch, and change the void loop() function to the following:

```
void loop()
{
    if (Serial.available())
    {
        flash(Serial.read()-'0');
    }
}
```

This code tells the Arduino that if it's able to read from the serial connection to take the first received integer (the '0') and send it as a parameter to the flash() function, which follows here. After the loop() function, enter the following into your sketch:

```
void flash(int n)
{
    for (int i = 0; i < n; i++)
    {
        digitalWrite(ledPin, HIGH);
        delay(100);
        digitalWrite(ledPin, LOW);
        delay(100);
    }
}
```

This function flashes the Arduino's onboard LED (hardwired to its pin #13) n number of times, which were passed to it as a parameter. As you can see, the concept is similar to the GPIO's OUTPUT functionality; first you declare the pin to be an output, and then write either a HIGH or LOW value to it to turn it on or off. Save the sketch again and re-upload it to your Arduino board. Then go back to your terminal, and in the same Python session type

```
ser.write('4')
```

and you should be rewarded with the Arduino's onboard LED flashing four times. Try it with different numbers and make sure it's working. Remember, however, that the Arduino is set up to read only the first integer sent to it. If you type

```
ser.write('10')
```

it will flash once, not 10 times.

Congratulations! You're now able to read and write to your Arduino from your Raspberry Pi!

# Running a Servo

Admittedly, flashing an LED on command is not the most impressive operation you can do with your Arduino/Pi combination. My main goal is to teach you how to get the two devices to communicate, and leave the possible uses and implications up to you, but let's discuss communicating with a servo connected to your Arduino.

As a matter of fact, all we need to do is modify our LED code just a bit, to interface with a servo rather than an LED. Clear the text from your pi_test sketch, and replace it with the following:

```
#include <Servo.h>
Servo myservo;

void setup()
{
    myservo.attach(9);
    Serial.begin(9600);
}
```

```
void loop()
{
    if (Serial.available())
    {
        drive(Serial.read()-'0');
    }
    delay (1000);
}

void drive (int n)
{
    if (n < 5)
    {
        myservo.write(50);
    }
    else
    {
        myservo.write(250);
    }
}
```

This code takes the integer you type into your Python prompt, translates it to one speed or another based on its value, and then writes that value to the servo as a speed. To test it, hook your servo's power wire to the Arduino's 5V pin, the ground wire to the Arduino's GND pin, and the signal wire to the Arduino's pin #9. Then save the code, upload it to your board, and—again in your Python prompt—experiment with typing different values of

```
ser.write('5')
```

from 0 to 9 into the prompt, and see how the servo responds.

Yes, it's a very simple code, but hopefully you understand the underlying concepts. Communicating with the Arduino over the Pi's serial interface is no different from communicating with, say, a GPS unit or another small breakout chip. The Arduino, however, is not only a bit more intelligent, but it is also infinitely more expandable, allowing you to add as many additional parts as the Pi does, if not more.

# The Arduino and the Gertboard

You may be wondering, since I've already discussed using the Gertboard with the Pi, how to interface with the Atmega chip on the Gertboard. The Atmega chip, after all, is the chip used on the Arduino, so it stands to reason that you could use the Arduino's IDE to interact with it.

The answer is that to use the Atmega chip on the Gertboard with the Arduino IDE, you need to install quite a bit of extra software and make some changes to the Pi's and the Arduino's configuration files. Finally (perhaps the most troubling), it requires four of your GPIO pins to communicate with the Atmega chip. Meanwhile, using an external Arduino is quite simple and doesn't require any of your precious GPIO pins to be sacrificed. If you want to install the Gertboard software, an excellent tutorial and walkthrough is available on Gordon Henderson's web page at http://bit.ly/1fgEFeo. Recall that Gordon is the developer of the WiringPi library I mention in Chapter 13, "The Gertboard." That library attempts to make it as easy to access the Raspberry Pi's GPIO pins as it is to access the Arduino's pins. Gordon has done some incredible work in writing and making available the software necessary to program the Gertboard's Atmega chip, and I highly recommend that you take some time to go through his site—he does a better job than I ever could of explaining the process.

# Summary

Although this chapter has provided just a short introduction to how to interface the Arduino with your Raspberry Pi, I hope you now realize that communicating with another board like the Arduino, especially via a serial connection, is a simple matter and no different than communicating with any other device. The main difference, of course, is that you can program the Arduino using its IDE, allowing it to base its actions on information provided to it from the Pi. Likewise, the Arduino can have sensors hooked up to it, act as a sensor network hub, and provide information to the Pi. This can allow you to offload some of the processing power to the Arduino and free up your Pi for more processor-intensive tasks.

In short, the Arduino and the Raspberry Pi don't *compete* with other, they *complement* each other. Each fulfills tasks in a different way, and they can be used together to do neat operations in your projects. Take some time to acquaint yourself with the interface—you'll be glad you did.

# Summary

# Index

# ■ E

Electronics
    9V battery electrocution, 52
    earth ground, 53
    electrical equations, 52–53
    fire extinguishers, 63
    first-aid kit, 63
    heat, 62
    ICs, 53
    inductance, 52
    lab safety outfit, 51
    Ohm's Law, 52
    parts storage organization, 64
    power, 52
    Python, 51
    resistance, 53
    robotics (*see* Robotics)
    sharp objects, 63
    soldering techniques, 66
    veins, 52
    ventilation, 64
    water circuit, 53
    wear safety glasses, 63

# ■ F

FFMPEG, 165–166

# ■ G

General Purpose Input/Output (GPIO) pins, 174–176
Gertboard
    Atmega chip, 203–204
    connected to Pi, 202
    converters, 204–205
    digital/analogue converters, 213–214
    GPIO pins, 202–203
    integrated circuits (ICs), 201
    I/O section, 205–206
    jumpers, 208
    LEDs, 210–212
    Microchip, 214
    motor controller, 206–207
    motor speeds and directions, 212
    open collector, 207–208, 213
    Pi's GPIO pins/RPi.GPIO, 209
    preliminary jumper, 209–210
    printed circuit board (PCB), 201
    Raspberry Pi project, 201
    WiringPi, 209
GPIO. *See* General Purpose Input/Output (GPIO) pins
GPS data, 164

# ■ H

H-bridges, 185
HDMI. *See* High definition multimedia
    interface (HDMI) port
High definition multimedia interface
    (HDMI) port, 5–7
Home security system
    description, 111
    dogs, 111
    Raspberry Pi, 112
    sensor network (*see* Sensor network,
        home security system)
HTML. *See* HyperText Markup Language (HTML)
HyperText Markup Language (HTML), 69

# ■ I

ICs. *See* Integrated circuits (ICs)
IDLE. *See* Integrated DeveLopment
    Environment (IDLE)
Integrated circuits, 53
Integrated DeveLopment
    Environment (IDLE)
    definition, 34
    icon, 34
    typing, 36–37
    window, 35
Inter-Integrated Circuit (I2C or IIC), 82–83, 179
I/O section, 205–206

# ■ J, K

Jumpers, Gertboard, 208

# ■ L

LED test side project, 183–185
Linux
    commands, 18–21
    description, 15
    kernel, 16
    LXTerminal icon, Pi desktop, 21–22
    package managers, 23–24
    Pi
        CLI, 16
        files and file system, 17
        Raspberry Pi terminal, 16
        root user *vs.* sudo, 17
    shells, 22–23
    text editors, 24–29
    users' playground, 15
Linux file permissions, 106

## ■ S

# Get the eBook for only $10!

Now you can take the weightless companion with you anywhere, anytime. Your purchase of this book entitles you to 3 electronic versions for only $10.

This Apress title will prove so indispensible that you'll want to carry it with you everywhere, which is why we are offering the eBook in 3 formats for only $10 if you have already purchased the print book.

Convenient and fully searchable, the PDF version enables you to easily find and copy code—or perform examples by quickly toggling between instructions and applications. The MOBI format is ideal for your Kindle, while the ePUB can be utilized on a variety of mobile devices.

Go to www.apress.com/promo/tendollars to purchase your companion eBook.